# Making Peace with the PLO

# Making Peace with the PLO

## The Rabin Government's Road to the Oslo Accord

David Makovsky

Published in Cooperation with
The Washington Institute for Near East Policy

WestviewPress
A Division of HarperCollinsPublishers

Copyright © 1996 by The Washington Institute for Near East Policy

Published in 1996 in the United States of America by Westview Press, Inc., 5500 Central Avenue, Boulder, Colorado 80301-2877, and in the United Kingdom by Westview Press, 12 Hid's Copse Road, Cumnor Hill, Oxford OX2 9JJ

Library of Congress Cataloging-in-Publication Data
Makovsky, David.
   Making peace with the PLO : the Rabin government's road to the Oslo Accord / David Makovsky.
      p.   cm.
   Includes bibliographical references.
   ISBN 0-8133-2425-4 (hardcover).—ISBN 0-8133-2426-2 (pbk.)
   1. Jewish-Arab relations.   2. Israel-Arab conflicts.   3. Israel—Politics and government.   4. Palestinian Arabs—Politics and government.   5. Israel. Treaties, etc. Munaẓẓamat al-Taḥrir al-Filasṭiniyah, 1993 Sept. 13.   6. Rabin, Yitzhak—1922–   I. Title.
DS119.7.M253   1996
320.95694—dc20                                                      95-39631
                                                                        CIP

The paper used in this publication meets the requirements of the American National Standard for Permanence of Paper for Printed Library Materials Z39.48-1984.

10    9    8    7    6    5    4    3    2    1

*To my father, Donald Makovsky,*
*with deep affection and respect*
*and*
*in loving memory of my mother,*
*Nancy Elbaum Makovsky*

# Contents

*Foreword*, Robert B. Satloff                                                    ix
*Acknowledgments*                                                                xiii

Prologue                                                                          1

I      The Unforeseen Peace Process                                              13

II     Drafting the Declaration of Principles                                    31

III    Upgrading the Oslo Talks                                                  45

IV     Brinkmanship                                                             59

V      The Israeli Political Environment                                        83

VI     International and Regional Changes                                      107

VII    Rabin's Personal Road to Oslo                                           117

VIII   The Lessons of Oslo                                                     129

Epilogue                                                                       143

*Appendix I: Security Council Resolution 242*                                  167
*Appendix II: The Camp David Accords*                                          169
*Appendix III: The Reagan Peace Initiative*                                     175
*Appendix IV: Reagan's Talking Points*                                          177
*Appendix V: The London Agreement*                                             181
*Appendix VI: The Shultz Initiative*                                           183
*Appendix VII: Israeli Government Peace Initiative*                             185
*Appendix VIII: The U.S.-Soviet Letter of Invitation*
  *to the Madrid Peace Conference*                                             191

*Appendix IX: The Israeli Labor Party Platform*     193
*Appendix X: U.S. Proposal for Israeli-Palestinian
Statement*     195
*Appendix XI: Rabin's Letter to Arafat Recognizing
the PLO*     199
*Appendix XII: Arafat's Letter to Rabin Recognizing
Israel's Right to Exist in Peace*     201
*Appendix XIII: Arafat's Letter to Norwegian Foreign
Minister Johan Jorgen Holst on the Intifada*     203
*Appendix XIV: The Israel-PLO Declaration of Principles*     205
*Appendix XV: Excerpts from Speeches at the Secret Oslo
Signing Ceremony*     219
*Apendix XVI: Rabin's Speech at the DOP Signing Ceremony*     223
*Appendix XVII: Arafat's Speech at the DOP Signing
Ceremony*     225
*Appendix XVIII: Clinton's Speech at the DOP Signing
Ceremony*     227
*Appendix XIX: Peres' Letter to Norwegian Foreign
Minister Johan Jorgen Holst on the Status of Jerusalem*     231
*Appendix XX: Senior Israeli Officials Who Report
Directly to Rabin*     233

*Chronology*     235
*About the Book and Author*     241

# Foreword

The long, tortuous history of the Arab-Israeli and Palestinian-Israeli conflicts has witnessed numerous tragic episodes, but rarely a moment as hopeful as the handshake between the leaders of the State of Israel and the Palestine Liberation Organization on September 13, 1993. Though other emotions were palpable among the well-wishers and onlookers on the White House lawn that day—including heavy doses of anxiety and trepidation—hope was the most powerful.

Indeed, could that moment have been frozen in time, a century of conflict that has left thousands dead and tens of thousands in mourning would be definitively over. Sadly, however, the conflict lives on and terror still claims the lives of innocents. But the accord signed between Israel and the PLO that day, along with the letters of mutual recognition that accompanied it, reshaped and redefined the conflict in fundamental ways.

This book offers the key element of the story behind that handshake—how and why the leaders of Israel abandoned a policy of rejecting the PLO as a terrorist gang bent on Israel's destruction for a diplomatic approach founded on the belief that the PLO and its longtime leader, Yasser Arafat, were essential partners in the experiment of peacemaking.

Others will no doubt dissect the Palestinian side of the equation. In *Making Peace with the PLO*, award-winning journalist David Makovsky brings to bear years of experience as a correspondent for the *Jerusalem Post* and *U.S. News and World Report*—during which he observed the mechanics of the Rabin government on a daily basis—to analyze and explain the Israeli side of the peace process. Along the way he sheds new light on the often combustible mix of policy, politics, and personalities that defines the Israeli decision-making process.

Through scores of interviews with Israeli, Palestinian, Egyptian, American, and Norwegian officials, Makovsky offers a glimpse inside the inner workings of a government during a period of intense national reckoning. From the decision to deport more than 400 Palestinian Islamic radicals to Lebanon in December 1992 to the popular "closure" of the West Bank and Gaza in March 1993 to the escalation against Hezbollah terrorism in Lebanon in July 1993, Makovsky presents a series of case studies in Israeli decision making that culminates with the historic breakthrough at Oslo.

Along the way, he sketches a political profile of Yitzhak Rabin and the narrow, Labor-led coalition he cobbled together following the election in June 1992. With an intimate knowledge of the Israeli political scene, Makovsky provides a primer on Rabin— soldier, strategist, politician, leader—that is second to none. His focus on the prime minister is particularly important given the personalized nature of the Israeli political system, which lacks any equivalent to the U.S. National Security Council.

Millions of words have already been written about the path to the Israel-PLO accord, but true to journalistic form, Makovsky has unearthed a handful of "scoops" that confirm some well-known elements of the Oslo process while forcing a wholesale rethinking of others. Among the revealing items:

• Israeli Foreign Minister Shimon Peres repeatedly blind-sided and circumvented Rabin, proposing numerous ideas to foreign leaders that went far beyond government policy. For example, Peres proposed to Egypt that Arafat take over Gaza and Jericho without ever having informed Rabin.

• Rabin, however, was no Peres dupe; on the contrary, Makovsky offers convincing evidence that the prime minister was informed of the Oslo talks from virtually the first discussion among academics and became intimately and personally involved in the subsequent negotiations.

• Domestic politics—namely, the fear that Israel's Labor-led coalition government might fall as a result of a corruption scandal unrelated to the peace process—compelled Rabin to conclude a deal in Oslo more quickly than he would have preferred.

• U.S. officials blithely accepted Rabin's dismissal of the PLO throughout the first half of 1993 and did not investigate numerous signs of clandestine Israel-PLO negotiations; largely, according to former Secretary of State James Baker, because they simply did not take Peres as seriously as they should have.

• A key factor in Israel's decision to strike the Oslo bargain was the PLO's repeated promise that they would subdue and control radical Islamic groups such as Hamas.

• Contrary to popular perception, then IDF Chief of Staff Ehud Barak was privy to all Oslo-related documents throughout the negotiating process and, along with chief Israeli negotiator in Washington Elyakim Rubinstein, led the charge against cabinet ratification of the eventual agreement.

These and other special findings lend spice to Makovsky's overall account of the Oslo process and provide a framework for drawing valuable and instructive lessons for the future of the peace process. His main contribution, however, lies elsewhere—in providing a dispassionate examination of a political system that revels in passionate debate. As much as anything, Israel's behavior in the Oslo process provides a lens through which to view democracy at work. Through dogged reporting and deft analysis, Makovsky keeps that lens sharp and clear.

*Robert B. Satloff, Executive Director*
*The Washington Institute*

# Acknowledgments

I would like to thank The Washington Institute for Near East Policy for providing me with the visiting fellowship that served as the basis for this project, and its executive director, Robert Satloff, for encouraging me to expand what was a short paper into a book. I would also like to thank the entire staff of the Institute for their help and for making me feel welcome during my stay.

There are two people without whom this book would not have been possible. As always, I am grateful to my uncle, Alan Makovsky, for his analytical insights and wisdom, and to John Wilner, who could not have been more helpful and generous with his support and patience. Wielding their respective pens, Alan and John brought clarity and shape to the book when needed.

The book also benefited from a variety of individuals who read the manuscript at different stages and offered helpful comments. Among those who were of assistance were William Quandt, Samuel Lewis, Ariel Weiss, David Hoffman, Ehud Ya'ari, Dore Gold, Joseph Alpher, Howard Goller, John Hannah, Yehuda Mirsky, and Varda Rosenblum.

I would like to thank two research assistants in particular, Gordon Lederman and Jennifer Sultan, for their dedication. I also thank the editors of the *Jerusalem Post*, who gave me both the opportunity to observe the peace process firsthand as a diplomatic correspondent and, along with the editors of *U.S. News and World Report*, time off to write a book about it.

Finally, I would like to thank the scores of Israelis, Palestinians, Americans, Egyptians, and Norwegians who gave freely of their time and advice. Many consented to being quoted by name without restriction, some allowed themselves to be quoted only selectively, and others requested that they not be identified. I thank them all.

*David Makovsky*

# Prologue

The conflict between Jews and Arabs in the Middle East predates the birth of the modern state of Israel. The two peoples, who had co-existed for years under a series of external powers, found themselves increasingly at odds as Jewish and Arab nationalism gained popularity and the ruling empires gradually declined and lost local control. Despite periodic efforts over the years to resolve the political dispute, and notwithstanding the 1981 ceasefire in Lebanon between Israel and the PLO, the Oslo accord marks the first comprehensive Israeli-Palestinian peace agreement in an almost 100-year-old conflict.

Although nationalism, socialism, and religious fervor contributed to the development of modern Zionism, it took a wave of anti-Semitism in Eastern Europe at the end of the 19th century to precipitate the first major wave of Jewish immigration to Ottoman-controlled Palestine. Between 1880-1914, some 60,000 Jews from Russia, Poland, and Romania settled in small enclaves that later became the major metropolitan areas of Israel. The Jews nonetheless remained a distinct minority in Palestine (except in Jerusalem) and encountered relatively little conflict from the Arab community.

The situation was aggravated, however, by Allied efforts to win local support against the Ottoman empire during World War I. Contradictory pledges of support for Jewish and Arab self-determination from senior British officials created incompatible expectations that manifested themselves in intercommunal strife that quickly escalated into full-scale anti-Jewish riots. The British authorities administering Palestine under the Mandate of the newly created League of Nations responded to the unrest by limiting further Jewish immigration.

The rise of Adolph Hitler and the Nazi movement in Germany, however, increased Jewish immigration to Palestine and the gradually shifting demographics prompted further Arab resentment and violence. The recommendation of the British government's 1937 Peel Commission—that Palestine be partitioned into separate Jewish and Arab states—was accepted by the Jewish community but rejected by the Arabs. The idea of partition remained dormant until the scope of the Holocaust, and Britain's decision to withdraw from Palestine, prompted a vote in November 1947 by the UN General Assembly, successor to the League of Nations, to divide Palestine into two awkwardly demarcated states and internationalize Jerusalem.

Taking its cue from the UN vote, the Jewish community in Palestine declared an independent state of Israel on May 14, 1948—the day the British Mandate officially ended—and was immediately attacked by the armies of Egypt, Syria, Jordan, Lebanon, Saudi Arabia, and Iraq. Israeli forces managed to repel the attack and even gain territory that had not been allotted to Israel in the original UN partition plan, but approximately 1 percent of the Jewish population was killed in the War of Independence. An estimated 600,000-700,000 Palestinian refugees fled the fighting and ended up in refugee camps in Jordan (both East and West Banks), Syria, Lebanon, and Gaza. Following their 1949 armistice agreements with Israel, Jordan annexed the West Bank and Egypt established a military administration in Gaza.

During this period, the remnants of the traditional Palestinian political leadership—in effect, the short-lived Palestinian Arab government—fell under the control of neighboring Arab states. The so-called "Palestinian issue" was quickly subsumed in the tumult of inter-Arab politics, and the Palestinians lost any independent decision making in their struggle against Israel. In 1958, Palestinian civil engineer and former student activist Yasser Arafat founded an organization called Fatah ("victory" or "conquest") in Kuwait that was dedicated to destroying Israel and returning Arab control to the whole of Mandatory Palestine. Six years later, the Arab League created a group with similar aims called the Palestine Liberation Organization (PLO) and appointed a Saudi diplomat of Palestinian origin as its chairman.

• • •

The 1967 Six Day War was a turning point in the Israeli-Palestinian conflict. Under the command of its then Chief of Staff, General Yitzhak Rabin, the Israel Defense Force (IDF) captured the Golan Heights, Sinai Peninsula, West Bank (including East

Jerusalem), and Gaza Strip. Although the war provided Israel with greater strategic depth and more defensible borders, it also made Israel responsible for the security and well-being of the more than 1 million Palestinian inhabitants of the occupied territories and created another 200,000 refugees.

The war also re-energized international efforts to end the Arab-Israeli conflict. In November 1967, the UN Security Council passed Resolution 242, which enshrined the notion of Israel's relinquishing captured Arab lands in exchange for peace and agreements on "secure and recognized borders." Israeli officials anticipated that the stunning defeat would bring the Arabs to the negotiating table, but the 1967 Arab League summit conference in Khartoum proclaimed that there would be neither recognition of nor negotiations with Israel.

Denied the political rewards of the Six Day War, Israel accepted the territorial status quo and began an ambitious program of settlement construction in selected areas to solidify its control over the occupied territories. During this period, former IDF commander Yigal Allon developed a blueprint for a peace accord that came to be known as the Allon Plan. The plan envisioned ceding most of the West Bank to a Jordanian-Palestinian state while retaining strategic areas for security purposes. Though never formally presented as a peace plan, successive Labor governments based their policies in the occupied territories on Allon's general tenets.

The military debacle of the 1967 War discredited the Arab governments and helped Arafat wrest the PLO from their control. Under his leadership, the organization launched increasingly bold attacks on targets in Israel and the West Bank from its bases in Jordan. The growing power of the PLO and severity of Israeli retaliation threatened the stability of Jordan and in September 1970 King Hussein ordered his army to restore control over the PLO enclaves. Driven from Jordan, Arafat and the PLO moved their headquarters to Beirut. The presence there and in southern Lebanon of thousands of Palestinian refugees from the 1948 War created a base for PLO operations against Israel.

In the meantime, efforts by U.S. Secretary of State William Rogers to mediate an Israel-Egypt peace accord based on Resolution 242 proved unsuccessful. To shatter Israel's sense of invulnerability, Egypt and Syria launched a surprise attack in October 1973. Though the IDF eventually regained the advantage on the battlefield, the war prompted further superpower diplomacy. Secretary of State Henry Kissinger used the negotiations on military disengagement as the basis for improving the relationship between Israel and Egypt—and between the United States and Egypt—thus laying the groundwork for the Camp David accords later that decade.

Supporting their mutual clients in the 1973 War had brought the United States and the Soviet Union close to conflict themselves, and Washington decided something needed to be done to advance the peace process. It cajoled Israel and moderate Arab states such as Egypt and Jordan to attend the first-ever Middle East peace conference in Geneva in December 1973. As would be the case in every diplomatic initiative until Oslo, the Palestinians were represented by someone else—in this case, Jordan. After an initial round devoted entirely to speeches, the conference adjourned into bilateral Israeli-Egyptian negotiations on disengagement and never resumed its plenary session.

A separate U.S. gambit to have Israel cede control of the West Bank town of Jericho to Jordan as a prelude to a more comprehensive peace treaty also failed. The Arab League reacted to the demise of the Jericho plan and the Palestinians' continued exclusion from negotiations affecting their fate by declaring at their October 1974 meeting in Morocco that the PLO was the "sole legitimate representative" of the Palestinian people. The following month, Arafat addressed the UN General Assembly. Israel, however, still refused to recognize or negotiate with the PLO and conditioned its agreement to the second phase of Sinai disengagement on a memorandum of understanding from Kissinger that Washington would neither recognize or negotiate with the PLO unless the organization first accepted UN Security Council Resolution 242 and Israel's right to exist.

• • •

In a March 1977 speech, newly elected U.S. President Jimmy Carter offered American support for a Palestinian homeland. Though he did not mention the PLO, his comments provoked a firestorm in Israel. Two months later, Israel's hawkish Likud party assumed power for the first time in the country's history, ending an almost thirty-year Labor monopoly. New Prime Minister Menachem Begin jettisoned Labor's vision of a territorial compromise with Jordan and instead claimed all of the West Bank and Gaza as Israel's biblical patrimony. The Likud encouraged massive Jewish settlement of the occupied territories in order to make territorial compromise much more difficult to contemplate or implement; it did not, however, annex any of the West Bank.

Military disengagement negotiations between Israel and Egypt after the 1973 War led to a series of secret meetings in Morocco in the fall of 1977 between senior Israeli and Egyptian envoys and ultimately to the discussion of the general outlines of a peace agreement in which Egypt agreed to sign a separate peace treaty with Israel in exchange for gradual but complete Israeli withdrawal from Sinai. The deal was not be made public until Egyptian President Anwar Sadat's historic visit to Jerusalem in November 1977, the symbolic gesture that pierced the wall of Israeli suspicion of Egypt by demonstrating that Sadat was willing to risk his standing in the Arab world to make peace with Israel. Sadat's visit set the stage for the historic Camp David accords, which nonetheless still required many more months of hard bargaining and mediation by Carter.

To refute criticism that he had sold out the Palestinians by reaching a separate deal with Israel, Sadat needed to show some progress on the Palestinian track. Begin obliged him during his first visit to Egypt in December 1977 by endorsing the idea of Palestinian autonomy in the West Bank. The United States developed Begin's idea of autonomy into an interim phase of civil power-sharing to be followed within a defined period of time by negotiations between Israel and a joint Jordanian-Palestinian delegation on the final disposition of the territories. The concept was subsequently broadened and incorporated into the Israel-Egypt peace treaty that was signed on the White House lawn in March 1979.

Washington dispatched a series of special envoys to the region over the next three years in an effort to advance the principle of Palestinian autonomy called for in the Camp David accords, but they made little progress and the talks ended permanently after Israel's 1982 invasion of Lebanon. Though Sadat was widely hailed outside the Middle East—and received the Nobel Peace Prize—for working to end Egypt's participation in the Arab-Israel conflict, Arabs in general and Palestinians in particular considered him a traitor who had forsaken Arab solidarity and the Palestinian cause by signing a separate peace treaty with Israel. In October 1981, militant Islamic soldiers assassinated Sadat as he reviewed a military parade commemorating the 1973 surprise attack on Israel.

• • •

In the early 1970s, the Palestinians began launching missile attacks and raids on northern Israel from southern Lebanon. which Israel responded with air attacks and occasional ground incursions. Egypt's separate peace with Israel at the end of the decade further isolated the PLO, which responded by initiating a cycle of attacks and retaliation in 1981 that threatened the stability of the Lebanese government and the fragile status quo between Israel and Syria. Fearing an uncontrollable escalation, the United States brokered a ceasefire between Israel and the PLO, the only known agreement between the two parties before Oslo.

Likud leaders such as Begin and Defense Minister Ariel Sharon believed that eliminating the PLO would leave Palestinians in the occupied territories with little alternative but to reach an agreement with Israel. The attempted assassination of the Israeli ambassador to Great Britain provided a pretext for the 1982 invasion of Lebanon, which led to a military clash with Syria and culminated in the Israeli siege of Beirut. In the end, another U.S.-brokered deal provided Arafat with safe passage to Tunis and scattered PLO forces in Arab countries throughout the Middle East, exacerbating long-simmering factional rifts within the organization. Sensing an opportunity, the United States offered a new vision of Palestinian autonomy known as the Reagan Plan but it was quickly rejected by Israel, the Palestinians, and the Arab states alike.

The PLO was now weaker and farther away from Palestine than ever before and Israel's invasion of Lebanon seemed to have achieved its primary goal. But it failed to achieve several of its key political objectives, including securing a viable peace agreement with Lebanon's Maronite Christian government and reducing support for the PLO in the occupied territories. At the same time, the war proved costly and divisive both at home and abroad. Mounting casualties in the largely reservist IDF brought public pressure to bear on the government for a withdrawal to a self-declared "security zone" in southern Lebanon. Television footage of the IDF pounding cosmopolitan Beirut and the subsequent massacre by Maronite militiamen of Palestinians in refugee camps around the city subjected Israel to further criticism and ruined any chance of reconciliation with the Palestinians in the occupied territories, who instead noted with admiration the fierce resistance of south Lebanon's Shi'i population to Israel's presence there.

Reeling from the Lebanon debacle, Arafat signed an agreement with King Hussein in February 1985 that for the first time since the 1974 Rabat conference acknowledged a Jordanian role in the peace process. The PLO wanted to participate in a joint peace delegation with Jordan, but the king's price for inclusion was acceptance of Resolution 242, renunciation of terrorism, and explicit recognition of Israel's right to exist. When at the last minute Arafat backed out of a commitment to fulfill these conditions, Hussein severed the accord a year after it was signed.

The 1984 Israeli elections resulted in a politically paralyzing arrangement known as a "national unity government," in which Labor and Likud agreed to share power rather than align themselves with less stable fringe parties. After serving as prime minister for two years in a rotational agreement with Likud leader Yitzhak Shamir, Foreign Minister Shimon Peres struck a deal with King Hussein in April 1987. Meeting secretly in London, Peres and Hussein agreed to an international conference (which Hussein believed was necessary to confer legitimacy on any agreement) that would serve as an umbrella for separate bilateral talks between Israel and its neighbors.

The so-called "London agreement" precluded the conference from imposing, vetoing, or otherwise hindering any solutions reached by the parties. Shamir remained implacably opposed to any kind of multilateral peace negotiations, however, and immediately rejected the agreement, proposing instead that a superpower-sponsored summit with Hussein serve as the basis for direct talks with Jordan. When Hussein rejected this idea, the London Agreement disintegrated and the Palestinian issue seemed to slip off the agenda of an Arab world increasingly preoccupied by the Iran-Iraq War.

• • •

Increasingly marginalized, local Palestinians took matters into their own hands and permanently changed the dynamic of their conflict with Israel. A December 1987 traffic accident in northern Gaza served as the catalyst for a series of riots that quickly erupted into a general uprising throughout Gaza and the West Bank. Misjudging the depth of Palestinian anger and desperation, Israeli officials initially dismissed the unrest as merely the latest in a series of periodic disturbances. When traditional crowd-control methods failed to curtail the demonstrations, Yitzhak Rabin (then defense minister) initiated a policy of "force, might, and beatings" designed to intimidate the mostly young, male Palestinian rioters.

The spontaneity of and broad participation in the uprising (known in Arabic as the *intifada*) undercut the claim by Israeli hardliners that Palestinian nationalism in the West Bank and Gaza was merely an instrument of PLO propaganda and political pressure and that, given a choice, most residents of the territories would actually prefer to remain under Israeli rule. Although the *intifada* did not threaten Israel's existence or even its overall control of the territories, it did undermine individual Israelis' sense of personal security and draw international attention to the plight of the Palestinians.

Citing the deteriorating situation, U.S. Secretary of State George Shultz proposed a modified version of the Camp David accords that came to be known as the "Shultz Initiative." Under Camp David, negotiations on the final status of the occupied territories were to begin after a three-year period of Palestinian autonomy. Palestinians worried, however, that Israel would be able to forestall final status talks indefinitely by delaying the implementation of the autonomy period. The Shultz Initiative sought to allay these fears by "interlocking" the two phases: final status talks would begin shortly after an autonomy agreement regardless of whether it was fully implemented. Other elements of the plan included the participation of local Palestinians (but not the PLO) in a joint Jordanian-Palestinian delegation, a role for the United States as an active partner in the negotiations (including even drafting its own plan for autonomy), and bilateral negotiations under the umbrella of an international conference that could not impose its will on the parties themselves.

Shamir rejected the Shultz Initiative on the grounds that the interlock effectively vitiated the interim autonomy phase and would pre-determine a territorial compromise, something he explicitly rejected. The PLO, which had been scrambling to take credit for and gain control of the spontaneous and indigenous uprising, balked at sharing power in a joint negotiating team with the Jordanians. With the *intifada* raging unabated and no signs of progress on the diplomatic front, PLO political aspirations were unexpectedly aided in July 1988 when King Hussein yielded to Palestinian nationalism and renounced Jordan's claim to the West Bank, effectively removing himself as a competitor to Arafat.

At the November 1988 meeting of the quasi-parliamentary Palestine National Council (PNC) in Algiers, the PLO took its first formal step toward recognizing Israel. It simultaneously declared an independent Palestinian state in the West Bank and Gaza and explicitly accepted both UN General Assembly Resolution 181 of 1947, the so-called "partition resolution" calling for a two-state solution to the conflict, and UN Security Council Resolution 242, which called for Israeli withdrawal from occupied land in exchange for peace. Though derided at the time as an essentially meaningless gesture, the PNC's acceptance of Resolution 181 marked an unprecedented acknowledgment of the legitimacy of Israeli statehood in Palestine.

At the same time, various private individuals and interest groups were working behind the scenes to try to initiate a peace process, while moderate Arabs and other leaders urged Arafat to comply with U.S. conditions for recognizing the PLO and initiating a dialogue with it. Palestinian-American Mohammed Rabie, for example, tried to arrange PLO acceptance of U.S. peace process terms in exchange for assurances of American support for Palestinian self-determination. And Swedish Foreign Minister Sten Andersson served as the intermediary in an effort by a group of American Jews to persuade the PLO to recognize Israel. Arafat's statements in the fall of 1988 came progressively closer, and in December he finally met the test and was rewarded with a public dialogue with Washington through U.S. Ambassador to Tunisia Robert Pelletreau.

●  ●  ●

The 1988 Israeli elections resulted in a second but less balanced national unity government in which the Likud had firm control over both the premiership and the foreign policy portfolio. Rabin remained defense minister and Peres was named minister of finance. With Shamir categorically rejecting a role for the PLO, the question that had long stymied the peace process—who would represent the Palestinians?—remained. During a visit to Washington in April 1989, Shamir said he favored holding elections in the West Bank and Gaza to choose a Palestinian delegation to negotiate an autonomy arrangement with Israel on the basis of Camp David (which he had voted against).

The Bush administration weighed in with its view— articulated in a speech in May 1989 by Secretary of State James Baker to the American-Israel Public Affairs Committee—that Israel needed to abandon its dreams of a "Greater Israel"

encompassing all of the territory between the Mediterranean and
the Jordan River and instead reconcile itself to eventually
relinquishing control over some of the occupied territories.

Egypt, which had been a pariah in the Arab world as a result
of the Camp David accords, gradually began to re-assert its pre-
eminent role in regional affairs in the 1980s and by 1989 was
perhaps best-positioned to mediate between Israel and the PLO.
Peres and his aides, who knew that the Palestinians in the
territories would not accept any deal that did not have the PLO's
imprimatur, accepted and even promoted an Egyptian role in the
peace process. Egyptian-Israeli cooperation reached the point that
Egyptian President Hosni Mubarak's ten-point plan to bridge the
gap between the Israeli and Palestinian positions was actually
formulated by Peres aides Nimrod Novik and Avi Gil.

Before agreeing to elections in the occupied territories to
choose a Palestinian negotiating team, the PLO wanted several
members of the Palestine National Council to participate in a
meeting with Israeli officials in Cairo in order to demonstrate that
Israel was actually dealing with the PLO. Foreign Minister Moshe
Arens worked out a deal with Baker to finesse the sensitive
question of whether East Jerusalem and *diaspora* Palestinians
would be involved in this so-called "Cairo Dialogue," but Shamir
ultimately rejected the idea as a diversion from his original plan,
which was specifically intended to bypass the PLO. To the Bush
administration, however, this merely confirmed a long-held view
that Shamir was not serious about his own plan or peace.

In response, Peres withdrew Labor from the unity government
in March 1990, ending its six-year partnership with Likud and
forcing a no-confidence vote. Though Peres appeared to have the
upper hand at the time, within three months Shamir was at the
helm of a Likud-led government that excluded Labor for the first
time in six years. Three months later, Washington terminated its
dialogue with the PLO because the organization refused to
condemn an abortive seaborne attack on a beach near Tel Aviv or
to punish its perpetrator, Mohammed Abbas (not to be confused
with senior PLO official Mahmoud Abbas), who was a member of
the PLO Executive Committee. The attack, and Washington's
response to it, seemed to undermine further the PLO's bid to
participate in the peace process.

● ● ●

Iraq's invasion of Kuwait in August 1990 and the subsequent Gulf War fundamentally altered the political landscape of the Middle East and made peace a genuine possibility. Iraq's defeat by a U.S.-led coalition of European and Arab countries neutralized the greatest potential threat to Israel (destroying its nascent nuclear arsenal in the process) and temporarily suppressed a major source of Arab radicalism. At the same time, the war sharply eroded the position of the PLO. The Palestinians had embraced Saddam Hussein's claims of pan-Arabism and his threat to the rich oil kingdoms of the Gulf, as well as his calls for the liberation of Jerusalem and use of Scud missiles against Israeli civilians during the war. In response to the former, Saudi Arabia and Kuwait cut off the aid that provided the bulk of the PLO annual budget and expelled Palestinian workers whose remittances sustained the economy of the occupied territories.

Recognizing the political upheaval in the Middle East as an opportunity to advance the peace process, Washington launched a diplomatic initiative in cooperation with Moscow that resulted in the Madrid peace conference in October 1991. Israel conditioned its attendance on the Palestinians' participation as part of a Jordanian delegation that excluded members of the PLO, residents of East Jerusalem, and *diaspora* Palestinians. It further insisted that any peace deal with the Palestinians be based on the two-phase approach stipulated in Camp David, without a Shultz-style interlock between the two phases.

Desperate to regain their footing and confident that they could control the Palestinian negotiators from PLO headquarters in Tunis, Arafat and his dominant Fatah faction grudgingly accepted these conditions and forced the decision on the rest of the organization. Supporters of the PLO's more radical factions, however, vehemently opposed participating from what they perceived as an Israeli-dictated position of subordination.

Although world attention was riveted on the ceremonial opening in Madrid, the conference adjourned immediately thereafter into separate bilateral negotiations between Israel and the Syrian, Lebanese, and joint Jordan-Palestinian delegations which quickly bogged down on each front. The Palestinians rejected Israel's proposal of "personal" autonomy as a substitute for control over designated areas in the West Bank and Gaza. The initial talks did not address substantive issues, as much of the discussions were taken up by Palestinian complaints about human rights in the territories.

U.S.-Israeli relations reached their lowest point in decades when the Bush administration linked Israel's request for $10 billion in loan guarantees needed to finance absorption of massive immigration from the former Soviet Union to a freeze in the construction of Israeli settlements in the occupied territories. The dispute became an issue in Israel's election campaign in 1992. Shamir believed that his insistence on maintaining settlement activity would appeal to Israeli voters who resented the Bush administration's arm-twisting.

Yitzhak Rabin's campaign took a different tack, stressing the need for a "new order of priorities" in which domestic concerns such as unemployment and infrastructure would take precedence over ideologically motivated spending in the territories. Rabin supported a settlement freeze in return for the loan guarantees. He accused Shamir of not being serious about making peace with the Palestinians and promised to reach an autonomy deal with the Palestinians within nine months of being elected.

Rabin's narrow victory in the 1992 election marked the first major shift of Israeli power since the Likud had come to power for the first time fifteen years earlier and would prove to have a major impact on the future of the Middle East peace process. Rabin and the members of his government were much more flexible on peace process issues and particularly territorial compromise and considered the Palestinian issue the heart of the Arab-Israeli conflict. Like the Likud, however, Labor's official position was that it would not negotiate with the PLO.

# I

# The Unforeseen Peace Process

In the midst of Israel's 1992 election campaign, Terje Larsen, a Norwegian sociologist who headed the Oslo-based Institute for Applied Social Sciences (known by its Norwegian acronym, FAFO), met with Yossi Beilin, then a member of the opposition Labor party in the Israeli Knesset. Larsen's purpose was to discuss a FAFO economic study on Palestinian living conditions in the West Bank and Gaza. Both men voiced doubt as to whether progress could be made in the Washington peace talks between Israel and Palestinians from the West Bank and Gaza, which had been stalemated since their inception following the Madrid peace conference in October 1991. They agreed that the "klieg lights" of the media had reduced the talks to public posturing and that Palestinian negotiators showed no inclination to make decisions independent of the PLO leadership in Tunis.

Beilin agreed with Larsen's belief that direct talks between Israel and the PLO were a prerequisite for peace and he suggested that Larsen talk to Yair Hirschfeld, a senior lecturer on Middle East affairs at Haifa University. Hirschfeld was interested in the political, social, and economic aspects of the conflict being explored by Larsen and also believed that Israel needed to talk to the PLO. Israeli law, however, banned contacts with PLO officials.

To circumvent the ban, Larsen suggested creating a secret "backchannel" to Faisal Husseini, a prominent East Jerusalem Palestinian who, though not formally a member of the PLO, was considered the organization's leading representative in the occupied territories. Husseini had been excluded from the Washington negotiations because then Prime Minister Yitzhak

Shamir believed that permitting a resident of East Jerusalem to participate would amount to an Israeli concession on the future status of Israel's capital.

Beilin and Hirschfeld had in fact maintained their own backchannel to Husseini since 1989 but they did not tell this to the Norwegians at the time. According to Hirschfeld, he served as the primary point of contact with Husseini and facilitated meetings for Beilin and Israeli Foreign Minister Shimon Peres as well. In the four years after the channel was initiated, Hirschfeld said he met with Husseini usually at least once a week, that Beilin met with him every few months, and that Peres met him eight to ten times. The meetings took place either in Husseini's home in the Silwana neighborhood of East Jerusalem or in a friend's apartment in the western part of the city.[1]

At a meeting among Larsen, Beilin, Hirschfeld, and Husseini at the American Colony Hotel in Jerusalem just days before the Israeli elections in June 1992, the three agreed that in the event of a Labor party victory, contact would be maintained in order to iron out differences at the Washington talks. Despite Labor's subsequent electoral success, the Norwegian backchannel did not materialize immediately. On September 9, Norwegian Deputy Foreign Minister Jan Egeland led a delegation to Israel. The thirty-seven-year-old Egeland, whose doctoral dissertation focused on Norway's potential role as an intermediary in the resolution of bilateral disputes, used the visit to offer his country's good offices in moving peace talks forward.

## The Norwegian Connection

Norway's interest in the conflict extended back at least to the late 1970s. The Norwegian Labor government had ties with Israel's Labor government during the 1970s through the Socialist International, and its links to the PLO date back to the deployment of Norwegian troops in 1982 as part of the UN peacekeeping contingent in southern Lebanon. With the approval of then Israeli opposition leader Peres, Norwegian Foreign Minister Thorvald Stoltenberg had tried in the early 1980s to bring

---

[1] Interview with Hirschfeld, June 20, 1994. At one point, Beilin, while still in the political opposition, got stuck at Husseini's home during a major snowstorm and had to call the Border Police to get his car out.

the Israelis together with moderate PLO official Issam Sartawi, but the attempt was thwarted in April 1983 when Palestinian radicals opposed to Norway's efforts assassinated Sartawi outside of a Socialist International meeting Stoltenberg was attending in Albufeira, Portugal.[2]

The Norwegians believed that precisely because they did *not* have major interests in the region—unlike the superpowers—yet were on good terms with both Israel and the Palestinians, they were uniquely suited to prod the talks along. As they also lacked the incentives and disincentives that superpowers traditionally use to change the equation of a negotiation, they settled for a more modest role as facilitators rather than mediators of negotiations.

Just as Jean Monnet inspired the post-war European Community by transforming the mutual hatred of France and Germany into a web of interdependent economic relationships, Norwegian leaders hoped the same phenomenon would occur between Israelis and Palestinians. "We invoked the experience of the European Community in transforming political relations by institutionalizing shared economic endeavor," said former Foreign Minister Johan Jorgen Holst, echoing sentiments often expressed by Peres.[3]

PLO representatives had already indicated that Norway had a role to play. Ahmed Qurai (known by his Arabic patronym as Abu Alaa), who headed the PLO's Samed investment arm and was sometimes referred to as the organization's "finance minister," had traveled to Oslo in January 1992 for talks on bilateral economic cooperation. During a meeting with Egeland and later with Larsen, Abu Alaa informally raised the idea of having Norway's Labor government assume the role once exercised by the Swedish Labor government in mediating Middle East peace. Swedish Foreign Minister Sten Andersson had been instrumental in persuading the Palestine National Council (PNC), the PLO's parliament-in-exile, to declare its support for a two-state solution in November 1988, and had initiated a dialogue between American Jewish peace activists and Arafat one month later in Stockholm before losing power in the 1991 elections.[4]

---

[2] Interview with Stoltenberg, November 11, 1994.

[3] Holst speech at the Columbia University School of International and Public Affairs, September 28, 1993, as printed in *Middle East Insight*, September/October, 1993.

[4] Attempts over the years by third parties—ranging from diplomats to

In a meeting with Stoltenberg (who served as foreign minister until being replaced by Holst in April 1993) and his top aides in August 1992 following Rabin's electoral victory, Arafat aide Bassam Abu Sharif reiterated Abu Alaa's request for Norwegian intervention. The Norwegians informed Israel of the request through Israeli Ambassador to Oslo Yoel Alon, but it was almost immediately rebuffed. It remains unclear whether Alon ever forwarded the message to Jerusalem.

Efforts were renewed in September 1992 when, after a dinner in his honor, Egeland, Larsen, and Larsen's wife Mona Juul (a member of Stoltenberg's personal staff who had also served in the Norwegian embassy in Cairo) held off-the-record talks with Beilin and Hirschfeld. Egeland reiterated Larsen's suggestion from the previous April about the possibility of Israeli-PLO negotiations. Beilin responded that Israeli law precluded official contacts, and instead he favored private talks with Husseini.

Despite the Norwegians' best efforts to schedule a more substantive meeting with Husseini either in Jerusalem or Oslo, none took place. The Norwegians were puzzled by the lack of progress. In reality, Beilin had become nervous about the

---

academics to journalists—to mediate between Israel and the PLO are too numerous and varied to discuss in detail here. These and other conduits were also frequently used to pass messages. In an interview on August 18, 1994, Israeli Foreign Minister Shimon Peres said his preferred channel was the Egyptian government. This was particularly true in the months preceding the collapse of Israel's so-called "national unity government" in March 1990. Peres wanted the PLO to allow Palestinians from the occupied territories to meet with Israeli officials in Cairo and sent messages to Tunis through Egyptian Ambassador to Israel Mohammed Bassiouny and presidential adviser Osama el-Baz.

In his 1994 memoirs, *The Road to Oslo*, senior Arafat aide Mahmoud Abbas (known as Abu Mazen) wrote that the PLO had a short-lived contact with Israeli Brigadier-General (Res.) and Health Minister Ephraim Sneh in the months before Israel's June 1992 elections. He said that Sneh, who was head of the Israel's civil administration in the occupied territories during the 1980s, held some thirty meetings with Said Kanaan, leading PLO supporter from Nablus, that focused primarily on increasing votes for Labor among Israeli Arabs.

Kanaan reportedly also gave Sneh a note from the PLO that read: "(1) We are satisfied with the party platform. (2) Whatever you want, we will help you. (3) We want to hold meetings with Yitzhak Rabin or whomever he authorizes." As Kanaan was talking to Sneh, Rabin walked in the room. "We are serious" about making peace, Rabin reportedly said. "Do not leak [information about the existence of] these meetings. I am ready to discuss additional messages. Watch your statements, because we will monitor them closely."

The story caused a political furor in Israel, and Abu Mazen subsequently disavowed the account in his own book. Sneh confirmed meeting Kanaan once, as well as having had some discussions with PLO aide Nabil Shaath in Washington in the first half of 1993, but was unaware of the secret Oslo talks.

endeavor. It was one thing to hold private conversations, but quite another to conduct what would be tantamount to backchannel negotiations. In addition, shortly after his September meeting with Egeland and Hirschfeld, he learned that Rabin had vetoed a request from Peres to hold private meetings with Husseini. Beilin saw the Rabin veto as a cue to avoid controversy, and so he also refrained from meeting Husseini.

## Laying the Foundation for Oslo

Even as Beilin and the Norwegians were trying to negotiate indirectly with the PLO through Husseini, senior Israeli security and political officials were receiving reports from another secret backchannel to the organization: meetings in London and later Rome on the security aspects of peace that were being conducted between former PLO and Israeli security officials. Participating in the meetings were Nizar Amar, at one time a senior member of the PLO's Force 17 commando group; Ahmed Khalidi and Yazid Sayegh, two UK-based Palestinian academics with PLO affiliations; Shlomo Gazit, former head of Israeli military intelligence; Joseph Alpher, deputy head of Tel Aviv University's Jaffee Center for Strategic Studies; Aryeh Shalev, a senior research associate at the Jaffee Center; and *Ha'aretz* military commentator Ze'ev Schiff, who eventually replaced Shalev.

The first of four rounds took place October 8-10 in London. In order for the Israeli participants to comply with the ban on contacts with PLO officials, the talks were held quietly with minimum third-party participation during the off-hours of an academic conference on Middle East security issues hosted by Harvard professor Everett Mendelsohn under the auspices of the American Academy of Arts and Sciences (AAAS). According to Alpher, Mendelsohn knew the conference was a guise, but believed that it was the best away to bring security-minded Israelis and Palestinians together. Among the ideas discussed over a period of about nine months was the long-time proposal for an Israeli withdrawal from Gaza.

There was no official Israeli input in the talks. They were a dialogue rather than a negotiation but served as a valuable conduit to understand positions of well-informed Israelis and Palestinians. Amar, a subordinate to PLO Executive Committee member Mahmoud Abbas (better known by his patronym Abu

Mazen), made clear that he was speaking on behalf of the PLO and was authorized by Arafat to provide the PLO leader's view on issues. According to Israeli officials, the information derived from the AAAS meetings later proved helpful to them in Oslo.

"The purpose of the [AAAS meetings] was to familiarize the two sides with the security thinking as it was," said Alpher. "By distributing reports [of the meetings] to thirty top members of the security and political establishment, we tried to engage the leadership of both sides to begin thinking about and planning security arrangements and security arrangements within the framework of an interim settlement." He theorized that the PLO saw both the Oslo and London/Rome channels as a means of demonstrating to Rabin that the organization was intent upon playing an active role in any Israeli-Palestinian negotiations.[5]

Ironically, the two parties most popularly associated with the Oslo channel—Beilin and the Norwegians—were not in fact its initiators. Israeli government officials were hesitant to meet Husseini, but Hirschfeld and Ron Pundik, an expert on Jordan at Hebrew University's Truman Institute, were enthusiastic believers in an Israel-PLO dialogue and thought they could be useful in breaking the deadlock in Washington.

Hanan Ashrawi, the Palestinian spokeswoman at the Washington negotiations, urged Hirschfeld to travel to London on December 4 to meet Abu Alaa, who was coordinating Palestinian participation in the steering committee for the five sets of multilateral peace talks, which dealt with regional issues such as arms control, economic development, and the environment.[6]

Though initially noncommital out of concern about Israeli laws that prohibited contacts with PLO officials, Hirschfeld eventually agreed to the meeting. He had read that shortly after the Madrid conference Abu Alaa had called publicly for economic links with Israel and he considered him a realist. Hirschfeld asked Larsen, who was in London coincidentally on an unrelated trip, to handle the logistics for the meeting with Abu Alaa.

The meeting took place at the Cavendish Hotel in London. Hirschfeld suggested holding quiet talks in Norway, noting Oslo's

---

[5] Interview with Alpher, March 22, 1995.

[6] Hanan Ashrawi, *This Side of Peace* (New York: Simon & Schuster, 1995), p. 220. Since Israel's participation in the multilaterals was contingent upon the PLO's not attending the talks, Abu Alaa operated from a hotel a short distance from where they were being held.

willingness to be of assistance. Before a second meeting that evening, he consulted with Beilin, who had been unaware of the earlier encounter. "Beilin gave me the okay to hold talks with Abu Alaa in Norway," Hirschfeld later recalled.[7] During the subsequent conversation that evening at London's Ritz Hotel, Hirschfeld told Abu Alaa that he had received the backing to go further without mentioning Beilin by name. Abu Alaa accepted.[8]

As a result of the Hirschfeld-Abu Alaa meeting, Beilin, during a break between multilateral sessions the same day, asked U.S. officials their views of Israel's possibly holding talks with the PLO. Apparently wary of getting caught between Rabin and the dovish Beilin, then Assistant Secretary of State for Near East Affairs Edward Djerejian and his deputy, Daniel Kurtzer, said such a move would be premature. Hirschfeld was less elliptical, telling Kurtzer on December 5 that he had met Abu Alaa and that they had agreed to hold talks in Norway. According to Hirschfeld, Kurtzer said such talks could be useful as long as they remained unofficial. This marks the first of many occasions on which the United States was informed about Oslo.[9]

Discussions under the cover of FAFO intrigued Beilin and offered three potential benefits. First, the participation of private Israelis in a seminar under FAFO auspices would not violate Israeli law. Second, the nature of such discussions would be more academic than political, thereby allowing the exploration of PLO views without Israeli commitments. Finally, the backchannel could operate on FAFO funds, rather than Israeli funding that would have required an official government decision to conduct the talks. In fact, to avoid any appearance of official sanction, Beilin insisted that all Israeli documents given to the Palestinians be written on FAFO stationary.

## Lifting the Ban on PLO Contacts

In November 1991, long before the Norwegian mediation proposal and Rabin's selection as the Labor candidate for prime minister, Beilin's dovish Mashov faction had engineered the

---

[7] Interview with Hirschfeld, June 20, 1994.
[8] Ibid.
[9] Ibid.

adoption at a party convention of a resolution that called for the repeal of the six-year-old Knesset ban on private Israeli contacts with the PLO. Peres, who maintained a solid grip on the party apparatus, overrode opposition from Rabin and others and pushed the resolution through and into the party platform. Shortly after Rabin's victory in the Israeli election, Peres called upon him (at Beilin's behest) to implement the party decision and have the Knesset reverse the ban. In addition, the coalition agreement with the leftist Meretz party stated that were the ban not lifted within six months, Meretz would be free to put forward its own bill to do so.

Because the Meretz bill would legalize meetings between private citizens without affecting the taboo on government contacts, Rabin did not see it as particularly harmful. He was concerned, however, about the timing—particularly, according to aides, given the upcoming U.S. elections. Rabin appreciated the Bush administration's forceful intervention against Iraq during the Gulf Crisis and had been a supporter of Republican administrations since his tenure as Israel's envoy to Washington during the Nixon years. Nevertheless, he feared that the Bush administration would exploit the lifting of the ban to resume its dialogue with the PLO that had been suspended after an abortive terrorist attack on the beaches of Tel Aviv by followers of PLO Executive Committee member Abu Abbas.[10]

When Bush lost the election in November 1992, Rabin no longer worried about the ramifications of repealing the ban, and on December 1 the Knesset gave preliminary approval to do so. Rabin himself did not show up for the vote, however. This may have been the first of many indications that the premier had no grand design to initiate negotiations with the PLO. Hirschfeld was following the progress of the Knesset bill closely and deliberately asked the Norwegians to schedule the first Oslo session for January 20, the day after it was to become law. Despite the bill's passage, Rabin pledged there would be no governmental contacts.

---

[10]In December 1988, incoming Bush administration officials had helped to convince outgoing Secretary of State George Shultz to utilize his unimpeachable credentials with Israel and the American Jewish community to start such a dialogue.

## The First Round of Talks in Oslo

The secret negotiations between Israel and the PLO can be divided into at least two stages. There were five rounds of exploratory "pre-negotiations," the first of which was held over the weekend of January 20-22 under the guise of an academic conference at the estate of the Borregard paper company in Sarpsborg, 100 kilometers southeast of Oslo.[11] It began with a lecture on Palestinian living conditions in the West Bank by FAFO associate Marian Heiberg, wife of Norwegian Defense (and soon to be Foreign) Minister Holst. The Norwegians adopted the conference format because they were not certain that the Knesset would rescind the ban on contacts with the PLO; under the old law Israelis were allowed to attend only academic seminars with representatives of the organization.

Hirschfeld led the Israeli side, joined by Pundik, who recalls being given a "long leash" to conduct the talks. The two had received only minimal instructions from Beilin, who thought the value of the backchannel was less what the Israeli academics could convey than what they could learn from their Palestinian counterparts. On his own initiative, Beilin told Hirschfeld and Pundik to try to divine the PLO's thinking, test its seriousness, and determine where gaps could be bridged, while making clear that they were not authorized to speak for the Israeli government.

Beilin later admitted that he doubted the talks would amount to more than passing conversations, similar to those between Israeli doves and PLO officials over the years at various peace symposia in Europe. At most—and this would have been a worthwhile contribution indeed—the two sides might reach compromises on deadlocked issues that could then be brought to the Washington peace talks (unbeknownst to the negotiators there) under the guise of American proposals, and therefore be more readily accepted. Beilin did not believe that Rabin would accept the notion of direct Israel-PLO negotiations.

The Palestinians were led throughout by Abu Alaa, who was joined by Maher al-Kurd, a member of PLO chairman Yasser Arafat's office and longtime associate of Abu Alaa; and Hassan Asfour, who had been tracking the progress of the Washington talks for Abu Mazen. More than any other senior PLO figure, Abu

---

[11] The subsequent four rounds were held on February 11-12, March 20-21, April 30-May 1, and May 8-9.

Mazen had established contacts with Israeli liberals. He headed the PLO's Israel desk and had written widely on the relationship between the Palestinians and the Israeli left-wing.

Considered the PLO's top political pragmatist, Abu Mazen was determined to reach an agreement with Israel in order to obtain Palestinian rights. He had proposed secret talks with the Rabin government immediately after it was elected, broaching the idea with the Egyptians as early as September 1992 only to have it go nowhere. Though he never attended the Oslo talks, participants considered Abu Mazen the Palestinian architect of the accord and it was he who ultimately signed the accord for the PLO at the White House ceremony in September 1993.

At the outset of the January 20 meeting, the two sides established the ground rules—no dwelling on past grievances, total secrecy, and retractibility of all positions put forward in the talks. The Norwegians served as facilitators but did not mediate disputes; they remained outside of the negotiating room, receiving separate briefings from each side before and after meetings.[12] Larsen and Juul stressed the need to create an informal atmosphere during the talks and used a variety of means to achieve that end, including having the two sides share meals.

The role of this Norwegian husband-and-wife team as backchannel facilitators cannot be overstated. They devoted at least a year to the Israel-PLO talks and were largely responsible for holding the Oslo channel together. On the most basic level, they ensured that the talks were discrete and the atmosphere amiable and offered continuous encouragement to both sides. Larsen was in daily contact with Jerusalem and Tunis between sessions, passing messages between the parties between rounds and ensuring that momentum was maintained even when there were serious disagreements. Juul served as the liaison to the Norwegian government, keeping officials in Oslo informed and urging them to nudge the talks forward when necessary.[13]

---

[12] This did not prevent each side from complaining to the Norwegians about the negotiating position of the other, in part as a tactic intended to soften each other's positions.

[13] Larsen and Juul played a behind-the-scenes role after Israel and the PLO signed the DOP on September 13, 1993. They passed messages during impasses in implementation talks over the subsequent eight months. Larsen was later appointed UN coordinator to the Palestinian Authority in the Gaza-Jericho, and Juul was assigned to the Norwegian embassy in Tel Aviv.

## Peres Becomes a Player Again

In the very first round of talks, Hirschfeld and Abu Alaa agreed on three main ideas: Israeli withdrawal from Gaza, gradual devolution of economic power to the Palestinians based on proven cooperation and leading to Palestinian economic institution-building, and a "Marshall Plan" for international economic assistance to the nascent Palestinian entity in Gaza. Given the interests of Abu Alaa and Hirschfeld, it is not surprising that they spent much time on economics. Within the first round, the elements of the Oslo accord were falling into place.

Hirschfeld briefed Beilin regularly throughout the Sarpsborg talks. After reviewing detailed minutes of the negotiations, Beilin decided to present Peres with the notes of the proceedings. They agreed that Peres should broach the subject of Oslo with Rabin, who confirmed that Peres informed him about the talks in the first week of February; Peres said he persuaded Rabin to allow the talks to continue by arguing that the backchannel provided valuable information about PLO positions without obligating the Israeli government.[14] Their enthusiasm was tempered, however, by the fact that Abu Alaa was relatively unknown in Israel even to experts, and it remained unclear how authoritative he was.[15]

Prior to informing Rabin about the Oslo initiative, Peres had played almost no role in the new government's peace efforts. The prime minister believed that he could single-handedly guide the peace process himself without help or interference from Labor party rival Peres, with whom he disagreed on both tactics and the strategic principles underpinning Israel's negotiating positions.

Shortly after his election, Rabin made two moves designed to marginalize Peres and maintain personal control over Israeli decision making in the peace process. Realizing that the defense minister's authority over the occupied territories afforded him enormous input in negotiations, he took the defense portfolio for himself. (Rabin had held the post from 1984 to 1990 in so-called "national unity governments" with the Likud and clearly relished the post, enjoying the details of security more than the political demands of being prime minister.)

---

[14] Interviews with Rabin, October 4, 1993, and Peres, December 31, 1993.

[15] A senior Israeli official recalled that when Rabin asked the intelligence community for an assessment of Abu Alaa, he discovered that the file was only four-and-a-half pages long.

Peres' strong standing within the Labor party prevented him from being completely ignored, however, and so Rabin offered his rival a truncated position as foreign minister in which Peres would be excluded from the bilateral negotiations that were the centerpiece of the peace process, as well as much of U.S.-Israel relations, and relegated instead to the multilateral talks on regional issues. Only Rabin, riding the wave of an electoral victory in which he brought Labor back to dominance after fifteen years, could have succeeded in so marginalizing Peres.

Rabin eventually brought Peres back into peace process decision making to deal with the unexpected consequences of his decision in December 1992 to deport 415 Islamic militants (mostly members of the Islamic Resistance Movement, known by the Arabic acronym Hamas) from the occupied territories to southern Lebanon. The deportations were a response to the killings of eight Israeli soldiers in a 12-day period, culminating in the kidnapping and murder of a member of the border patrol in central Israel.

Though intended primarily to calm the Israeli public in the aftermath of the attacks, Rabin hoped the deportations would also reduce the intimidation of moderates in the occupied territories and allow Palestinian negotiators in Washington to be more flexible. He dismissed prescient warnings from Maj.-Gen. Danny Rothschild, head of Israel's civil administration in the West Bank and Gaza, and Elyakim Rubinstein, chief negotiator with the Palestinians in Washington, that the Arabs would respond by boycotting the Washington talks and that the United Nations could threaten sanctions. (Peres, who was in Tokyo at the time, subsequently told confidantes that the deportations would never have occurred if he had been in the country.)

Rabin's strategy ultimately boomeranged. Although Israeli intelligence reported that the Palestinian delegation in Washington was quietly gleeful about the action against the PLO's militant Islamic rivals, their private satisfaction did not translate into a freer hand at the negotiating table. On the contrary, they felt compelled not only to defend the deportees publicly, but to boycott the talks as well. Instead of advancing the peace process, the deportations effectively stopped it dead in its tracks.[16]

---

[16] At a cabinet meeting in early January, Rabin predicted that the Syrians would still attend the Washington talks, citing a public statement by Syrian Foreign Minister Farouq al-Shara at an Arab League meeting calling on the Palestinians to boycott the multilateral peace talks instead. The prime minister's hopes were

The prime minister felt he was in a bind. Two months after vetoing a Peres-Husseini meeting, Rabin reversed his decision and allowed the foreign minister to meet with Husseini to try to coax the Palestinians back to the table. In so doing, he gave Peres a foothold in bilateral talks that the foreign minister would not relinquish. Peres and Husseini held four secret meetings (including some at Peres' home), but could not reach an agreement.[17]

Peres grew increasingly exasperated by rising Palestinian violence in the aftermath of the deportation imbroglio and, having informed Rabin in early February about the existence of the Oslo talks, appealed privately to him on February 9 to negotiate directly with the PLO and reach an agreement that would allow Arafat to serve as the head of Palestinian self-rule. It was the second time in a month that Peres had urged Rabin to accept the inclusion of the PLO, and the third since the start of the Labor government. Peres said he told Rabin that

> as long as Arafat remained in Tunis . . . he represented the 'outsiders,' the Palestinian *diaspora*, and would do his best to slow down the peace talks. I suggested that we propose to Arafat and his staff that they move to Gaza. Once there, they would have the right to vote and to stand in elections; and if elected, they would represent the Palestinians directly in the negotiations with Israel. My criticism of the Washington talks was that we were trying to reach a declaration of principles without any reference to specific territorial issues.[18]

Rabin did not accept Peres' appeal regarding Arafat, but agreed to allow Hirschfeld and Pundik to continue their contacts in Oslo, particularly since Israel could plausibly deny official involvement in them. He asked Peres to delay the talks until the end of the month, however, because U.S. Secretary of State Warren Christopher—who was hosting the Washington talks—

---

quickly dashed, however. Instead of rejoining the talks and thereby isolating the Palestinians, Damascus joined the boycott, which lasted until April. It was the first indication since the start of the Madrid conference that the Palestinians had the political clout to prevent the Syrians from negotiating with Israel.

[17] The meeting did have one benefit, however; in his report to Tunis on the meeting, Husseini noted the presence of Hirschfeld and Pundik along with Peres, which helped to establish their *bona fides*.

[18] Shimon Peres, *Battling for Peace* (London: Weidenfeld and Nicolson, 1995).

had scheduled a trip to the region a couple of weeks later. But Peres had already approved the academics' return to Sarpsborg for another round of talks two days later, and he ignored Rabin's request. This minor bit of insubordination was soon followed by another example of Peres' penchant for willfully circumventing Rabin.

The foreign minister believed that permitting Husseini to join the Palestinian delegation in Washington would break the deportation-induced logjam, and in an extraordinary move designed to maneuver Rabin into adopting his negotiating strategy, he raised this possibility during a meeting with Christopher in Washington on February 16, suggesting that Rabin would be much more likely to accept Husseini's participation if the Americans—rather than Peres—proposed the idea. Peres' subterfuge proved successful when, during the prime minister's first trip to Washington in early March to meet with President Bill Clinton, Rabin assented to "Christopher's" proposal to include Husseini in the talks.[19]

### The United States Overlooks Oslo

Like the Israelis, the Norwegians informed the United States about the Oslo track before it was completely underway. Egeland and Larsen first raised the idea of a Norwegian-sponsored backchannel with Dan Kurtzer shortly after their meeting with Beilin in September 1992. Although they knew that U.S. policy officially looked askance at the PLO, the Norwegians expected encouragement from the State Department "dove" often credited with drafting the 1988 U.S. decision to initiate a dialogue with the PLO.

Instead, Kurtzer told them repeatedly that Arafat was an unreliable negotiating partner and that the Oslo talks would have little value without Rabin's backing. Kurtzer's pessimism left the Norwegians with the sense that he did not want anyone to intrude on the U.S.-led peace process. A more likely explanation is that,

---

[19] Peres often tried to utilize the Americans to introduce proposals that he thought would be rejected if he were recognized publicly (or even by Rabin) as their source. In fact, after the Oslo agreement was concluded in August, Peres flew to see a vacationing Christopher in California and asked him to present the accord as a U.S. document; Christopher rebuffed the request as a transparent fiction.

though Kurtzer did not mind a certain amount of well-intentioned "meddling" by Israeli academics such as Hirschfeld, he was wary of the participation of a foreign government.

At the NATO talks in Brussels in February 1993, Stoltenberg briefed Christopher on Norway's role in engineering a meeting between PLO officials and Israeli academics "with political connections" in Jerusalem.[20] Stoltenberg presented the Oslo channel not as a competing track to the Washington talks but as a supplementary opportunity to resolve impasses in the official negotiations. Christopher responded positively, promising follow-up discussions that never took place. When they did not hear from U.S. officials after several weeks, Egeland and Juul contacted Kurtzer again about the talks, and even went to the U.S. embassy in Oslo on several occasions to speak to him on a secure phone. At the end of March, the Norwegians sent Kurtzer a declaration of principles (DOP) drafted by Hirschfeld and Abu Alaa.

U.S. officials did not seek additional information on Oslo, apparently content with hints and general briefings. Even when Holst (who had become foreign minister in April 1993) informed Christopher at the end of May that Israel had upgraded the talks to the official level, this startling fact failed to draw a U.S. response. (Before meeting Christopher, Holst contacted Beilin to ask how much he could tell the United States. Beilin replied that Holst could say the talks had been upgraded, but could not provide names or indicate how senior the officials were.)

In early July, prior to the arrival in Jerusalem of U.S. Special Middle East Coordinator Dennis Ross, Peres told U.S. *charge' d'affaires* William Brown that Israel was going to reach a deal with the PLO. Brown passed the information along to his superiors, but neither he nor they followed up on it. After Ross' trip ended, Kurtzer met privately with Beilin, who waxed enthusiastic about prospects for a breakthrough but gave few details. During Christopher's visit to the region in early August, two weeks before the Oslo agreement was initialed, Peres updated him about Oslo.

When the secretary of state raised the subject in a subsequent meeting with Rabin, however, the prime minister dismissed the news with a wave of his hand, saying he doubted anything would come of it. Although this response probably reflects Rabin's view of the prospects for Oslo's success rather than disingenuousness

---

[20] Interview with Stoltenberg, November 11, 1994.

on his part, it also demonstrates that the Clinton administration viewed Rabin as the sole Israeli decision maker on the peace process and accordingly took its cues from him.[21]

Given Rabin's well-known pro-U.S. orientation and penchant for centralized control of events, U.S. officials dismissed the Oslo backchannel as a Peres vision that stood no chance of winning Rabin's backing.[22] This degree of trust is perhaps surprising, considering Rabin's pattern of secretiveness. He had not consulted with or even informed U.S. officials prior to several major Israeli security actions or foreign policy decisions such as the Hamas deportations in December 1992, the closure of the territories in March 1993, and "Operation Accountability" in southern Lebanon in July 1993.

A second reason for the Americans' dismissive attitude toward the Oslo talks lies in the frequency with which U.S. officials heard of secret contacts. They had no reason to believe Oslo was any more serious than other oft-touted tracks such as the AAAS meetings or those between Member of Knesset (MK) Ephraim Sneh and PLO official Nabil Shaath in Washington and at several international symposia on the Middle East.[23]

---

[21] Upon becoming prime minister, Rabin had made clear that U.S. envoys should conduct peace process business only with him.

[22] "The [Clinton] administration just did not take Shimon [Peres] seriously during Oslo," former Secretary of State James Baker lamented in an interview on March 13, 1994. Two weeks before Peres initialed the accord in Oslo, Christopher paid only the most perfunctory courtesy call to the Foreign Ministry while visiting Rabin, asking Peres only three questions in their half-hour session.

[23] While Holst was in the United States, State Department Policy Planning chief and former Ambassador to Israel Samuel Lewis coincidentally convened a gathering of top U.S. policymakers and former senior officials on May 27, 1993, to discuss the impasse in the Washington negotiations. In an interview on June 22, 1994, Edward Djerejian, then the leading U.S. policymaker in charge of the Middle East peace process, recalled the scene. "I said, 'Given the Norwegian Foreign Ministry channel and the two to three other channels that we are aware of with the PLO, wouldn't it be ironic if the talks in Washington were a facade and Israel and the PLO are dealing [directly] with one another?' There was nervous laughter in the room."

Some U.S. officials reluctantly admit to a third reason for their lack of interest. The United States had masterminded a world-class feat in getting Israel and its Arab neighbors to sit around a single table at the Madrid peace conference, which served as the basis for the Washington talks. In the aftermath of Madrid, the United States simply believed it was indispensable. "When you invent the wheel, you believe nobody else can have a car," one U.S. official observed.[24]

---

[24] For all these reasons, American officials received but did not follow up on a major hint of progress in Oslo. In talks with Christopher in East Jerusalem during early August 1993, the Palestinian delegates to the Washington talks took the unusual step of rejecting U.S.-proposed "bridging" language for a declaration of principles within minutes of receiving it. During a meeting of State Department officials in the U.S. consulate in East Jerusalem following the disappointing session with the Palestinians, Kurtzer opined to his colleagues that the Oslo channel must be delivering substantive progress because Arafat would have never instructed his delegates to dismiss a U.S. draft without offering an alternative. Although the Palestinians subsequently gave Christopher a counterproposal orginating in Tunis and vaguely mentioning Gaza and Jericho, the U.S. peace team apparently did not realize its significance and went ahead with a scheduled vacation.

# II

# Drafting the Declaration of Principles

In February, Beilin began to believe that the only way to understand PLO thinking fully was to draft a DOP for the interim period of Palestinian self-rule, and Abu Alaa quickly agreed to do so. Since the ground rules permitted either side to retract an offer at any point, he saw no danger in incorporating ideas that had not been previously raised by Israel in the stalled Washington talks. The drafting process began at the second round of Oslo talks at the Borregard mansion in Sarpsborg from February 11-12 and concluded at the third round on March 20-21.

The six-page document that emerged, entitled Sarpsborg III, contained fifteen articles and was accompanied by annexes on the status of Jerusalem in Palestinian elections, Palestinian economic development, and regional economic development. Many of these provisions either remained in or served as the basis for the final version of the Oslo accords, sometimes to the chagrin of subsequent Israeli negotiators who found it difficult to amend previously agreed elements.

Several elements stood out as departures from existing Israeli policy. First, Israel agreed to withdraw completely from Gaza within two years, at which point a "trusteeship" of some sort would be established to govern the territory. Although the nature of this trusteeship was not defined in the document, Hirschfeld proposed a Namibia-like UN administration of Gaza (to ensure a gradual withdrawal) that essentially meant consenting to the eventual establishment of a Palestinian state.[1]

---

[1] Hirschfeld's proposal elicited a furious response from Israeli policymakers,

Second, Israel for the first time ever explicitly agreed to negotiate the status of Jerusalem, its self-declared eternal and indivisible capital, as well as settlements, sovereignty, and borders in future talks on the final status of the occupied territories (although sovereignty and borders were removed in later drafts).[2] In an accompanying annex, Israel agreed that Palestinian residents of Jerusalem could both vote and stand as candidates in elections for a council to administer self-rule.

The Labor party position prior to Oslo was that Palestinians in Jerusalem would be allowed to vote in the elections (just as Americans living in Paris are allowed to cast absentee ballots in U.S. elections) at polling places outside the city, but would not be permitted to run for office because that implied Palestinian jurisdiction over the city. Under the draft DOP, the Palestinians would be allowed to cast their ballots at polling stations within Jerusalem (Muslims at the al-Aqsa Mosque, Christians at the Church of the Holy Sepulchure) as opposed to the West Bank cities of Ramallah and Bethlehem. The Israeli academics believed that stationing the polling booths at religious sites would somehow put the issue of elections in the context of Palestinian religious and not political rights to the city.

Third, the DOP did not enumerate the powers of or constraints upon Palestinian jurisdiction in the West Bank, thereby suggesting that it would be total. Moreover, it suggested that East Jerusalem would be part of the area under Palestinian self-rule, and thus there would be no impediment to establishing the self-rule headquarters there.[3]

---

who feared it would serve as a precedent for UN involvement in Israeli administration of the occupied territories, something Israel has consistently fought. The Palestinians quickly agreed to drop the idea, which they feared would slow Israeli withdrawal from Gaza.

[2] In a post-Oslo interview, PLO official Nabil Shaath said that until the Sarpsborg talks, the Israelis had "never accepted that the final status of Jerusalem [should] be on the agenda of the permanent status negotiations. . . . In a way, [doing so] calls into question the legality and finality of their annexation." See *Journal of Palestine Studies* 33 (Autumn 1993): 7.

[3] Palestinian jurisdiction in Jerusalem was left somewhat vague. The Palestinians insisted on making the city their administrative headquarters, no doubt to lay the groundwork for its eventual transition to capital of a Palestinian state. The DOP said that self-rule would be administered by "existing Palestinian institutions," a cryptic reference to Orient House, a building in East Jerusalem owned by Faisal Husseini's family since 1897 that had served as the headquarters for Palestinian political activity since the 1991 Madrid peace conference. The issue would remain the last major sticking point in the Oslo negotiations.

Fourth, the draft DOP accelerated the timetable for beginning negotiations on final status by severing them from elections for the self-rule council that were scheduled to take place three months after it was signed. Under Camp David, final status negotiations were to begin two years after the elections; under the Oslo agreement, the clock began ticking after the DOP was signed. The change reflected the negotiators' uncertainty over whether elections would ever occur, due mostly to the PLO's fear that they would lead to defeat or power-sharing with Hamas.

In addition, both sides realized that the new timetable gave them the flexibility to skip self-rule altogether and move directly to final status negotiations if they so chose. Final status talks before the Israeli elections in 1996 would minimize the risk that the ultimate disposition of the territories would be in the hands of a Likud-led government. Looming Israeli elections would also provide the Labor government with leverage against the Palestinians in times of impasse, since stalemated negotiations could lead to the election of a Likud government that would have a negative attitude toward the entire Oslo accord.

Fifth, in an extraordinary departure from past policy, Israel agreed to binding arbitration of disputes when negotiation and mediation had failed. Under Article 15, the arbitration panel would consist of Israel, the Palestinians, and Madrid conference co-sponsors Russia and the United States. The implication was monumental: Israel could be coerced into ceding sovereignty.

The remaining annexes of the Sarpsborg accord focused on economics. Annex II dealt with the establishment of Palestinian economic institutions, and Annex III called for the help of the top seven industrialized states and the Organization for Economic Cooperation and Development (OECD) to fund infrastructure and other regional projects such as desalination. It also called for an Israeli-Palestinian-Jordanian body that to coordinate exploitation of the Dead Sea, a move that angered the Jordanians when the final DOP was revealed.

Certain elements of the Sarpsborg III DOP that contravened long-standing Israeli policy would come back to haunt Israeli negotiators when the talks were later upgraded to an official level. Israeli officials were forced to make concessions in the ensuing four months just to retract positions that the academics already agreed upon. Though some of the concessions made early on in Sarpsborg were probably necessary if a deal were ultimately to be achieved, the question was one of timing. Offering them early deprived Israeli negotiators of bargaining chips after negotiations were upgraded. As invaluable as the academics were in establishing the Oslo channel, in retrospect it appears that they should have taken a backseat once the drafting process began.

To be fair, Hirschfeld and Pundik received little guidance from officials such as Beilin and later Peres. Beilin said he had no way of knowing at the start that the Oslo channel would develop the way it did, and thought that giving Hirschfeld and Pundik broad latitude would enable them to discern more easily the positions of the other side. The fact remains, however, that individuals essentially representing the Israeli government put forward positions that were at variance with accepted Israeli policy. This vacuum was possible only because the Rabin government did not have ready-made policies for dealing with the long-shunned PLO.

### "Gaza First" Becomes "Gaza Plus"

For more than a decade, Peres and Beilin had advocated a "Gaza First" approach in which Israel would cede control of the teeming, poverty-ridden Gaza Strip to the Palestinians before tackling the more difficult issue of the West Bank. Like most Israelis, the two men saw Gaza as a burden to be jettisoned. If, for domestic political reasons, Israel could not make major concessions on the West Bank, "Gaza First" would still satisfy Palestinian demands that an interim phase include a transfer of *territorial* authority—jurisdiction over a specific geographic area.

As such, early withdrawal from Gaza represented a departure from previous interim solutions dating back to the Camp David accords, all of which had focused on an Israeli transfer of *functional* authority to the inhabitants—in other words, Palestinians would be given control of various government functions prior to any Israeli withdrawal from specific territory. The Palestinians were wary, however, that a "Gaza First" agreement would prove to be an Israeli ruse to get rid of Gaza without moving toward a solution on the West Bank; in short, they feared that "Gaza First" would become "Gaza Only."

Rabin downplayed the significance of the Oslo channel in part because he did not believe the PLO really wanted Gaza; after all, they had rejected the idea in the past and their interests seemed best served by having the area remain a festering sore, thereby underscoring the urgency of settling the entire conflict in all the territories. Peres agreed with Rabin's appraisal, and unbeknownst to Rabin he decided to add something to sweeten the deal.[4] In a meeting with Egyptian officials on November 16, 1992, Peres proposed the idea of "Gaza Plus"—ceding to the Palestinians Gaza *and* either Jenin or Jericho, two West Bank towns without Jewish settlers, as a "downpayment" on Israel's intention to deal with West Bank territorial issues.

According to Peres (and contrary to popular belief) it was he and not the PLO who proposed adding Jericho to the Gaza deal.

> I preferred to offer Jericho as a sign of our intent to continue negotiations, even if 'Gaza First' would be the main policy. There were no Jewish settlements in the immediate Jericho area, therefore there would be no need to discuss their fate. We proposed an administrative center to be set up in Jericho to take pressure off Jerusalem, especially since Jericho is not far from Jerusalem. Its proximity to the Jordan River opened a preferred solution in my eyes for the future, a confederation between Jordanians and Palestinians . . . [5]

Peres believed Rabin would agree to the idea because withdrawal from Jericho had long been envisioned in mainstream Labor party thinking, going back to a plan formulated in 1968 by Yigal Allon, former commander of the Palmach, the pre-state Israeli commando unit, and Rabin's mentor.[6]

---

[4] Interview with Peres, August 18, 1994. Rabin's view of Gaza was unambiguous: "I want Gaza to sink into the sea," he told a delegation from the Washington Institute for Near East Policy in Jerusalem on September 2, 1992. Israelis stress that he did not mean the remark literally but simply saw Gaza as strategically unimportant and even a liability. Rabin quickly added that since Gaza will not disappear, Israel must deal with it.

[5] Shimon Peres, *The New Middle East* (New York: Henry Holt, 1993), p. 23.

[6] In 1974, domestic pressure forced newly elected Israeli Prime Minister Yitzhak Rabin to reject Secretary of State Henry Kissinger's proposal that Israel cede the Jericho area to Jordan in the context of post–Yom Kippur War disengagement agreements between Israel and Egypt and Syria. In a July 29, 1994, interview in *Yediot Aharanot*, Israeli statesman Abba Eban blamed Jordan's loss of its claim to the West Bank at the Arab League conference in Rabat on Rabin's refusal to yield Jericho.

According to an interview with Allon (Israel's foreign minister at the time of the Jericho Plan) published posthumously in *Davar* on August 30, 1994, Jordan's insistence on delaying the plan—which it had already accepted—caused it to fail. "They thought that a majority at the Rabat conference would support them as the Palestinian representative and guardians of the administered territories, and therefore they thought it would be easier to attend the conference without the

### "Bringing Arafat to Gaza"

Peres was not entirely surprised when the PLO rejected his "Gaza Plus" proposal in November 1992. Although the offer was intended in part to divide the PLO from the local Palestinians, the foreign minister suspected that Arafat would not accept responsibility for Gaza unless he were also allowed to head the Gazan political authority.[7] This view was confirmed by reports from Israeli participants in the third AAAS meeting, which took place on March 26-27, 1993, in Rome.[8]

So, for the third time in six months, Peres used a third party to circumvent Rabin and try to jumpstart stalled talks. Without the prime minister's authorization, he asked veteran Egyptian Ambassador to Israel Mohammed Bassiouny to test the idea of offering territorial (as opposed to merely functional) jurisdiction over both Gaza and Jericho directly to Arafat and the PLO. Bassiouny discussed the idea with Egyptian President Hosni Mubarak, who in turn raised it with Arafat.[9]

---

burden of a compromise with Israel. Only after receiving the mandate of the Arab League could they go straight to concrete negotiations" on Jericho.

[7] In an interview on December 31, 1993, Peres said he met with Rabin shortly after Labor's election in June 1992 and suggested that Israel hand Gaza over to Arafat, but that the prime minister demurred.

[8] During that session, Nizar Amar told his Israeli counterparts that Arafat was no longer seeking behind-the-scenes control and that, rather than have local Palestinians in charge, he wanted to administer self-government personally. During the last AAAS session June 17-19 in Rome, Amar told the Israelis that their focus on security would be meaningless if Arafat were not included in the deal. Israel cannot get rid of Arafat, he said, unaware that Israeli officials were already meeting with members of the PLO in Oslo. In response to questions from the Israelis, Amar dismissed reports of secret talks in Oslo as false.

[9] Peres had long viewed Egypt as the main conduit for obtaining the views of the PLO, particularly because of the 1989-90 U.S. attempt to broker the "Cairo dialogue" between the Likud-Labor national unity government and pro-PLO Palestinians. While the Knesset's ban on PLO contacts was in effect, Cairo gladly filled this role, proud of its close contacts with both sides. Veteran Egyptian national security adviser Osama el-Baz, a champion of the Palestinian cause, served as the point man throughout. Peres had an additional reasons for using the Egyptians to convey his offer to the organization. At the second AAAS meeting in London on January 29—just a week after the first Oslo session—Nizar Amar cited Arafat as saying that Israel should use Egypt as a conduit for any future diplomatic initiatives.

Though the advent of the Oslo channel ended the Egyptians' virtually exclusive role in linking Israel to the PLO, their importance to the Oslo track should not be underestimated. El-Baz helped Abu Mazen draft Palestinian replies to Israeli proposals at Oslo—a delicate role for the Egyptian, who was also in charge of contacts with Syria. Despite numerous conversations with

Using the Egyptians to forward the proposal became even more significant when Rabin scheduled a summit meeting with Mubarak in Ismailiya on April 14. Two days before the summit, Arafat informed Mubarak that he had accepted Peres' unauthorized proposal, although the map he put forward delineated PLO control over the bridges linking Jordan to the West Bank, the Rafah crossing point linking Gaza to Egypt, and an "extraterritorial" road across Israel's Negev desert to link Gaza to the West Bank. In so doing, Arafat reversed his rejection of the "Gaza Plus" proposal five months earlier, apparently because the new offer allowed him to return to Palestine and thus implied Israeli recognition of the PLO.

At the Ismailiya meeting, Mubarak adviser Osama el-Baz showed a surprised Rabin the document indicating Arafat's readiness to assume control of Gaza as part of a package deal that would include Jericho and control of key arteries. Since Peres had not informed Rabin about his proposal, it was the first time—at least in diplomatic discourse—that Rabin had heard of the "Gaza-Jericho" idea.[10]

According to several sources, Rabin was both intrigued and depressed by the PLO document. On the one hand, it was the first sign that Arafat was in fact willing to take control of Gaza. The price for removing that thorn from Israel's side, however, was the loss of Jericho under terms Rabin considered unacceptable. He saw Palestinian control over the two key bridges as a dangerous security risk because it would prevent Israel from controlling the flow of Palestinians and weapons into the territories.

Peres recalled that Rabin was furious and "jumped to high heaven" when he heard the details of Arafat's demands.[11] Senior Israeli officials say Peres sought to calm him by claiming that this was merely the basis for further negotiations; that if Rabin agreed to Arafat's control over Gaza and Jericho, Peres could convince the PLO to drop its other demands; and that, as prime minister and ultimate decision maker, he could reverse the whole process. "In meetings with Rabin, Shimon would minimize the importance

---

Syrian President Hafez Assad, el-Baz apparently never revealed the existence of the Oslo backchannel.

[10] Peres claims he broached the idea of ceding Jericho (minus the bridges) to the PLO in one of his early meetings with Rabin; see *Battling for Peace*, p. 331. Rabin had no idea, however, that Peres had raised the idea with the Egyptians or through them to the PLO.

[11] Interview with Peres, August 18, 1994.

of the whole gambit," said a senior Peres aide. "He wouldn't say, 'We're doing something revolutionary,' he'd say, 'Let's try this. If it doesn't work, it doesn't work. But why not try?' "

According to Peres, it took months of conversations to convince Rabin of the need to reach a deal with the PLO, and it was only in "late June or early July," after testing the *bona fides* of PLO negotiators, that the prime minister finally agreed.[12] Rabin insisted on excluding Jericho from the negotiations, however, despite Peres' contention that Arafat could probably be convinced to drop his demand for control of the bridges, and that ceding Jericho might divert Palestinian attention from Jerusalem—a mistaken assumption. He finally agreed in mid-July to include Jericho apparently only after he became convinced that the PLO felt that obtaining a foothold in the West Bank was vital for the accord, and then only if the Palestinians dropped their insistence on control of the bridges and an extraterritorial road linking Gaza and Jericho.

### Disillusionment with the Washington Track

The Washington peace talks reconvened in April after the United States brokered a series of deals in which Israel offered the immediate repatriation of some Hamas deportees and the return of the rest by the end of the year. Nonetheless, Rabin remained pessimistic about the talks. He told his negotiators before their departure to Washington that he saw no potential for movement on the Palestinian track because Arafat would not allow the Palestinian delegation to make progress as long as he was excluded from the process.

A critical element in Rabin's decision to pursue the Oslo track seriously was the fact that Husseini showed no inclination to make new proposals when the Washington talks resumed; half the time the talks were in session, Husseini was in Tunis at Arafat's behest. According to Rabin confidant and then Health Minister Haim Ramon, this was the pivotal moment for the

---

[12] Interview with Peres, December 31, 1993. Rabin was concerned that the Oslo channel was not presenting him with a full picture of the PLO's position, since Ismailiya was the first time he heard of Arafat's demand for Jericho and an artery connecting it to Gaza. This led Rabin, apparently still unaware of Peres' behind-the-scenes role, to devise a series of tests for Palestinian negotiators in Oslo to ascertain whether they were acting under the authority of the PLO leadership.

premier. "Rabin became convinced in April and May that we needed to talk to the PLO after Faisal [Husseini] did not rise to the occasion and be the leader that people said he was," Ramon said. "His sitting out part of the round in Tunis symbolized the fact that the people in the territories were subordinate to Tunis."[13]

Rabin's analysis was essentially correct: Arafat had instructed the Palestinian delegation to do just enough to sustain the Washington talks without moving them forward. As a result, progress was often measured procedurally rather than substantively. One Israeli delegate to Washington said they considered it "progress when the Palestinians agreed to hold a committee session with us, even though virtually no substantive changes were made." At a symposium at Bir Zeit University in Ramallah in June 1993, Palestinian delegate Saeb Erakat reportedly said that Palestinian strategy was to block progress in Washington in order to prompt Rabin to deal directly with Arafat.

PLO strategy was not the sole reason for the lack of progress in Washington, however. Though several of the Israeli delegates to Washington later grumbled that they could have reached a similar deal as the negotiators in Oslo had they had been allowed to offer the same concessions, another delegate candidly observed that the dynamics of the two negotiations were very different. "Many if not all of the Palestinian delegates [to Washington] had either been deported or jailed" by Israel in the past, he noted. "The PLO people sitting in Tunis did not have the trauma of someone such as [chief Palestinian delegate] Haider Abdul-Shafi, whom we deported in 1967. Every day he would bring up Jewish settlements and human rights. Those talks hardly moved."

One factor that contributed to the relative success of the Oslo process was an agreement by both sides to avoid delving into polemics and historical grievances that would have paralyzed the talks. This allowed negotiators to focus on creating a blueprint for the future. Similarly, there is no evidence that external events such as the Hamas deportations, the closure of the territories after a wave of stabbings, or Israel's bombardment of southern Lebanon had any impact on the Oslo process.

In early April 1993, Peres aide Avi Gil took home two thick notebooks containing transcripts of the Washington talks held since the Rabin government took over negotiations the previous

---

[13] Interview with Ramon, November 15, 1993.

August. Gil's reading led him to the conclusion that the two sides had been talking in circles up until the suspension of talks in December. Senior U.S. officials privately bemoaned "the politics of the weak," in which Palestinian negotiators from the occupied territories said they had no authority to compromise because they were not elected officials. There had been so little progress, commented Gil only half-jokingly, that it would be impossible to put an undated version of the transcripts in chronological order.

Although they had informally agreed at the first session in August 1992 to hold elections in the territories in April, the two sides had not resolved the main issues: the nature of self-rule, security arrangements, jurisdiction, and authority over settlements. Moreover, the Palestinians would not agree to an interim accord unless it guaranteed the eventual establishment of an independent state. That was not a price Rabin was willing to pay, a view enthusiastically shared by Rubinstein, a holdover from the Shamir government. Both wanted to "keep options open" in the interim period by not agreeing to anything that would prejudice final status talks. This meant defining Palestinian jurisdiction in functional rather than territorial terms. As a result, Palestinians complained that the Rabin government's positions were essentially the same as those of Shamir's.[14]

At least one member of Israel's delegation to Washington disagreed with this approach. When Eitan Bentsur, deputy director-general of the Foreign Ministry and Rubinstein's deputy on the negotiating team, returned to Israel in October 1992, Peres asked for his personal assessment of the talks. Reading from a handwritten memo, Bentsur said the Palestinian delegation was "divided," making "the most extreme position" the lowest common denominator and progress therefore unlikely.

Under the heading of "options to consider," Bentsur told Peres that Israel should consider making "direct or indirect contact" with the PLO, hoping the organization would place its own "imprimatur" on the talks. He noted that Nabil Shaath was already an adviser to the Palestinian delegation in Washington, hinting that it would be easy to make contact should Israel choose.

---

[14] The Rabin government's definition of self-rule was in fact a modification of Shamir's functionalist view of "personal autonomy," but with an added quasi-territorial dimension that enabled the Palestinians to exercise virtually full authority within (but not beyond) municipal borders. The Palestinians dismissed this as inadequate.

This idea was apparently never pursued. Bentsur later said he did not reiterate the suggestion in consultations with the Israeli delegation because he believed Rubinstein would veto the idea before it reached Rabin's desk.[15]

Beilin, Gil, and Foreign Ministry Director-General Uri Savir shared Bentsur's frustration. "Israel is neither speaking to the right people nor speaking about the right things" in Washington, Gil told his boss. "The Labor party does not believe in 'keeping all options open'" until final status talks by pretending that the Palestinian delegation is independent of the PLO and insisting on discussing only functional autonomy. "Rather, it believes in territorial compromise. So why is it afraid of putting forward new positions in peace talks? Does anybody believe, for example, that we would stake a claim to Gaza in final status talks? The Washington talks are a waste of time."

Peres and his aides were not the only ones who thought the Washington talks were going nowhere. In March 1993, military intelligence chief Major General Uri Saguy reportedly told a closed session of the Conference of Presidents of Major American Jewish Organizations that attempts to promote an independent Palestinian authority within the territories had failed. More important, Rabin gave a similar assessment to Christopher during a visit to Washington that same month. U.S. aides listened carefully to Rabin's analysis of regional trends because they sensed it was a direct window on his state of mind.

In remarks that surprised American officials, Rabin admitted that only Arafat could make a deal for the Palestinians because the Palestinians living in the territories were not willing to defy him. Ross, who at the time was an adviser on the peace process, seized on Rabin's admission. Asked under what conditions he would talk to Arafat, Rabin's dismissive reply—that there was no way he could talk to Arafat—did not match the conclusions of his own analysis. Peres' people, who realized that Rabin's analysis was ahead of his operative conclusion, attributed this discrepancy to simple "inertia" and fear of public opinion.

---

[15]Interview with Bentsur, January 10, 1995.

## Testing the Oslo Channel

As skeptical as Rabin was of the potential for success in the Washington talks, he was also not convinced of the viability of the Oslo track either and in any event did not want it to become the only venue for negotiations. To keep his options open, Rabin wanted to use Oslo as it was originally conceived: to broker compromises on issues that were obstructing the official non-PLO channel in Washington.

After learning of Arafat's acceptance of the Gaza-Jericho proposal through Mubarak, however, Rabin became suspicious of the PLO negotiators in Oslo, who had never raised the Jericho option. Before proceeding any further with the Oslo negotiations, he decided to test Abu Alaa's authority.

He instructed his negotiators to inform their PLO counterparts that continuation of the Oslo channel would be contingent upon resumption of the Washington talks, the return of Husseini (whom Arafat had "benched" shortly after the Israelis finally consented to his inclusion), an end to verbal dueling in the multilateral talks, and the removal from one of the plenary meetings of PNC member Yusef Sayigh, whose presence had caused Israel to boycott the talks. Arafat complied with the Israeli ultimatum.[16]

The Palestinian negotiators made other concessions to demonstrate the utility of the Oslo channel. At the end of fourth round of talks held from April 30-May 1, Abu Alaa informed Hirschfeld that the PLO had agreed to exclude Jerusalem from interim self-rule, although there was a dispute over whether he would put it in writing.[17] The PLO apparently also agreed to finesse the issue of whether Palestinian residents of East Jerusalem could both stand as candidates and vote in elections for the interim self-rule authority; the final text of the agreement said

---

[16] Peres, *Battling for Peace*, p. 284. Israel did not want public contact with PNC members, whom it viewed as synonymous with PLO officials, and indeed Sayigh did not attend the next plenary session in May. But Arafat's acquiesence to Israeli conditions caused friction among the Palestinians. Unaware of the Oslo track, Husseini and others did not understand why he ordered them to resume the Washington talks. Relations between Arafat and his Washington negotiators came to a boil at an August meeting in Tunis, when Palestinian delegates challenged Arafat's tactics and threatened to resign before finally backing down.

[17] Interview with Hirschfeld, December 1, 1993. In an interview on June 20, 1994, Singer said that "keeping Jerusalem out was not put in writing, but Hirschfeld said he received a verbal promise from Abu Alaa."

ambiguously that Palestinians from Jerusalem could "participate" in elections.[18]

The concession on Jerusalem carried a price for Israel, however, as the PLO began to demand that it was time for the Israeli negotiators to demonstrate their *bona fides*. According to Larsen, Abu Alaa had spoken of his "ministerial rank" within the PLO at the very first session in January, intimating that his interlocutors should be of equal status. During the third round of Oslo meetings from March 20-21, Larsen sought to convey Hirschfeld's authority to Abu Alaa by saying, "I can confirm that Yair is working with the authorization of the political echelon in Israel."[19] But having agreed to resume the Washington talks, Arafat wanted to be sure that Israel would not use the backchannel merely to extract concessions it could not obtain in Washington. In early May, Abu Alaa told Larsen that the Oslo talks would end unless Israel upgraded the negotiations to an official level.[20]

---

[18] Even as Abu Alaa was conceding the issue in Oslo, however, Arafat was instructing the Palestinian delegation in Washington to insist that East Jerusalem be included as an integral part of any interim agreement. This diplomatic masterstroke—taking contradictory positions in different venues—achieved two objectives simultaneously. Raising the issue of Jerusalem in Washington alarmed the Israeli public and brought those talks to a screeching halt, providing the PLO with breathing time to negotiate in Oslo.

[19] Interview with Hirschfeld, June 20, 1994.

[20] Interview with Larsen, November 23, 1993. He had traveled to Israel a few weeks earlier to confirm that Beilin stood behind the talks, but Abu Alaa was not satisfied by these assurances and insisted on official negotiations. Hirschfeld, however, denies that Abu Alaa issued a threat.

# III

## Upgrading the Oslo Talks

On May 13, Rabin and Peres met to discuss upgrading the Oslo talks. Although Israeli negotiators felt the PLO had demonstrated some goodwill and both sides believed they were near an agreement, Israel's decision to raise the level of its participation in the talks was motivated primarily by the PLO threat to terminate the Oslo backchannel. Peres offered to lead the Israeli delegation in Oslo, but Rabin rejected the idea, saying that such a move would raise the level of the talks too quickly.

He preferred to send a bureaucrat but agreed to let Peres name the envoy, a decision that suggests that, though Rabin had become more actively involved in the Oslo talks, he still wanted to maintain some distance from them. He approved the choice of Savir, who had served as government spokesman during Peres' 1984 stint as prime minister and whose closeness to Peres had resulted in his appointment at age forty-one as the youngest-ever director-general of the Foreign Ministry.

Upgrading the talks had significance beyond procedural wrangling and proved to be a pivotal turning point. It transformed the Oslo track from academic, exploratory discussions to genuine, official negotiations. To Abu Alaa, it was an unmistakable sign that Rabin and not just Peres stood behind the Oslo channel.[1] In effect, the secret Oslo backchannel became the main channel for Israeli-Palestinian negotiations.

The change also gave the PLO significant tactical leverage, in that they could threaten to disclose the negotiations publicly. Even

---

[1] Interview with Abu Alaa, January 5, 1994.

if the talks later collapsed, Israel would no longer be able to dismiss the PLO as a terrorist organization beyond the pale of civilized discourse and deserving to be ostracized by the world community. Thus official negotiations made an Israeli decision to publicly recognize the PLO more a matter of "when" than "if."

### Recognizing "Red Lines"

PLO officials believed that upgrading the talks meant essentially finalizing the March 21 Sarpsborg III DOP. Rabin's instructions to Savir (relayed by Peres), however, were far less ambitious. Savir received no mandate to negotiate a deal at Oslo but was told merely to recommend whether Israel should launch into detailed negotiations. He was to keep Jerusalem outside the interim accord, temporarily set aside Jericho, and ensure Israel's right to veto the use of arbitration in the case of an irreconcilable dispute. In addition, the prime minister insisted on maintaining the Washington talks and total secrecy about Oslo.

Savir and Abu Alaa held thirteen hours of talks during that weekend. Abu Alaa viewed the participation of a senior Israeli official as a sign that Rabin himself was involved in Oslo, since it would have been too risky for Peres to make such a move on his own. He told Savir that this finally convinced him that Israel was serious about reaching an agreement. He stressed that an Israeli-Palestinian breakthrough would usher in a new era of cooperation between the two sides and throughout the Middle East. Though he conceded that there would be divisions within the PLO over accepting a deal with Israel, Arafat and Abu Mazen could be counted upon to deliver.

Savir said an agreement would be possible if certain changes were made in the Sarpsborg DOP but stressed that Oslo could not serve as a replacement for the continuation of Washington talks. Both men understood that any deal they reached in Oslo would be presented to the negotiators in Washington as an American proposal. For Abu Alaa, this meant that it would be the so-called "inside" Palestinians (those residing in the occupied territories) and not the PLO who would sign the deal with Israel.

At this point, mutual recognition was not being considered. Savir and Abu Alaa believed that the biggest obstacle to a peace deal would be the shock such an announcement would create among the Israeli and Palestinian people, who had not been prepared for such a bold move. Abu Alaa bluntly pointed out the need for a public relations plan to sell peace to both populations.

The personal chemistry between the two men was immediately apparent. Savir was impressed with Abu Alaa's focus on economic interdependence with Israel, while Abu Alaa noted that Savir spoke privately of the Israeli occupation of the West Bank as running counter to human rights. Second, and more significantly, the two men cut quickly to the heart of the matter and recognized each other's bottom lines.

"The Palestinians needed to know that autonomy could lead to a state, while we needed to know it would bring security," recalled Savir in a subsequent joint interview with Abu Alaa. "Once the 'red lines' were understood, everything else could be negotiated. But if they were not understood, we could have negotiated for years without results."[2] In a private interview, Abu Alaa went further, indicating that the Palestinians viewed the Oslo accord as leading inexorably to statehood and wanted the Israelis to accept the notion of a Palestinian state as an eventuality rather than a distinct possibility. "We needed to know the Israeli view of whether the interim agreement [would determine the scope of] final status," he said. "This was the most key point."[3]

Hirschfeld seems to take a middle position between Abu Alaa and Savir. "In private conversations, we told the Palestinians in Oslo that if there is security, stability, and economic cooperation, then the interests of the two parties will be to go beyond an interim agreement," he said.[4] Another senior Israeli official said a decision was made to break with past policy by offering concessions that enabled the Palestinians to establish many of the elements of sovereignty.

"We never guaranteed the PLO a state," he said. "But we told them, 'If you want a state, you begin by establishing institutions that are consistent with that principle, such as control of land, police, and administration, not to mention linking [PLO headquarters in] Tunis and the territories.' " These kinds of Israeli statements undoubtedly led the Palestinians to believe that compliance with the interim agreement would result inevitably in Palestinian statehood.

---

[2] Joint interview with Savir and Abu Alaa, January 5, 1994.

[3] Interview with Abu Alaa, January 5, 1994.

[4] Interview with Hirschfeld, June 20, 1994.

With their "red lines" in place, Savir and Abu Alaa were able to reach agreement on many of the basic elements of the Oslo accord in only three weekends of negotiations. They decided to add a security annex to the DOP according to which Gaza would be demilitarized (to allay Israeli fears of the power vacuum being filled by heavy weaponry), the Palestinian police force would disarm all groups perpetrating terror against Israel (Abu Alaa apparently wanted this tied to Israeli economic gestures such as allowing 120,000 Palestinians to return to their jobs in Israel), and the Israel Defense Forces (IDF) would redeploy outside of Palestinian population centers in the West Bank as called for in the Camp David accords.

Abu Alaa agreed with Savir's request to set aside the issue of Jericho for the time being. He confided to Savir that he did not believe Israel would yield on its opposition to Arafat's demands for extraterritorial roads and control over bridges, but voiced his hope that Jericho would ultimately be part of the negotiations. In return for Palestinian concessions, Savir expressed his belief that Israel could withdraw most of its forces from Gaza in far less than the two years called for in the Sarpsborg DOP, although it could not evacuate them completely during the interim period due to the continued presence of 4,500 Israeli settlers. He also accepted Abu Alaa's proposal that the United States and Russia sign the DOP to demonstrate that the PLO was not totally reliant on Israeli goodwill in the case of disputes.

Despite their rapport and rapid progress, sharp differences remained on a range of issues. Savir rejected his request for the release of some 200 Palestinian prisoners and deportees before an upcoming Muslim holiday as an Israeli gesture to bolster PLO moderates, saying they must deal with the disease and not the symptoms of the Israeli-Palestinian conflict. Similarly, Abu Alaa countered Savir's request that the Palestinians end the uprising in the occupied territories known in Arabic as the *intifada* (literally, "shaking off") as a preliminary step in the peace process by saying that Israel would first have to recognize the PLO as the representative of the Palestinian people that is empowered to end violence.

Nonetheless, Savir returned to Jerusalem confident that Israel could reach a deal with the PLO, and he wrote an enthusiastic memo to Rabin, Peres, and Beilin claiming that the Oslo talks offered Israel a historic opportunity to reconcile with the Palestinians. Savir's confidence stemmed from his belief that the difference between the two sides could be surmounted, that Abu Alaa's ties to Arafat made him an authoritative interlocutor, and that the economic cooperation with Israel the Palestinians saw as essential for the success of their new entity would provide Israel with leverage even after it had made political concessions. Savir added an unofficial note calling for Israel to assent to mutual recognition with the PLO, arguing that recognition would lead the PLO to renounce terrorism and temper its other demands.

## Rabin Expands His Role in the Oslo Talks

In his post-Oslo memo, Savir also recommended assigning a legal expert to the talks to assist in drafting the final DOP.[5] Beilin aide Shlomo Gur, until then the only Israeli lawyer involved in Oslo, agreed that legal expertise was needed and recommended Joel Singer, an Israeli attorney working at a Washington, D.C. law firm who had served in the IDF Advocate-General's department for almost two decades. Singer's legal experience included promulgating military ordinances as legal adviser to the senior IDF officer in charge of the occupied territories, as well as work on the Israel-Egypt disengagement agreement, the Camp David accords, subsequent Palestinian autonomy negotiations with Egypt in the early 1980s, and issues connected to the Israeli occupation of the territories.

Singer had come to Beilin's attention during Israel's 1987 negotiations with Egypt over Taba, a disputed fleck of territory adjacent to Israel's southern tip at Eilat. More critically (and unbeknownst to Beilin), his military work had made him known to Rabin, who had served as defense minister for a good part of the 1980s. Rabin trusted Singer's objectivity and wanted his assessment of whether Oslo was worth pursuing. With Singer's arrival in Oslo, the prime minister became more actively involved in the negotiations and for the most part guided the Israeli negotiating team.

Contrary to the public perception that the Oslo talks were conducted exclusively by Peres, who then presented the prime minister with a *fait accompli*, Rabin in fact quickly asserted his

---

[5] Savir also sought an economic expert and proposed Freddy Zach, a top official in the Civil Administration, and bankers Yossi Chechanover and Emanuel Sharon. None was contacted, however, due perhaps to fear of press leaks.

authority as chief decision maker on Oslo. More accurately, there was a classic division of labor between the two senior statesmen, based on their respective personal temperaments. Rabin was a cautious analyst who became animated by nuts-and-bolts issues, while Peres remained a more conceptual visionary who, sources say, became detached and uninterested when the discussion turned to details. (Peres is capable of handling minutiae when necessary, however, as demonstrated by his role toward the end of the Oslo talks and during the negotiations on implementation.)

Upgrading the talks to official negotiations led to the creation of an informal "steering group" to develop Israel's negotiating strategy. Savir, Singer, Hirschfeld, and Pundik briefed and discussed strategy with Beilin, Gur, and Gil. The group formulated option papers whose conclusions Peres modified to reflect his own ideas and then took to Rabin. Though not initially considered Rabin's representative in the negotiations, Singer and Beilin joined most of "at least a dozen" meetings with Rabin and Peres to discuss the substance of the negotiations before, in between, and after the subsequent Oslo rounds.[6] Savir did not attend so as to preserve an informal "balance of power" between Rabin and Peres.

Since Israel has no American-style National Security Council—and due perhaps to his long stint as defense minister—Rabin often relied on the IDF for staff work on security issues. In the case of Oslo, however, he excluded senior IDF officers, intelligence officials, and Arab affairs experts from this inner circle (military intelligence chief Maj.-Gen. Saguy found out about Oslo through his own means).[7] Even Jacques Neriah, a veteran military intelligence officer who served as Rabin's diplomatic adviser and in-house Arabist, was apparently kept in the dark about Oslo.[8]

---

[6] Interview with Singer, June 19, 1994, and Beilin, November 25, 1993.

[7] Rabin's penchant for compartmentalizing aides is strikingly similar to the style of his Likud predecessor, Yitzhak Shamir.

[8] Neriah did play a cameo role late in the negotiations by translating a letter to Rabin from the PLO in Tunis, but he was unaware of its context. Neriah and then-Health Minister Haim Ramon were tipped off by PLO adviser Ahmed Tibi about a possible deal with the PLO involving mutual recognition, and on August 15th, just days before the Oslo deal was initialed, Ramon urged Neriah to draft a declaration of principles as the basis for a deal. In a June 14, 1994 interview, Neriah recalled that Ramon had presented his declaration of principles to Rabin, and asked that the two be permitted to pursue secret diplomacy in Tunis. Without revealing the Oslo talks, Rabin's reply was to dampen enthusiasm. "Let's wait a little," he told Ramon and Neriah and put the document away

Rabin apparently informed IDF Chief of Staff Lieutenant General Ehud Barak, a close aide believed by many to be his preferred successor, about the secret backchannel. "The prime minister showed me all the papers coming out of Oslo," Barak later recalled.[9] It remains unclear, however, how much influence Barak had on Rabin's thinking. His negative remarks to the cabinet when the issue was brought to a vote would suggest that, although Rabin may have sought Barak's advice, it was neither decisive nor adopted.

Since everyone on the steering group was deeply involved in the Oslo talks, and Rabin had no unbiased personal staff to assist him, the prime minister lacked both military advice and an independent intelligence assessment, and ended up vetting every line of the DOP himself.[10] According to Barak, Rabin made the final decision to proceed with Oslo on his own personal responsibility in order to avoid politicizing the IDF. Though he became increasingly involved in the substance of the talks, Rabin remained far from certain they would succeed, in part because he was not sure whether the Palestinians would accept Israeli terms.[11]

Singer characterized his attitude toward Oslo as a pendulum. "Sometimes you sat with him and you thought he really believed it would work, other times it seemed clear that he did not believe in it," he recalled.[12] Peres described Rabin's approach as being linked to the his temperament. "Rabin, by disposition always cautious, moved slowly and warily. He was skeptical about the Oslo talks; sometimes he wholly disbelieved in them. When asked later why he did not share the secret with any of his close aides, he replied frankly that he doubted anything would come of Oslo. Nonetheless he gave me, and the talks, a chance. And ultimately, when the final goal became attainable, he did not draw back."[13]

---

without looking at it.

[9] In an interview on December 8, 1994, Barak added that "the prime minister was waiting to see which channel would deliver results, either Oslo or Elyakim" Rubinstein in Washington, admitting that it was not much of a contest since the Israelis in Oslo had a much broader mandate.

[10] Interview with Singer, June 19, 1994.

[11] Interview with Rabin, October 4, 1993.

[12] Interview with Singer, January 10, 1995

[13] Shimon Peres, *Battling For Peace* (London: Weidenfeld & Nicolson, 1995), p. 330.

### Government Negotiators Replace Academics

Singer joined the Oslo team in early June and immediately began to criticize the draft DOP prepared in March at Sarpsborg, which he felt had been written by laymen who sorely lacked legal precision. "I thought the first draft was catastrophic," recalled Singer in typically blunt fashion. "First, I wanted to get rid of the UN trusteeship idea. It created a very bad precedent. Second, I wanted the part about Jerusalem being outside of the deal in writing, and not just a verbal promise."[14] He drafted a legal opinion for Rabin and Peres indicating that the UN trusteeship would be legally tantamount to the designation of a Palestinian state and equivalent to the process of decolonization in cases such as Namibia. Singer complained that the existing formulations and understandings constrained him and led him to draft accompanying "minutes" that sometimes sharply qualified clauses in the preliminary DOP.

"If someone who is not a doctor is performing an appendectomy and in the middle of the operation he turns it over to you, you cannot just start from scratch," he said. "You have to work around things" that have already been done.[15] Israel ultimately insisted that these minutes be signed, published, and given equal weight along with the rest of the DOP. Singer said his role was particularly dicey because the Israelis and Palestinians who had been negotiating in Oslo were both ready to sign the DOP. Abu Alaa had apparently been informed that Savir was coming to Oslo to place his imprimatur on the accord and then actually sign it. "Uri [Savir] told me that I should insist on [changing] only the really important things, since we were close to signing" the DOP.[16]

Singer's presence in Oslo disrupted the relaxed atmosphere the Norwegians had taken great pains to create. According to both Israelis and Palestinians who were present, Singer often acted like a prosecuting attorney conducting cross-examination. At his first

---

[14] Interview with Singer, June 19, 1994.

[15] Ibid.

[16] Ibid. In an interview on June 20, 1994, Hirschfeld did not dispute Singer's characterization, but described the first five rounds of discussions with PLO officials in Oslo as "pre-negotiations," implying that the participants knew there was more work to be done. Singer, he said, "likes to say that proposals put forward [in that period] were not 'fully baked.' I would say that the earlier talks created the 'dough' so the 'bread' could later rise."

Oslo appearance on June 11, several participants say he angered Abu Alaa by asking no less than 200 questions on DOP-related issues. However, Singer's explanation that Rabin had instructed him to ask these questions convinced both Abu Alaa and Arafat that Oslo was not merely a Peres plan. This was the first time that an Israeli negotiator had invoked Rabin's name and thereby confirmed that the prime minister had authorized the talks.

Moreover, both sides recognized that Singer's questions brought analytic clarity to the informal talks. Whereas Savir avoided potential diplomatic land mines, Singer headed directly for them in an attempt to resolve them. And despite his confrontational style, Singer clearly shared his colleagues' enthusiasm for pursuing a deal.[17] He took the lead in finalizing the DOP and relied on Savir to overcome impasses through private meetings with Abu Alaa. Hirschfeld and Pundik became notetakers and analysts who participated in internal Israeli strategy sessions. As far as can be determined, Abu Alaa remained the principal negotiator for the PLO, though Palestinian legal adviser Mohammed al-Kosh replaced Maher al-Kurd.

The PLO realized from the outset that any deal with Israel would turn on the issue of security. Throughout the Oslo talks, Abu Alaa told his Israeli interlocutors that Arafat was uniquely capable of ending terror against Israel, that the Palestinian police would enforce Arafat's will on the street, and even that the very entry of Arafat into Gaza would create "shock waves" among the Palestinian population and cause the public to turn against Hamas—in short, that Arafat had both the capability and will to end terror against Israel. "They kept saying all the time that Arafat could and would stop terrorism. We heard this from May 1993 to (post-Oslo) May 1994—that Arafat would make the difference."[18] The Israelis took these remarks at face value, and Rabin became fond of saying that the PLO would be able to handle Hamas because it would not be hampered by civil liberties constraints such as injunctions by the High Court of Justice.[19]

---

[17] When Singer briefed Peres on his initial talks in Oslo during a United Nations human rights conference in Vienna, participants said he told the foreign minister, "If we don't make peace with these people, we are idiots."

[18] Interview with Singer, February 20, 1995.

[19] Rabin had information to the contrary. At the March 26-27 AAAS meeting in Rome, Amar said that Arafat's agreement to a ceasefire would not apply to the *intifada* or attacks by rejectionist groups like Hamas over whom the PLO had no control. At an earlier meeting in January, Nablus academic Khalid Shkaki

Both sides communicated with their superiors during the course of negotiations—which often ran late into the night—and sometimes blamed intransigence on the part of those at home as a way of extracting concessions from the other side. After his first round of talks, Singer told Rabin he thought a deal could be reached. Upon hearing this, the prime minister authorized Singer to incorporate favorable answers from Abu Alaa in a new draft DOP, much of which was written at the Washington law firm where he was working before taking the position of Foreign Ministry legal adviser.

Singer also told Rabin emphatically that he favored negotiating mutual recognition with the PLO because it would likely be the result of the negotiations anyway, and therefore Israel should use it early on as a bargaining chip to extract concessions on issues that it deemed important. Surprisingly, Peres disagreed. Negotiating two breakthroughs simultaneously would ensure that neither was successful, he said. Instead, Peres favored using mutual recognition as Israel's ultimate trump card at the end of the negotiations in order to extract final concessions from the Palestinians.

Pundik said the Israelis discussed the new elements of the DOP with the Palestinians at the June 25-27 session and actually gave them a written draft—the first formal document produced by an official Israeli delegation and the PLO—during the next session in Gressheim, a town about sixty miles north of Oslo, on July 4. In fact, several different drafts, still on FAFO stationery, were revised during an intense forty-eight hour period during which negotiators say they essentially did not sleep.

Although it was assumed that each side would take the draft back home for the approval of their superiors, by the end of the session in early July both sides felt they had made major progress and were on the verge of an agreement, with only a few issues yet to be resolved.[20] In several areas, the Gressheim DOP superseded the Sarpsborg document. Israel formally agreed to withdraw from Jericho and Gaza (except for the bloc of settlements at the southern end of the strip) within three months after the DOP was signed, compared to the two-year period stipulated in Sarpsborg. There was no mention of trusteeship.

---

(brother of Islamic Jihad leader Fathi Shkaki) quoted Hamas leaders as vowing to continue violence against the IDF and Jewish settlers after a peace agreement.

[20] Interview with Hirschfeld, December 1, 1993.

The Palestinians maintained their insistence on full jurisdiction throughout the territories, but in the accompanying minutes (drafted by Singer to cover aspects that the Palestinians found hard to swallow in the actual DOP) they agreed to exempt settlers, settlements, Israeli visitors to the territories, and military locations from their control. These were important points for Rabin, who wanted broad language that would enable him to claim jurisdictional exemptions in final status talks for "security zones": swaths of occupied territory that would ultimately remain under Israeli control.[21]

In addition, Israel succeeded in limiting the PLO's functional jurisdiction beyond Gaza-Jericho to five areas of so-called "early empowerment": education, health, tourism, welfare, and taxation. Palestinian administration of any other civilian functions in the territories required mutual agreement, effectively providing Israel with a veto. Moreover, whereas the PLO agreed to cede control over Israelis living in or traveling through Gaza and Jericho as well as external security, Israel insisted on retaining responsibility for internal security in the Palestinian entity itself. This would remain a key area of dispute throughout the Oslo process.

At Gressheim, Savir and Singer retained Hirschfeld's commitment at Sarpsborg to redeploy IDF forces outside of Palestinian population centers in the West Bank after withdrawing from Gaza, a commitment first made in the Camp David accord. Redeployment was important to the Palestinians because it would provide a tangible sign of Israel's willingness to withdraw eventually from at least part of the West Bank, and thus allow the PLO to refute charges that the "Gaza first" proposal would ultimately amount to "Gaza only." Redeployment is also a "hot button" issue for many Israelis, because the presence of the IDF is the only thing that protects Israeli settlements in Arab-dominated and far-flung areas.

The commitment to redeploy has far more profound implications now, however, than when Begin first accepted the idea in 1978. At that time, there were only about 5,000 Jewish

---

[21] In an interview on June 19, 1994, Singer said that in subsequent meetings with Israeli officials, Rabin defined military locations as virtually the entire Jordan Valley. During the post-Oslo implementation talks concluded in May 1994, Rabin attained something that he did not reach in the negotiations in Norway: a definition of clusters of settlements as contiguous areas or "blocs" (like the Gush Katif area in Gaza), as opposed to individual "islands" of Israeli authority isolated from one another in a sea of Palestinian jurisdiction.

settlers clustered together in the occupied territories, and a redeployed IDF could have served as a buffer between them and the Palestinians without much difficulty. In an effort to pre-empt future attempts at a territorial solution (e.g., partition), successive Likud-controlled governments had encouraged some 120,000 Israelis to settle in enclaves throughout the West Bank, with the most ideological settlers deliberately establishing outposts in or near Arab population centers.

Though 70 percent of the settlers live within roughly a dozen miles of the so-called "Green Line" (Israel's pre-1967 border), including in the immediate vicinity of Jerusalem, it is virtually impossible to redeploy the IDF and still maintain the security of the more isolated settlements. However desirable partition may have been, domestic political constraints forced Rabin to defer the thorniest issues—in this case, dismantling certain settlements—until final status talks. Thus, instead of negotiating a divorce from the Palestinians, the Rabin government found itself trying to arrange some form of cohabitation. Thus, instead of retaining *full* control over *some* of the land through a partition deal, Israel accepted *partial* control over *most* of the land.

Political and security considerations also led Rabin to seek a more ambiguous commitment on redeployment. In a June 10 meeting with his top aides, he insisted that redeployment be made a "matter for Israel's sole discretion. The Declaration [of Principle] could include a requirement for 'consultation' with the Palestinians, the Prime Minister said, but not for 'agreement' with them. The detailed deployment of Israeli troops for strategic defense or for the protection of Israeli settlements and Israeli civilians would not be conditional on the other party's agreement."[22]

Singer's June DOP lacked Rabin's unilateral tone and was intentionally vague on the subject of redeployment. To bridge the gap between Camp David and the realities of the post-*intifada* West Bank, it proposed an initial IDF redeployment on the eve of Palestinian elections (without specifying a withdrawal from every population center) and linked further pullbacks to Palestinian performance on security. The language, which was incorporated in the final Oslo accord, said "further redeployments to specified locations will be gradually implemented commensurate with the

---

[22] Peres, *Battling for Peace*, p. 62.

assumption of responsibility for public order and internal security by the Palestinian police force . . ."

The entire issue of redeployment could have been moot, however. Throughout the secret Oslo talks, senior Israeli policy makers were never certain that the interim accord would reach the second phase involving elections in the rest of the West Bank and thus the majority of the Palestinian population. "There were various hints during the Oslo process that the elections might be deferred or might not be held at all," Peres later recalled. "I did not see [elections] as necessary a condition [for making peace]. I do not believe democracy can be imposed artificially on another society, though I do believe that the Palestinians could potentially become the first truly democratic Arab society and that nothing would be a greater boon to Arab life than true democracy."[23] Peres was not the only skeptic. Two sources say that Rabin and "to some extent" Beilin did not believe that an interim redeployment would ever occur because Arafat's anti-democratic tendencies would lead him ultimately to cancel elections.[24]

At PLO insistence, the Gressheim DOP proposed that Palestinian institutions in East Jerusalem be combined into a defined area and placed under the jurisdiction of the new Palestinian entity. The apparent extraterritorial status of an enlarged Orient House compound—tantamount to ceding a small chunk of East Jerusalem to Palestinian control—constituted a sharp departure from previous Israeli policy, and was rejected by Rabin. In a departure from the Sarpsborg DOP, there was no longer any mention of allowing East Jerusalem Palestinians to be

---

[23] Ibid., p. 339. Shortly after Oslo was announced, senior Israeli officials said privately that canceling the elections would be an indirect way of effectively canceling the second phase of the Oslo accord because the DOP explicitly links redeployment to the holding of elections. They argued that a convergence of interests between Arafat and Israel could lead both sides to simply muddle through until the negotiations on final status. With the passage of time, however, this seems less likely, since the PA does not want to forgo an opportunity to expand its control in the West Bank and the Palestinian elite increasingly view elections as an important means of curbing Arafat's autocratic tendencies.

[24] In post-Oslo meetings with government officials, Barak voiced opposition to wholesale redeployment due in part to doubts that Palestinian police could control the areas in question, which include such highly volatile places as Hebron, where militant Jews and Islamic fundamentalists live uneasily side-by-side, and Ramallah, where settlers drive through the city to get to work each day. Sources who participated in meetings with Barak say he believed it would be tactically unwise to yield on redeployment during the interim period, as this would mean Israel would have fewer bargaining chips during final status talks.

elected to the self-rule council. Israel attempted to similarly abandon Sarpsborg's agreement to negotiate Jerusalem in final status talks, but the Palestinians stood firm on this hard-won concession and the Israelis eventually reaffirmed their previous commitment.

Although critics complain that the Rabin government gave away too much in the Oslo negotiations, some of Israel's concessions were practically pre-ordained. The PLO benefited from the fact that a blueprint for Palestinian self-rule already existed: the 1978 Camp David accords, which had been hammered out between Israel and Egypt with U.S. mediation as Egyptian President Anwar Sadat's price for a separate peace treaty with Israel. Though they dismissed the pact at the time as a sellout, the Palestinians used certain components of Camp David to their advantage in Oslo. After all, they argued, if Likud leader and Camp David signatory Menachem Begin could accept certain elements of the accords, certainly Israel's Labor-led government would not find them objectionable.

Thus, although the Gressheim DOP did not explicitly commit Israel to negotiate settlements and 1948 refugees in final status talks as the Sarpsborg version had (these issues were added in subsequent drafts), it did require the creation in the interim phase of a panel comprised of Israel, the Palestinians, Jordan, and Egypt to discuss the return of persons displaced by the 1967 war as called for in the Camp David accord. Israel said approximately 200,000 were displaced at the time, but the Palestinians claim that this figure has mushroomed to 800,000. (The Palestinians apparently told their Israeli counterparts that only a fraction of that number could be absorbed in the new entity given the difficult economic conditions in the occupied territories.)

# IV

## Brinkmanship

"Everyone went home smiling" from the July 5 meeting, Hirschfeld later recalled, "and then the brinkmanship began."[1] When talks resumed on July 10 at the Halvorsbole hotel outside of Oslo, the Palestinians sought no less than twenty-six revisions of the Gressheim DOP, apparently withdrawing concessions made at the end of June and early July. They wanted to insert into the DOP key parts of the Arafat document that had been presented to Rabin in Ismailiya in April—including control of the Allenby Bridge and extraterritorial roads between Gaza and Jericho (and adding an air corridor). The new draft called for the Gaza and Jericho crossing points to be "under the responsibility of the Palestinian authorities, with international supervision and in cooperation with Israel."

Although Israeli negotiators saw this as an indication that, for the first time, Arafat was concentrating on all the details of the accord, they feared that the Palestinians were returning to their opening positions and complained that the changes would effectively vitiate the DOP. Arafat's personal involvement was confirmed during that session when Abu Alaa delivered the PLO chairman's first direct message to Israeli negotiators. Sounding conciliatory, Arafat nonetheless made clear that he wanted Palestinian residents of East Jerusalem to be eligible as candidates in elections for a self-rule council. The Israelis thought this controversial issue had already been finessed by saying that they could "participate" in self-rule elections.

---

[1] Interview with Hirschfeld, December 1, 1993.

Savir threw the latest Palestinian version of the DOP back at Abu Alaa, telling him it was simply unacceptable. Everything that had been said about the Palestinians was true, he said; they never missed an opportunity to miss an opportunity. The changes created an atmosphere of crisis that permeated the negotiations for several weeks. PLO officials believed that adopting a tougher line was fair because Israel had done so when its officials took over from the academics after Sarpsborg. "We had [agreed to] a document with Hirschfeld, and then suddenly you came with a new proposal," Abu Alaa reportedly responded to Savir. "We felt the same then as you are feeling now. We have the right to do what you did to us."[2] Savir refuted this assertion, noting that there had been many hours of negotiation and compromise since Singer had presented his first draft on June 25.

The Israelis viewed the Palestinian negotiating strategy as an inversion of the standard model, wherein both sides start from maximalist positions and gradually move toward a compromise somewhere in the middle. According to Singer, the Palestinians began with a relatively centrist position and then moved *backward* as the opposing party moved toward them. "The Palestinians put forward their opening position," Singer later recalled, "but then instead of moving toward you, like in any other negotiation, they move *beyond* their opening position, so that you are almost at their opening position as negotiations move on."[3]

On July 11, a day after talks started at Halvorsbole, Norwegian Foreign Minister Holst (who had replaced Stoltenberg in April) used an official visit with Tunisian president General Zine el-Abidine Ben Ali as a cover for his real business in Tunis, a meeting with Arafat.[4] Accompanied by Larsen and Juul, who briefed him on the crisis at Halvorsbole, Holst tried to resolve the negotiating deadlock between Israel and the PLO by assuring him that Israel was committed to reaching an agreement in Oslo and by trying to resolve the logjam on the issue of the extraterritorial road and air corridor between Gaza and Jericho. Knowing that Israel would not accept an actual physical corridor, he convinced Arafat to accept "safe passage," otherwise known as "guaranteed access."

---

2   Jane Corbin, *Gaza First* (London: Bloomsbury, 1994), p. 117.

3   Interview with Singer, December 30, 1994.

4   Ben-Ali, who had Holst chauffeured to Arafat's office, was apparently aware of the Oslo channel but remained quiet.

Like the Palestinians, the Israelis sought assurances from the Norwegians about the extent of the other side's commitment to the Oslo channel.[5] They wanted to know whether Arafat was fully engaged in the details of the secret talks and committed to the negotiations' success. More critically, they were concerned that the Oslo talks had been doomed by the impasse in the previous round and wanted an authoritative view of whether the deadlock was intractable. "The Israelis asked us to come [to Jerusalem] because they were about to end the [Oslo] channel," recalled Juul.[6]

Holst dispatched Juul and Larsen to Israel on July 12 with a letter assuring Peres that the negotiations were worth pursuing. "The letter was partly substance, noting that Arafat was no longer discussing extraterritoriality," she explained. "But it was also psychological. Holst stressed his impression that Arafat was very much behind the Norway talks. He was involved in the details and dedicated to the talks' success. This made an impression on the Israelis."[7] In addition, Larsen and Juul briefed virtually every Israeli involved in Oslo about their meeting with Arafat.

At a private lunch with the Norwegians the next day at the Laromme Hotel in Jerusalem, Peres resumed discussions on the details of a deal. After insisting that they not divulge anything to the Palestinians, he told his guests that Israel would allow Arafat to come to Gaza and Jericho "as long as he does not call himself 'president'," Juul said.[8] She and Larsen returned to Tunis with a letter from Peres to Holst seeking clarification of the PLO leader's intentions. Holst passed it to Arafat, who conceded on issues of extraterritoriality, and Rabin permitted talks to continue. "I think [our assurances] helped keep the talks going," Juul said.[9]

---

[5] Egyptian presidential adviser Osama el-Baz served the same role for the PLO as they sought independent confirmation of Rabin's involvement in the backchannel. Following a meeting with Rabin and his advisers in Israel at the end of June, el-Baz requested a private session with the prime minister. Apparently unaware of el-Baz's mission, Rabin declined, citing a full schedule. According to sources, el-Baz said rather indignantly, "Mr. Prime Minister, all I want is five more minutes of your time. If you are not willing to grant it, there was no reason for you to invite me here." Rabin conceded. In their subsequent *tete-a-tete*, el-Baz asked him whether he was aware of everything going on in Oslo and committed to its success. Rabin replied in the affirmative on both counts, and el-Baz returned happily to Cairo and informed Arafat.

[6] Interview with Juul, October 8, 1994.

[7] Ibid.

[8] Ibid.

[9] Ibid.

The lunch with the Norwegians marked the first known occasion on which Peres or any other Israeli involved in Oslo confided to a third party that Israel would allow Arafat himself to return to Gaza. Although the DOP would not be officially linked to mutual recognition, it was clear by now to both Peres and Rabin that the former would not happen without the latter.

Nonetheless, most senior Israeli officials were apparently wary of how the Israeli public would react to an explicit deal with the PLO and wanted the Palestinian negotiators in Washington to sign the final deal—though they had no doubt that PLO officials would be in charge of the new Palestinian entity once mutual recognition occurred.

Rabin had reason to believe that the public would support a peace deal even if Arafat were involved. Pollster Kalman Geyer had conducted a poll for the prime minister indicating that the public was willing to support a deal with the PLO. Though he refused to say whether it was specifically intended to determine public attitudes toward a Oslo breakthrough, Geyer said that Rabin "had enough information at that time . . . [to tell him that] the public would back him up. The Israelis wanted to get out of Gaza so much, they were willing to accept Arafat as long as he agreed to end the state of war and amend the [PNC] Charter."[10]

Gil, for example, had long supported direct negotiations with the PLO, but even he was concerned that Arafat's return to Gaza could doom the deal, because the Israeli public viewed the PLO leader as the Devil incarnate. Since the Gulf War, however, many Israelis had begun to perceive Arafat as a weakened figure who feared being eclipsed by indigenous leaders such as Husseini on the one hand and Hamas on the other. Arafat considered his return to Gaza not merely the symbolic embodiment of Palestinian nationalism but vital for his personal and institutional survival. Thus, although Arafat's approval was a *sine qua non* for any deal, the symbolism of his return was a chip that Israel could use to extract substantive concessions.

Savir had cabled his superiors from Oslo saying that the Palestinians wanted a "package deal"—the DOP in exchange for mutual recognition. For tactical reasons, however, Rabin and Peres had repeatedly rejected proposals to put mutual recognition on the negotiating table. Rabin wanted the DOP to stand

---

[10] Interview with Geyer, February 27, 1995.

independently of mutual recognition, and Peres worried that by pursuing both objectives simultaneously, they would "overload the wagon" and achieve neither.[11]

Both men knew, however, that mutual recognition was essential to the PLO (and thus to reaching a deal), and they decided that negotiations on the two elements should be handled sequentially rather than simultaneously. Rabin authorized Savir to mention recognition in passing during the July 11 session and then to offer specific terms for mutual recognition during the July 25-26 meeting, but only as an off-the-record personal initiative outside his role as an official representative of the Israeli government.[12] Nonetheless, allowing an Israeli negotiator to offer Israel's terms for mutual recognition was a crucial step down Rabin's road to negotiating with the PLO. It represented his recognition that Arafat was going to be his partner.

At the July 25-26 meeting at the Halversbole Hotel, the PLO used substantive objections to the DOP as a means of forcing the issue of mutual recognition. Although Arafat had abandoned his insistence on control of an extraterritorial road after Holst's intervention, the Palestinians continued to demand almost all of their other twenty-six amendments to the DOP. The Israelis were furious and refused to discuss the revisions; Abu Alaa announced he was resigning from the talks. Both sides made farewell remarks, saying that history would judge them poorly for failing. Yet each side knew that Middle East diplomacy thrived on brinkmanship; halting talks or threatening to do so is an integral part of negotiations. Having deferred discussion of substantive areas of disagreement to the end, no final breakthrough could occur without some kind of crisis.

As Abu Alaa was leaving, Savir realized he might not get another opportunity to float the idea of recognition. In a private meeting between the two, he took out of his pocket a single sheet of paper listing seven pre-conditions for mutual recognition with the PLO. Savir told Abu Alaa he would try to obtain Rabin's approval for mutual recognition if the PLO would agree to the seven points and yield on eight areas of dispute in the DOP, for which he would try to obtain eight Israeli substantive concessions to match. It had to be a package deal—the "seven points" and

---

[11] Interview with Peres, December 31, 1993.
[12] Interview with Peres, June 19, 1994.

"eight for eight" concessions—or there could be no deal, Savir said.

The seven points were PLO recognition of Israel's right to exist in peace and security; its commitment to resolving the conflict on the basis of UN Security Council resolutions 242 and 338; repeal of the provisions of the PLO covenant calling for the destruction of Israel; renunciation of terrorism and cooperation with Israel in countering violence; ending the *intifada*; a commitment to resolve all outstanding issues with Israel peacefully; and Arafat's agreement to represent himself in meetings with Israelis in his capacity as chairman of the PLO and not as the president of Palestine. Hereafter, Israeli insiders referred to the idea of mutual recognition simply as the "seven points."[13]

### Ending the Stalemate

A series of Palestinian concessions that ended the impasse about ten days later seems to have been triggered both by Israel's willingness to put mutual recognition on the table and PLO concerns that Israel was refocusing its interest on negotiations with Syria—an impression that Israeli officials later admitted they reinforced by making positive public statements about prospects for progress in talks with Damascus.

In contrast, Israel's endgame strategy was influenced by concerns about the long-term viability of the Rabin government in the wake of a domestic political scandal involving a small but important member of the ruling coalition, the orthodox Shas party. Ultimately, both sides needed to clarify final issues through a secret exchange of letters between Arafat and Rabin—essentially a backchannel *within* the backchannel—in order to break the Oslo deadlock.

With hostilities flaring in southern Lebanon, Christopher was scheduled to visit the region in early August 1993 in an attempt to revive the Washington talks and initiate an indirect dialogue between Rabin and Syrian President Hafez Assad, on the theory

---

[13] The draft list of seven points that Savir handed to Abu Alaa omitted original text acknowledging that Arafat would head a PLO-administered Palestinian authority in the autonomous areas. Israeli officials apparently wanted to save this concession as a bargaining chip for later. It reinforces the view, however, that by July 1993 Savir knew that Arafat would be returning to Gaza.

that the negotiations between the low-level delegations in Washington were doomed without parallel contacts between senior officials.[14] Though Christopher's trip for the most part reflected his frustration at the deadlock in Israeli-Palestinian talks in Washington, U.S. and Israeli officials also saw it as an opportunity to re-ignite the stalled Oslo talks by reinforcing PLO fears of being excluded from a separate Israeli-Syrian deal.

To ensure that Arafat felt the heat, Ross suggested that Christopher return to Damascus after visiting Jerusalem, thereby creating the appearance of so-called "shuttle diplomacy" and thus of movement on the Israel-Syria track. Peres even wrote a letter to Holst that he hoped would be shared with the Palestinians, saying that if the negotiations were not completed, "the vacuum may be filled by opposing forces, or with other initiatives, including the possibility of desired progress between Israel and Syria. Secretary Christopher is at this very moment visiting our region."[15]

Arafat apparently got the message or at least realized the need to keep the United States engaged until (and prepare the local Palestinians for) the outcome of the Oslo process. In a meeting with Mubarak prior to Christopher's arrival in Cairo, he promised to have the local Palestinians who comprised the delegation to the Washington talks give the secretary of state a counterproposal to previous U.S. compromise language during a meeting in Jerusalem. Mubarak passed this information on to Christopher.

Arafat's proposal, which according to Ashrawi included a vague reference to initiating Palestinian self-rule in Gaza and Jericho but did not mention the PLO or other issues the local Palestinians felt were vital, was the final straw in a long list of grievances they had against the chairman. When Arafat refused to amend it, the local Palestinians threatened to resign. At an initial meeting with Christopher, they told him the document was not ready, putting the secretary of state in the unusual position of having to remind them of their responsibility to obey the PLO chairman, whom Washington did not officially recognize.[16]

---

[14] His trip took on new urgency just days before departure when in late July Israel began an intense bombardment of southern Lebanon known as "Operation Accountability" in response to escalating violence there and Katyusha rocket attacks on northern Israel by the Iranian-backed Hezbollah Islamic militants.

[15] Peres, *Battling for Peace*, p. 343. In the same letter, Peres writes that "the limits of maneuverability have been tested. Now the time is ripe for decisions. . . . The biggest risk of all is the inability to take risks."

[16] Hanan Ashrawi, *This Side of Peace* (New York: Simon & Schuster, 1995), p.254.

Arafat insisted that the local Palestinians transmit the proposal to Christopher, saying that they could travel to Tunis afterwards for an explanation. The delegates relented and, according to Ashrawi, had "the shortest, most somber meeting of all" with Christopher in which they handed him Arafat's authorized draft, "exchanged a few sad remarks about the cost of this document, and took our leave." Apparently neither they nor American officials understood the significance of the Tunis proposal.[17]

Efforts on the Syrian track were more than a mere negotiating tactic, however. Rabin dismissed a question from Christopher about the prospects for success in Oslo with a wave of his hand, and later gave the secretary of state a letter for Clinton asking for more U.S. involvement in the Syrian track. Singer said Rabin deliberately downplayed the viability of the Palestinian track when talking to Christopher because he did not want Washington to become involved in Oslo in case it failed.[18]

Rabin subsequently said, however, that he did not begin to believe the Oslo process might succeed until mid-August, when he was surprised by the growing list of PLO concessions. "On four or five major issues, they agreed to [things] I had doubted they would agree to," he said. "First, [keeping all of] Jerusalem under Israeli control and outside the jurisdiction of the Palestinians for the entire interim period. Second, [retaining all Israeli] settlements. . . . Third, overall Israeli responsibility for the security of Israelis and external security. Fourth, keeping all options open for the negotiations on a permanent solution."[19]

A secret exchange of letters between Rabin and Arafat also helped to break the stalemate in Oslo. Without disclosing the existence of the Oslo channel, Arafat apparently urged Israeli-Arab gynecologist and long-time confidante Ahmed Tibi to create an independent line of communication to Rabin in an attempt to revive the stalled talks. On July 17, Tibi met with his friend Ramon and urged him to ask Rabin to initiate a correspondence with the PLO in order to clarify its position on substantive peace process issues.

---

[17] Ibid., p. 255. Ashrawi, Erekat, and Husseini then flew to Tunis to submit their resignations, which Arafat refused to accept. Ashrawi said she asked him if there was another channel besides the Washington talks, and that he explained how he would build a Palestinian state from a Gaza-Jericho deal. See pp. 257-59.

[18] Interview with Singer, January 15, 1995.

[19] Interview with Rabin, October 4, 1993.

Two days later, Tibi traveled to PLO headquarters in Tunis with a letter from Rabin, returning August 4 with a letter from Arafat that he passed to Rabin via Ramon. Neither letter was addressed directly to the other party or signed by its author. According to Neriah, Rabin thought he was writing to Abu Mazen; Tibi said the PLO response was formulated by Arafat in a meeting with advisers. The clandestine correspondence marked the only known exchange between the two leaders during the Oslo process, and one that Israeli negotiators knew nothing about.

In his letter, Rabin sought to qualify the nature of Palestinian jurisdiction both functionally and geographically. He wanted Israel to retain final authority on all security issues in Gaza and Jericho and total freedom of movement for the IDF in the territories, so that it could intervene either preemptively or in retaliation as well as maintain "hot pursuit" of suspects. He opposed a clause in the DOP that gave the Palestinians unqualified jurisdiction over settlements and military locations in the territories beyond Gaza and Jericho, because it would have allowed the PLO to claim *de facto* sovereignty over the entire West Bank in final status talks.[20] Rabin also wanted to clarify the status of Jerusalem during the interim period because there had been some backsliding by the Palestinians during the July negotiations.

In his letter to Rabin, Arafat agreed to Israeli control over settlements, settlers, and Israelis traveling in the territories, but qualified Israeli jurisdiction as being responsible for "external" rather than (as Israel had insisted) "overall" or "comprehensive" security. The letter also signaled PLO willingness to exclude Jerusalem from the Palestinian self-rule area.[21] Critically, Arafat linked these favorable responses to mutual recognition between Israel and the PLO. This came as no surprise to the Israelis, who had floated the idea during the Oslo session in July. (Israeli negotiators had in fact drafted a memo in late July saying that the success of the backchannel—namely, the DOP—would require a "package deal" in which Israel accepted mutual recognition.)

Neriah, who translated the letter into Hebrew, said that although Rabin appeared to reject Arafat's response at the time, in

---

[20] To bypass the difficult issue of territorial jurisdiction in the Washington talks, American officials proposed a compromise called "early empowerment" that focused on the immediate transfer of certain noncontroversial elements of civil authority to the Palestinians in functional areas such as taxation and education.

[21] Interview with Tibi, November 22, 1993.

private conversations after the Oslo talks he described the exchange of correspondence as "the turning point" that led to the breakthrough.[22] Rabin apparently signaled Arafat in their exchange of letters that he would agree to mutual recognition as long as it was not formally linked to the DOP. Acting on Rabin's authorization, Ramon asked Tibi to seek modification of PLO demands for responsibility for "comprehensive security" and territorial control encompassing military areas. Tibi phoned Abu Mazen On August 7 from Ramon's kitchen, but the PLO would not change its position. According to Tibi, "the PLO favored flexible phrasing but would not give" in on those two issues.

At the same time, however, Rabin's apparent willingness to recognize the PLO (under certain conditions) and the "threat" (to the PLO) of progress on the Syrian track began to erode the stalemate. On the same day Tibi had phoned Abu Mazen, Israel and the PLO consented to a Larsen-Juul proposal for a "non-meeting" in Paris to finally end the impasse. To stress the unofficial nature of the meeting, the Israelis sent Hirschfeld instead of one of the official negotiators. Abu Alaa, who continued to represent the PLO, exhibited new flexibility and agreed to restart talks. "My job was to bring back to Jerusalem a new Palestinian [position] paper," Hirschfeld explained. "I saw that from the twenty-six changes they were seeking the month before, they were down to just two or three" issues relating to security and Palestinian institutions in Jerusalem.[23]

Israeli domestic politics unrelated to the peace process played a critical role in the resolution of the Oslo talks. Israel did not formally raise the idea of mutual recognition at the negotiating table until Rabin and Peres became concerned that a political scandal involving Arye Deri, the leader of the religious Shas party and Labor's junior coalition partner, threatened the long-term viability of the government and decided to hasten the Oslo process. Their sense of urgency increased further in mid-August 1993 when Israeli Attorney-General Yosef Harish called on Deri to resign his cabinet post due to a pending indictment.

Rabin and Peres feared that Deri might withdraw his party from the coalition in retribution, thereby threatening Labor's

---

[22] "I've heard him say after Oslo was over that the letter from Tunis was the turning point," Neriah recalled in a June 14, 1994 interview in Jerusalem. "But I saw his face while he read the letter, and he was not impressed."

[23] Interview with Hirschfeld, June 22, 1994.

narrow majority in the Knesset. Peres said they were extremely concerned about the Deri affair and "did not know whether the government would last."[24] Thus, domestic Israeli politics created pressure to conclude an agreement with the Palestinians as quickly as possible and proved to be the final push. "We must hurry or we may end up with a peace treaty but no government to sign it," Peres said he told Holst,

Apparently convinced that they were now in a race against the political clock, Rabin instructed his negotiators to place mutual recognition formally on the table at the next round of Oslo talks from August 13-15. As anticipated after the Paris meeting, most of the twenty-six revisions that the Palestinians had sought in the DOP disappeared. The remaining issues—the size of the Jericho area and control of Jordan-West Bank passage points—would bedevil negotiators through the eventual DOP implementation talks. Israel defined Jericho by its municipal boundaries, while the Palestinians referred to the "Jericho District," an area ten times larger than was demarcated under Jordanian rule.

To paper over the discrepancy, the two sides agreed to use the term "Jericho area" and left its precise borders to be decided upon during implementation talks. Similarly, the two sides could not agree on mechanisms for control of passage points linking Jordan and the territories (e.g., the Allenby Bridge) or Egypt and Gaza. Fearing unrestricted arms smuggling and Palestinian immigration, Israel made clear that it would not yield to the Palestinian demand to control the bridges, so the two sides agreed to "coordinate" arrangements.

The July crisis, in which the Palestinians suddenly demanded comprehensive changes in the DOP, was no less an attempt to wring last-minute concessions on self-rule from the Israelis than an opportunity to achieve mutual recognition, a long-sought PLO goal that would have a far-reaching psychological impact on both the Israeli and Palestinian publics. "Mutual recognition is more important than the DOP," Savir later explained, "because it is the center of the conflict. It turns the Israeli-Palestinian conflict from

---

[24] Interview with Peres, August 18, 1994. Without Shas, the Rabin government would have technically still had the minimum 61-vote majority needed to retain power in the 120-seat Knesset. However, this would have forced it to rely on the votes of Arab parliamentarians instead of the so-called "Zionist majority." When the Oslo accord was ultimately put to a vote in September 1993, Shas abstained, but Rabin enhanced his margin of victory due to the surprise abstentions of three members of the opposition Likud party.

an existential to a political conflict."[25] Mutual recognition was a *sine qua non* for cooperation between Israel and the PLO and had vital consequences for Arafat organizationally. For Rabin, it meant abandoning Israel's historic rejection of the PLO and concomitant efforts to separate Palestinians inside the territories from those outside.

**Endgame**

Aspects of jurisdiction, security, and Jerusalem remained sticking points to the very end, and were finally resolved in another Scandinavian capital, Stockholm, during a previously scheduled official visit by Peres. Holst flew in from Oslo on August 17 to help mediate the final issues by telephone with the PLO leadership in Tunis. So as not to divulge the true purpose of his presence to Swedish authorities, he told them he was meeting with Peres to resolve the long-standing issue of heavy water that Israel had allegedly stolen from Norway.

On the evening of August 18, Holst began a marathon seven-hour phone conversation with Arafat and Abu Alaa in Tunisia from the Swedish guesthouse where Peres was staying. The Israeli foreign minister remained in the background while Gil and Singer negotiated with the PLO via Holst, though they had to wake Peres three times during the night to consult with him on various Israeli positions.[26]

The formula upon which the two sides eventually agreed was consistent with the Rabin-Arafat letters. Rabin conceded to reduce Israel's security responsibility to control over borders (referred to as "external" security), and Arafat agreed to extend Israeli military protection to settlements, settlers, and other Israelis traveling in the self-rule areas. Israel also yielded to Palestinian demands on jurisdiction, but made clear in the "agreed minutes" attached to the DOP that jurisdiction involved only the specifically enumerated powers of transferred civilian authority and "any

---

[25] Address to Conference of Presidents of Major American Jewish Organizations, February 27, 1994.

[26] There were precarious moments during the phone conversation, such as when Peres threatened to shift Israel's peace-making efforts to the Syrian track, or when Holst—ignoring the likelihood that the line to Tunis had been tapped—read parts of the DOP over the phone, substituting the word "blurp" for "Israel."

other authorities agreed upon" later. The PLO wanted to keep the minutes secret, but Israel insisted and prevailed that they be published and given the same weight as the DOP.

Perhaps appropriately, the last major issue to be resolved was Jerusalem. Every scenario for Israeli-Palestinian negotiations had envisioned postponing the symbol-laden issue of Jerusalem until the end to prevent the talks from collapsing prematurely, and Oslo was no exception. The PLO felt that they had already made a concession by dropping their initial demand that the city be included in the self-rule area, and during the Stockholm telephone call they insisted that the draft DOP be modified to allow the Palestinian leadership to administer self-rule in Gaza and Jericho from Jerusalem.[27] The PLO's claim was bolstered by the July 5 Gressheim document, which said the Palestinian Authority would be allowed to control Palestinian institutions in Jerusalem, which would be grouped together in a special quarter.

Rabin and Peres, however, knew that Israelis would have enough trouble accepting Arafat's presence in Gaza and certainly would not tolerate having PLO headquarters located in Jerusalem, which would thus be perceived as the Palestinian capital. "If they had insisted on [maintaining a presence in] Jerusalem," said Peres, "we might not have had a government or an agreement."[28] He told Holst that the domestic situation was already precarious due to the Deri affair, and that the talks needed to be concluded as soon as possible. Israel refused to alter the status of Jerusalem and the Palestinians yielded, but they wanted something in exchange for their flexibility.

To mollify them, Peres (apparently with Rabin's authorization) agreed to issue a letter indicating that Israel would not deny the Palestinians access to Christian or Muslim holy sites in Jerusalem or close existing Palestinian institutions there, which he added were even to be "encouraged."[29] Fearful that the letter would offend Israelis and reduce public support for the accord, however, Peres insisted that the letter be written after the Knesset had

---

[27] Specifically, Article V of Annex II stated that "[t]he offices responsible for carrying out the powers and responsibilities of the Palestinian authority under this Annex II and Article VI of the Declaration of Principles will be located in the Gaza Strip and Jericho area pending the inauguration of the Council." The PLO wanted to add the phrase "or other places in the West Bank" after "Jericho area."

[28] Interview with Peres, August 18, 1994.

[29] See Appendix XIX.

approved the accord so he could tell its members that there were no secret written agreements.

When Peres finally wrote the Jerusalem letter in October, he addressed it to Holst rather than Arafat to avoid implying that the PLO chairman is the custodian of holy sites in Jerusalem, and it remained secret until Arafat divulged its existence in May 1994.[30] After the letter's revelation, Peres was excoriated less for its content than the fact that he had publicly denied that there were any secret deals with the PLO when the Oslo accords were debated in the Knesset, and then covered up the letter's existence until June 1994.[31]

The Stockholm phone call ended in the early hours of August 19 and clinched the negotiations, although minor modifications were made later that day before the DOP and accompanying minutes were initialed in a pre-dawn ceremony in Oslo on August 20. The event, videotaped for posterity by the Norwegian secret service, took place after an unrelated official dinner for Israeli diplomats at a government guesthouse known by its address, 44 Parkveirenin, where Peres was staying.

After those members of the visiting Israeli delegation who were unaware of the secret backchannel had gone to sleep, a small contingent of Palestinians filed into an ornate room and shook hands with Holst, Peres, and the other Norwegians and Israelis.[32] This was the first known meeting between Peres and a PLO official. Savir, Abu Alaa, Singer, and Asfour initialed the DOP, and then Savir, Abu Alaa, Holst, and Larsen gave speeches extolling the tremendous historical significance of the document.[33]

---

[30] Addressing a mosque in Johannesburg, Arafat divulged that he had been given a letter on Jerusalem. Two Likud MKs, Binyamin Begin and Dan Meridor, followed up on the remark and pressed Peres to release the letter, the existence of which had been denied just two weeks earlier from the Knesset podium by Police Minister Moshe Shahal.

[31] Since Orient House opened in 1991 under a Likud government, members of the opposition could not protest Rabin's commitment to maitain the status quo.

[32] Very few people were invited to witness an event that would affect millions. They included the Oslo negotiators (including Hirschfeld and Pundik), Mohammed Abu Khosh, Holst, Peres, Larsen, Juul, Heilberg, Gil, and Larsen confidante Geir Pedersen.

[33] See Appendix XV. Corbin notes that the desk used for the signing ceremony was brought in especially for the occasion and had historical significance in Norway. It was the same desk used by Christen Michelson to sign Norway's secession in 1905 after a century under Swedish rule. Aware of Israeli sensitivities, the Norwegians asked Peres if he would mind using the desk, and

Peres watched the ceremony but did not sign the DOP, since the Israeli cabinet had not yet authorized negotiations with the PLO. The ceremony lasted about an hour before adjourning for socializing. PLO officials congratulated Peres on his 70th birthday, but Israeli officials did not partake of the champagne due to the deaths of seven Israeli soldiers earlier that day in southern Lebanon. After a few hours rest, the negotiators reconvened later that day in Oslo to begin the next item of business: negotiating a mutual recognition agreement between Israel and the PLO.

## Informing the United States

Even after the DOP was initialed, Rabin mysteriously did not reveal the news to his own top aides immediately. Neriah learned of the accord while serving as a notetaker in a previously scheduled meeting between Rabin and Lester Pollack and Malcolm Hoenlein, two officials of the Conference of Presidents of Major American Jewish Organizations. "The prime minister said he had reached an accord with the PLO and that Arafat would be coming to Gaza and Jericho. I almost fell off my chair," Neriah later recalled, adding that Pollack and Hoenlein sat in stunned silence with their mouths agape.[34]

As press reports of the Oslo agreement began to leak out—the *Jerusalem Post* headline declared, "Israel and PLO Near Historic Understanding on Gaza-Jericho"—Rabin was forced to break the news to the members of the Israeli delegation that had been conducting talks with the Palestinians in Washington. This was particularly difficult in the case of delegation head Eliyakim Rubinstein, whom the prime minister had deliberately misled when confronted about rumors of a secret backchannel with the PLO. "Leave it alone, it's all multilateral," sources say Rabin had responded dismissively, implying that the talks dealt only with regional issues such as the environment.

The other key party that needed to be briefed about the Oslo DOP was the Clinton administration, particularly in view of its role in brokering the Washington talks and the need by all parties to ensure that the United States would support the new deal. After a brief stop in Israel, Peres, Holst, and their top aides flew to

he agreed.
[34] Interview with Neriah, June 14, 1994.

a naval air station in southern California on August 27, 1993 to brief Christopher and Ross, who were vacationing nearby.[35] Before getting into specifics, Peres explained to Christopher and Ross why he had not consulted with Washington about Oslo.

Sounding like a man settling old scores, Peres vented his resentment at the United States for not supporting him six years earlier after he had reached the secret London agreement with Jordan's King Hussein. Although it was Shamir who had actually blocked the agreement, Peres blamed the Americans. "I learned my lesson from the London agreement," he declared. "[Secretary of State at the time George] Shultz got cold feet at the last moment. Shamir sent [then Foreign Minister] Moshe Arens to Shultz to stop him from coming out to the region—and everything was destroyed."[36]

Afterward, the three were joined by aides. Christopher and Ross, who had already been informed about the accord by Egyptian officials, complimented Peres and Holst on its scope and resolution of thorny issues. When Ross asked pointedly whether the DOP was linked to mutual recognition, Peres insisted it was not—although the exchange of letters between Rabin and Arafat made clear that there could be no DOP without mutual recognition. Christopher wanted to know the Oslo accords' implications on U.S. policy toward the PLO.

Peres told the Americans that a letter from Arafat renouncing terrorism was forthcoming, and therefore Israel hoped the PLO Commitments Compliance Act of 1989 (known by its authors' names as the Mack-Lieberman Act) would be repealed. Christopher responded that the administration would work with congressional leaders to repeal the ban. He indicated that the support of the American Jewish community would be important, and was happy to hear that Rabin had already broken the news of the accord to Pollack and Hoenlein.[37]

---

[35] Rabin had phoned the secretary of state in advance of Peres' arrival and Christopher called him back after Peres left to make sure that the foreign minister's version corresponded with the prime minister's.

[36] Peres, *Battling for Peace*, p. 352. American officials do not recall his statement.

[37] In a working-level meeting, Ross and Singer reviewed the text of the Mack-Lieberman Act, which had been passed after the Reagan administration announced in late 1988 that it would inaugurate a political dialogue with the PLO. Ross noted that the law required the PLO not only to renounce terrorism but also "evict or otherwise discipline the individuals or groups taking acts in contravention of the Geneva commitments." Therefore, he suggested that the

Peres and Holst expressed their belief that an official signing ceremony in Washington would provide international credibility and demonstrate the U.S. commitment to the Oslo accord. Yet there could be no White House signing ceremony if PLO officials were barred from U.S. soil by an act of Congress. If the PLO fulfilled Israel's conditions for mutual recognition and each side recognized the other, Christopher said, the United States would not object to having a PLO official come to Washington to sign the accord. If mutual recognition were not concluded before the signing ceremony, Singer said, PLO officials had assured the Israelis that they would instruct Husseini to sign the Oslo accord without making any changes.

Though the world's attention would be riveted on the signing ceremony on the White House lawn a little over two weeks later, the event was hardly discussed during the meeting in California. The main topic was the role of the Washington talks in concluding the Oslo agreement. U.S. officials rejected as transparent Peres' suggestion that the accord be presented as an American proposal in order to defuse the anticipated shock to Israeli and Palestinian public opinion. Instead, Ross drafted a statement announcing that Norway had facilitated progress in talks between Israel and the Palestinians, and that negotiations would now reconvene in Washington. As news of the accord leaked in Israel, however, and a deal on mutual recognition was reached a little over a week later, the fiction of dealing with Husseini or resuming peace talks in Washington was quickly jettisoned. Israel would sign the DOP with the PLO.

At the end of the meeting with Christopher, Peres raised two issues that the Israelis believed were vital to the success of the Oslo accord. The Palestinian entity would require sufficient funding to be viable, he said, and suggested that money be raised from the Scandinavians and the Europeans; the idea of convening an international donors conference came later. Second, public support for the Oslo accord in Israel would be contingent upon a "peace dividend," Peres said, and he urged the United States to push pro-Western Arab states such as Tunisia, Oman, and even Saudi Arabia to recognize Israel and establish diplomatic relations.

---

PLO letter include a phrase that the PLO not only renounced violence but would also "discipline its violators," language that Singer readily embraced.

## Getting the Green Light

On August 30, Rabin presented the accord to his cabinet for approval. The ministers were astonished by the scope of the agreement. Rabin made clear that no amendments could be made, but he gave Rubinstein a chance to present twenty-one objections to the Oslo accord, the overriding theme of which was that Israel could no longer enter into final status talks with all options open. Rubinstein was not the only senior Israeli official in that cabinet session who had serious reservations about the agreement; Barak weighed in with his primary concern that Israel would no longer have overall security responsibility for Gaza and Jericho.

Barak's objections to the security component of the Oslo deal may have been one reason that Rabin did not seek his advice while conducting the secret negotiations. As the senior military official responsible for Israeli control over the West Bank and Gaza, Barak did not like the deleterious effect on IDF readiness that resulted from continuous police duties in the occupied territories, and he certainly did not favor their annexation. To the contrary, he advocated ceding a good chunk of the territories in an eventual political settlement. In the cabinet meeting, however, Barak warned that, despite its political advantages, the Oslo interim arrangement would force the IDF to protect settlers and other Israelis in the territories while simultaneously relinquishing jurisdiction over the Palestinians.

Barak argued that, according to the Oslo accord, the IDF would have to rely on the Palestinian police to hand over armed fugitives who might be hiding in refugee camps. Moreover, Israel's internal security service (known by its Hebrew initials as Shin Bet) would lose significant intelligence-gathering assets and the coercive leverage of administrative authority—control over a variety of permits, for example—to elicit Palestinian cooperation and compliance. Under those conditions, he complained, the IDF could not guarantee the security of the main roads through the occupied territories, much less provide military escorts to Gaza settlers driving their children to ballet or judo lessons beyond their settlements, who would quickly find themselves dependent primarily on Palestinian troops for protection.

When the topic turned to how Israel would handle a potential collapse of the Oslo agreement and the ensuing chaos, Barak warned cabinet ministers who estimated that the IDF could retake control over Gaza in a day (including some who spoke privately about using air strikes) not to disregard the effect of the international reaction to such a move. In the end, with Rabin situated to the political right of most of his own cabinet, he had little trouble wining approval for the accord. Indeed, the entire cabinet voted in favor, except for Economics Minister Shimon Shetreet of Labor and Deri of Shas, who both abstained.

The terms of the Oslo accord were also unpopular with the Palestinians who had been involved in the negotiations in Washington. By her own account, Ashrawi confronted Abu Mazen over what she considered to be the unfavorable terms of the accord, telling him sharply that it was "clear that the [Palestinians] who initialed this agreement have not lived under occupation."

"You postponed the settlement issue and Jerusalem without even getting guarantees that Israel would not continue to create facts on the ground that would preempt and prejudge the final outcome," she continued. "And what about human rights? There's a constituency at home, a people in captivity, who rights must be protected and whose suffering must be alleviated. What about all our red lines? Territorial jurisdiction and integrity are negated in substance and the transfer of authority is purely functional."

Abu Mazen's reaction revealed the PLO's priorities in the Oslo talks. "All these [things] will be negotiated," Ashrawi reports his retorting. "We got strategic political gains, particularly the fact that this agreement is with the PLO and not just a Palestinian delegation and the recognition of the Palestinians as a people with political rights. We got . . . a commitment to discuss the refugee issue and Jerusalem in [subsequent negotiations on] permanent status. We're going to discuss boundaries and that means statehood. Could you have gotten more?"

"Its not who makes the agreement, but what's in it," Ashrawi shot back. "I have no ego problems being excluded or kept in the dark, or even about being used. My main concern is about substance. I think this agreement has many potentially explosive areas and could be to our disadvantage. . . . Strategic issues are fine, but we know the Israelis and we know that they will exploit their power as occupiers to the hilt, and by the time you get to permanent status [negotiations], Israel will have permanently altered realities on the ground."[38]

---

[38] Ashrawi, *This Side of Peace*, p. 261.

It is a testament to Israel's highly personalized decision-making process that so few could make such a momentous decision for so many, essentially short-circuiting top-level security institutions—and more critically—with virtually no cabinet debate. It is ironic that, although Israel is a highly contentious society whose public is very interested in politics, Oslo demonstrated that it also gives its elite enormous discretion to make public policy. The very fact that Rabin and Peres have dominated the Labor party for twenty years and have each been involved in sensitive security positions since the 1950s demonstrates that the Israeli elite are trusted enough to change the contours of policy on such a key issue as making peace with an organization widely branded as terrorists.

Some have joked that Israel's decision-making process is just like Syria's: virtually a one-man show. In fact, Israel is a boisterous democracy, as any reading of the Israeli press demonstrates. However, perhaps due to an arcane electoral system that puts a premium on the role of the party and minimizes accountability to citizens, the Israeli public all too often does not believe it can influence individual government decisions. (Unlike Americans, Israelis believe the system can be beaten but not changed.) Instead, the public is willing to grant its leaders the benefit of the doubt as long as they are perceived to be safeguarding Israeli security. It is probably not surprising that a country that has existed for decades under siege is naturally more willing to let the elite make such choices, even in a society as contentious as Israel.

The thunderous level of political discourse in Israel creates a two-tiered debate that is apparently welcomed by the decision-making elite. While the public is engaged in partisan bickering, the upper rungs of officialdom have a much freer reign to debate policy options. Once a course of action is thrashed out within the ruling circles, the public—and even those who do not agree with the government's policy—will generally support its decision.

For example, polls taken before the Gulf War showed that a large majority of Israelis favored retaliating if Iraq fired Scud missiles at Israel. Once the government invoked its restraint policy, however, 80 percent of those polled supported non-involvement in the war. Similarly, there was virtually no public debate about whether Israel should spend approximately $2 billion to upgrade the F-15 plane. The public tends to trust the government to act wisely on security issues, unless it is proven otherwise.

As Israel matures as a democracy, one can expect a more vigorous and perhaps less intensely partisan public policy debate. Despite the leeway the elite have in Israel, trust can be squandered if officials are seen as not protecting the national security interest. If the Oslo process is widely considered to be undermining Israeli security, Rabin and Peres will be constrained from making grandiose peace process decisions with its Arab neighbors in the future.

## Pomp and Circumstance

Before the DOP could be formally signed, the details of mutual recognition needed to be resolved. Holst played a key role in working out acceptable language. Arafat balked at including an explicit call for an end to the armed struggle and the violence of the *intifada*, saying he could only control his own people, not Hamas. Moreover, the PLO wanted both sides to declare an end terrorism and violence. After Israel rejected this, the Palestinians tried to dilute their recognition letter by having it simply recall Arafat's 1988 renunciation of terrorism and violence in Stockholm. That, too, was rejected by Israel. "We wanted a one-way letter that was clear and not shrouded by other statements," Singer said.[39]

In the two weeks prior to the signing ceremony, the two sides were busier selling the DOP to their own constituencies than concluding the last piece of unfinished business, mutual recognition. Desultory talks were held but differences remained. Savir, Singer, and Abu Alaa met in Paris on September 4 and after two days of intensive negotiations they reached an agreement in which Israel won some of the seven points it had sought and compromised on others.

Arafat recognized Israel's right to exist in security (after Israeli negotiators argued that recognizing Israel's mere existence was insufficient), renounced terrorism, and assumed responsibility for preventing acts of terrorism by "all PLO elements and personnel" and "disciplin[ing] violators" of the agreement. Israel originally wanted Arafat to assume responsibility for the acts of all Palestinians, including those not affiliated with the PLO (i.e., members of Hamas), but the PLO would not agree.

---

[39] Interview with Singer, June 19, 1994.

Arafat also made a commitment to amend the provisions of the 1964 PNC charter calling for the destruction of Israel, although no timetable was specified. PNC rules require a two-thirds majority to amend the charter, and Arafat said he did not have enough support to do it immediately. He apparently told the Israelis that once he arrived in Gaza, he would try to bring in new members who would enable him to muster a majority.

On the issue of the *intifada*, Israel settled for a letter from Arafat to Holst saying that the PLO would "take part in the steps leading to the normalization of life, rejecting violence and terrorism, contributing to peace and stability, and participating actively in shaping reconstruction, economic development, and cooperation."[40] In turn, Rabin wrote a letter stating that Israel recognized the PLO as the representative of the Palestinian people. Holst flew to Tunis on September 9 to obtain Arafat's letter to Rabin, which he presented to the prime minister in Jerusalem the next morning. Rabin's reply was faxed to Arafat and later delivered in person by Holst. On September 10, President Clinton announced that the United States was resuming its own dialogue with the PLO.

With the issue of mutual recognition settled, everything was set for the formal signing of the DOP. On the lookout for a foreign policy victory, the Clinton administration wanted the ceremony to be as high-profile as possible. President Clinton himself urged both leaders to attend, phoning Rabin personally on September 9. Although officials in Jerusalem grumbled that Clinton's move forced Rabin into a corner, the prime minister was not completely opposed. According to a source who read the transcript of a phone call Clinton made to Rabin from Air Force One during a trip to Cleveland, the prime minister clearly wanted to oblige the very supportive American administration but was wary of according Arafat the status of a head of state.

The issue was resolved the next day, when Arafat, who for much of his political life had been branded in the West as a terrorist and thus barred from contact with U.S. officials, seized the opportunity to be photographed with Clinton on the White House lawn. Christopher phoned Israel to convey the news of Arafat's planned attendance and reiterated Clinton's invitation to the prime minister. Against the advice of aides who feared the

---

[40] See Appendix XIII.

event would be politically unpopular at home and elevate Arafat's international stature, Rabin complied. Though known for his battle-hardened toughness, Rabin later admitted to reporters that he had "butterflies in his stomach" about agreeing to appear with Arafat in Washington and accepting a deal with the PLO.

In classic Middle Eastern fashion, bargaining continued up until the signing ceremony itself, and actually delayed it for about fifteen minutes. Tibi notified Peres on the morning of September 13 that the PLO chairman and his entourage were "packing their bags" unless Israel agreed to last minute changes in the DOP. The main alteration they sought was to have the term "Palestinian delegation" replaced throughout the document with "PLO." Mutual recognition did not mean merely that Arafat would direct the new Palestinian entity, but that Israel recognized the PLO more broadly as the representative of the Palestinian people empowered to implement the DOP. Israel consented to the change.

Standing across from Arafat on the White House lawn, Rabin's body language seemed to communicate virtual physical pain. He twisted and turned constantly and the expression on his face— particularly when he reached out to shake Arafat's hand— remained an uncomfortable grimace throughout the ceremony. In his remarks, Rabin conveyed some of the *angst* he felt on the occasion:

> Let me say to you, the Palestinians: We are destined to live together on the same soil in the same land. We, the soldiers who have returned from the battle stained with blood; we, who have seen our relatives and friends killed before our eyes; we, who have attended their funerals and cannot look into the eyes of parents and orphans; we, who have come from a land where parents bury their children; we, who have fought against you, the Palestinians; we say to you in a loud and a clear voice— enough of blood and tears. Enough.

# V

# The Israeli Political Environment

The Oslo deal did not occur in a political vacuum. For more than a year prior to the signing ceremony on the White House lawn, important changes in Israeli politics and the thinking of the Israeli government had begun to take shape, creating an environment for making peace with the PLO. The critical elements in that evolution included Rabin's election, the strategic government decisions that led to Oslo, and the shifting relationships among key personalities.

Rabin's stunning victory in the Israeli elections in June 1992 marked the first time in fifteen years—in fact, since the previous Rabin government—that the Likud was completely excluded from power. The public perception of Rabin as a security-minded centrist won him the support of crucial "swing" voters in the middle of the Israeli political spectrum, who normally voted for Likud because its tough approach to security issues contrasted with Labor's center-left image.

The key to Rabin's return to power was Labor's drive to democratize. Having made his career in the IDF, Rabin was never attracted to party politics and distrusted politicians, who he felt do not think in rigorous, analytic terms and tend to leak the contents of sensitive meetings in order to ingratiate themselves to the press. In contrast to party rival Peres' tight grip over the Labor apparatus, Rabin lacked a genuine base within the party and instead derived his support from the broad public.

Peres had failed in four consecutive attempts to bring Labor back to power (he won a plurality in 1984 but was forced to form a so-called "national unity government" with the Likud), and his public image as a schemer had been reinforced by his role in bringing down the Likud-Labor alliance in 1990. The latter fiasco, publicly labeled by Rabin as a "stinky maneuver," led to calls to broaden Labor decision making and in 1991 the party adopted a system of internal primary elections to select the candidate for prime minister.

In February 1992, some 108,000 party members—about 65 percent of those eligible—participated in Labor's first primary. Rabin received 40 percent of the vote, and Peres 34 percent. Had Labor followed its traditional approach, Peres undoubtedly would have been selected as Labor's nominee in 1991 for the fifth time. The Labor party rank-and-file, however, more closely resembled the profile of the country at large, which was undergoing a major transition, moving away from some of its pioneering ideological moorings and becoming a more middle-class society. At forty-four, Israel had clearly reached middle age and, like Rabin, prided itself on its pragmatism.

These changes were also reflected in the Labor party's campaign themes. In the months before the election in 1992, the Bush administration threatened to withhold $10 billion in U.S.-backed loan guarantees for the absorption of Soviet Jewish immigrants unless then Prime Minister Shamir agreed to freeze the expansion of settlements in the West Bank. A deep-seated ideologue, Shamir was convinced that in the showdown with Bush, Israeli voters would rally around the candidate who chose ideology over money. He rejected American conditions and U.S.-Israeli relations sunk to their lowest ebb since the Carter administration.[1]

Rabin, however, realized that settlements were becoming increasingly unpopular with Israel's growing middle class, who were more concerned with the improvements in quality of life

---

[1] In an interview in the *Jerusalem Post* on April 17, 1992, just two months before the election, Shamir was asked if he considered himself an ideologue or merely a hard bargainer. "Without ideology, you can't achieve anything serious," he replied. "Tacticians [who lack] ideology will not achieve anything. Someone with ideology has the possibility of getting help from tacticians, but the top priority is ideology." Though he did not endorse their goals, Shamir expressed admiration for communist ideologues Lenin and Mao Zedong. "Lenin succeeded in getting events under control and directing their course as he desired," he said. "Lenin was a genius [who] can only be compared to Mao Zedong. He orchestrated everything theoretically in his brain and he acted according to his theoretical model. . . . [T]he ideals were inflated and unjustified—it's a fact where they led to. But Russia is still waiting for [another] man like this."

than the loan guarantees could provide. His campaign slogan emphasized the need to change "national priorities" by shifting resources away from settlements that he charged were costing Israel close to $1 billion annually and into improved infrastructure such as roads, schools, and better immigrant absorption.[2]

Remarkably, not once during the election did Rabin mention swapping land for peace, even though the Labor platform called explicitly for territorial compromise and Rabin himself repeatedly railed against the possibility of Israel's being turned into a binational state. Instead, he campaigned for increasing Palestinian self-rule without yielding swaths of the West Bank and insisted that security in the occupied territories would remain in Israeli hands. He also pledged the Israel would "not come down" from the Golan Heights. In perhaps one of his greatest contributions to more than a quarter century of political debate in Israel, Rabin hammered home the theme that Palestinian terror did not constitute an existential threat to the country, but rather was an issue of personal security, which would be enhanced not by *combating* the Palestinians, but by striking a deal with them.

Rabin cited the killing of Helena Rapp, a teenage girl from Bat Yam, just before the election in 1992 as proof that Likud policies were undermining the personal safety of ordinary Israelis. Israel essentially needed to separate itself from the Palestinians if it wanted to be safe, he said; autonomy would mean fewer Gazan workers in Israel and thus fewer opportunities for attacks on Israelis. This appeal was targeted specifically at the secular, middle class Israelis who lived primarily along Israel's narrow coastal heartland and were the backbone of his electoral base.

Rabin made a tacit compact with these voters: If they supported his peace polices, there would be no terror inside the Green Line. The perennial struggle with terror would be confined to the occupied territories, to which the residents of Tel Aviv would be bystanders. He would later return to the theme of separation when his peace policies came under attack after a series of terrorist incidents within Israel infuriated the public and made them skeptical of Arab intentions.[3] While making clear that the

---

[2] The idea that one of the central roles of government was to provide better social services was virtualy alien to Shamir. In his farewell speech to the Knesset on July 13, 1992, the day the Rabin government was sworn in, Shamir termed such thinking "nihilistic."

[3] In a rare televised address to the nation on January 24, 1995 (in the aftermath

ultimate goal was coexistence between Israelis and Palestinians, Rabin stressed that his immediate concern was to separate the two distinct religious, ethnic, and political entities as much as possible.

In the only pre-election debate, the television moderator asked both Rabin and Shamir whether, as prime minister, they would be willing to give up the Gaza Strip, which Israelis of nearly every political stripe regarded as an undesirable burden. Rabin indicated that he would, saying "Gaza [belongs to the] Gazans." Shamir demurred, saying Gaza was part of *Eretz Yisrael*, the land of biblical Israel, and thus could not be abandoned.

With his emphasis on social services and immigrant absorption, Rabin won nearly 75 percent of the Russian immigrant vote, while Shamir's biggest losses occurred in the middle class suburbs between Haifa and Tel Aviv.[4] As dramatic as Rabin's victory was, however, it was narrower than most observers realize. Had roughly 40,000 more people in a country of 5 million voted for Likud or parties to its right (like the Orthodox), he would have been forced into another paralyzing national unity government. Rabin avoided making the election a referendum on the idea of trading land for peace, and he did not confuse the Israeli public's willingness to probe the seriousness of potential Arab peace interlocutors with a desire to make sweeping *a priori* territorial concessions.

The combination of pragmatism and military credentials made Rabin perhaps the only Israeli leader capable of seizing the opportunity to make peace that Oslo presented. Politicians to his right (like Likud leader Benjamin Netanyahu) had the credibility but not the will to make territorial concessions and recognize the PLO; politicians to his left (like Peres) had the will but lacked the credibility. Rabin had both attributes. Just as Nixon was able to go to China and Charles De Gaulle could withdraw French troops

---

of a double suicide bombing near Netanya that claimed the lives of twenty-one Israelis, all but one of whom were young soldiers), Rabin sought to regain flagging public support by returning to the theme of separation. He declared that Israel must continue negotiating in order "to bring about a separation between Israelis and Palestinians, but not [along] the pre-1967 borders. Jerusalem must remain united forever, and the security border of Israel must be the Jordan River."

[4] Ironically, Shamir's willingness to attend the Madrid peace conference vitiated the old argument that "there is no one to talk to" among the Arabs about peace. This robbed some ideologists of their main contention to the broader public, namely that no peace process involving territorial concessions was feasible, let alone desirable.

from Algeria, Rabin had the security credentials needed to convince the Israeli public of the wisdom of the Oslo deal.

By deriving his base of support not from his party but from the public-at-large, however, Rabin was obliged to respond to public sentiments, perhaps more so than any previous Israeli prime minister. His advisers knew that regardless of the political views of individual Israelis, nothing would weaken Rabin's political support as quickly as the perception that he was soft on terrorism. Having emphasized personal security in his campaign, Rabin was obliged to take terrorism seriously. Although not a threat to the existence of the country, it imperiled something more immediate—the viability of his government.

Thus, the three important decisions Rabin made prior to Oslo—the Hamas expulsions, closure of the territories, and air strikes in Lebanon known as "Operation Accountability"—were not made with an eye toward a breakthrough with Arafat, but rather to calm a restive public following a wave of Arab violence and in so doing to ensure the political survival of a government committed to the peace process. Regardless of the efficacy of the measures themselves, Rabin's tough stance on security gave him the domestic credibility that enabled the Israeli public to accept Oslo.

Eitan Haber, the prime minister's top personal aide, speech writer, and perhaps only personal friend, coined a succinct motto for the premier: "If you want to make drastic concessions on peace, you must show the public you can take drastic measures for security."[5] Rabin declared that Israel would pursue peace as if there were no terrorism, and fight terrorism as if there were no peace process. Haber was charged with ensuring that Rabin paid attention to the domestic side of foreign policy and was not publicly perceived as veering to the left alongside Peres. Haber, who comes from a Revisionist (i.e., right-wing) Zionist family, believed that "the public voted [for] Rabin, but thinks [like] Likud."[6] Even normally dovish Meretz ministers said privately that the government could not make concessions on peace and survive domestically unless it took tough measures to ensure the personal safety of citizens.

---

5  Interview with Haber, October 19, 1993.

6  Ibid.

## The Hamas Deportations

The temporary deportation of 415 senior Hamas activists on December 17, 1992, followed the killings of eight uniformed Israeli officers in a twelve-day period, culminating in the kidnapping and murder of border patrolman Sgt. Nissim Toledano outside his home in central Israel. For nearly a year, Barak had been advocating deportations as a tool to fight terrorism (including after an attack during the Likud's tenure, only to have then Justice Minister Dan Meridor reject the idea), and he created a public storm abroad when he recommended it again in an appearance before the Knesset Foreign Affairs and Defense Committee in early January 1992.

Characterizing the idea as "food for thought" rather than an operational recommendation, Barak suggested that as many as 1,200 Palestinians be expelled for fixed periods of up to eighteen months. In a confidential memo to Rabin months later, Barak expressed his view that the adverse reaction anticipated from the international community would be mollified by explaining that the deportees would be allowed to return to the occupied territories once the terrorism subsided. If, for example, the Jabalya refugee camp in Gaza became calm, its deportees would be allowed to return.

Rubinstein warned that the deportations would prompt the Arab participants to boycott the negotiations. Rothschild anticipated that the UN would impose sanctions. He reminded Rabin that they could not predict the response of newly appointed Lebanese Prime Minister Rafik Hariri, who might even shoot the deportees and bring the world's condemnation down upon Israel. No high-level official anticipated the eventual outcome: that Hariri would simply refuse to accept the deportees and thus provide the international media with weeks of television footage of people stranded on snow-capped mountains.[7]

---

[7] Some lower-level military officers reportedly feared this would occur and one source claims that Barak received their analysis and failed to pass it along to the prime minister. Rabin later admitted that he thought Lebanon would accept the 415 as it had accepted smaller numbers of deportees in the past, and he railed against the military for poorly executing the operation, a problem exacerbated by bad weather conditions.

## The Closure of the Occupied Territories

As some analysts predicted, the Hamas deportations did not put an end to extremist violence. In March, a wave of fatal stabbings by Palestinians once again sowed panic among the Israeli public, particularly because the attacks occurred largely within the Green Line. Moreover, they appeared to be spontaneous attacks conducted by independent Islamic militants among the day laborers from the occupied territories, rather than an organized terrorist cell that could be penetrated by Israel's domestic security service.

Rabin, who had rejected repeated calls from a minority of ministers for sealing Israel's border with the occupied territories in response to past terror attacks, now decided to implement such a measure. The defense establishment was almost universally opposed to the idea, arguing that it would prevent 120,000 Palestinian day laborers from entering Israel, thus depriving the territories of needed revenue and encouraging increased extremism. To counteract this, Rabin ordered a large-scale public works program in the territories that increased Palestinian employment there from 8,000 to 40,000.

At the same time, a growing mood of gloom in Israel was exacerbated by a tabloid war among mainstream newspapers, in which the afternoon daily *Ma'ariv* sought to compete with rival *Yediot Ahronot*'s sensationalist headlines. One gory front page ran a photo of a dagger protruding from one of the victims, with the headline blaring, "Stabbed in the Back." Holding up copies of the offending newspapers, Rabin complained at a Knesset Foreign Affairs and Defense Committee meeting that the headlines were three times the size of those on the eve of the Six Day War.

Although not intended as such, the closure of the territories proved to be the Rabin government's most significant strategic decision apart from Oslo itself. It forced the Israeli public to become accustomed to the idea that it might be safer by resurrecting the Green Line—in other words, divesting itself of the territories. The separation of the two populations proved very popular in Israel. As one former Likud minister summed up the general sentiment, "The public just doesn't want to be knifed," he said. "It cares less about where the border is than the fact that it exists and the Arabs are on the other side."

Despite their traditional tough line on security, Likud officials opposed closure because the military checkpoints and Palestinian entry permits effectively resurrected the Green Line and thus the idea that the territories are somehow distinct from the rest of Israel. They were also concerned that closure would encourage the development of an independent Palestinian economy and thus less dependence on Israel. This provided Labor with a rare opportunity to employ tougher rhetoric than Likud—sometimes to the point of crudeness. "The difference between Likud and Labor," said Ramon during a Knesset speech, "is that the Likud wants the Arabs over here, and we want them over there."

No less significant was Rabin's attempt to drive a wedge between the settlers and the rest of the Israeli population by saying that "96 percent" of Israelis were happy with the closure, implying by contrast that only settlers were not. Despite the concerns of the IDF that the move would turn the territories into a pressure cooker and feed Palestinian anger and resentment, attacks on settlers did not increase. This was largely due to efforts to alleviate Palestinian unemployment in the territories and the fact that the closure made it easier for the IDF to chase Palestinian militants involved in the terrorist acts. Rabin's distinction between Israelis within the Green Line and settlers in the occupied territories would reassert itself in the future, however.

## Operation Accountability

Israel's assassination of Lebanese *sheikh* Abbas Musawi in February 1992 led to a cycle of retaliation with the Iranian-backed Hezbollah guerrilla group that escalated into a major border skirmish in July 1993. Hezbollah fired Katyusha rockets at population centers in northern Israel in retaliation for civilian casualties from IDF bombings of guerrilla installations in villages beyond Israel's self-declared security zone in southern Lebanon. If Lebanese civilians were susceptible to attack, Hezbollah warned, so were Israelis.

Rabin's initial response was to pass messages to Assad through Ross warning that Israel would take decisive action to end the rocket attacks. Syria serves as a conduit for Iranian weapons and is widely believed to acquiesce to, if not actually encourage, attacks on Israel and its allies in southern Lebanon. Assad, however, insisted to Ross and other U.S. officials that Hezbollah had the right to resist the Israeli presence in southern Lebanon in order to liberate their country.

As the Katyusha attacks continued, public pressure mounted for a massive Israeli response. Rabin turned to the military, and Barak laid out a complex plan to bomb the south and create a mass exodus of Lebanese refugees fleeing northward. The pressure of thousands of Lebanese congregating in Beirut would force Hariri and President Elias Hrawi to plead with Damascus to rein in Hezbollah. At that point, Syria would turn to the United States to broker a ceasefire.

In a single morning meeting on July 26, 1992, the cabinet approved the plan with very little debate or dissent (except from Environment Minister Yossi Sarid), and the operation played out exactly as Barak had anticipated. "The billiards ricochet shot worked just as he said," Ramon recalled.[8] Indeed, shortly after the Israeli offensive began Secretary of State Christopher traveled to the region to resolve the conflict, in much the same way as he put forward a compromise during the deportation crisis. A ceasefire was worked out within five days, and Rabin scored points with Israeli public opinion, leading several U.S. officials to say privately that the United States had "bailed out Rabin and Barak."

Under the terms of the ceasefire, Hezbollah committed itself to refrain from hitting Israeli towns on the northern border, as long as Israel did not bomb villages outside of the security zone unless it could pinpoint the exact military installation whence an attack had been launched. In general, the opposing forces in the security zone became what Barak publicly described as "boxers in a ring."[9] Israel's allies in southern Lebanon were angered by the deal, which they said legitimized Hezbollah attacks on them without triggering Israeli retaliation beyond the security zone.[10] And though Lebanese villagers had been warned that support for Hezbollah would result in IDF retaliation, in the aftermath of Operation Accountability Hezbollah could offer their supporters immunity from Israeli strikes.

---

[8] Interview with Ramon, November 15, 1993.

[9] Interview on Israel Television, August 19, 1993.

[10] A senior Defense Ministry official insisted privately that Israel could have done more to aid its south Lebanese allies by prolonging Operation Accountability for another week. "We could have improved the terms" of the agreement, one said, "but Rabin wanted to end the whole operation before Christopher was scheduled to arrive in the region a few days later."

## The Rabin-Peres Relationship

One of the more remarkable aspects of the Oslo breakthrough was the degree of symbiotic cooperation between legendary rivals Rabin and Peres. The two men had vied for the leadership of the Labor party since 1974, their personal animosity fueled over the years by dissimilar pasts, differing strategic visions of Israel's future, contrasting management styles, and sharply distinctive personalities. Once Beilin initiated the backchannel, however, their individual strengths combined to make Oslo possible.

Peres had the vision to recognize the need for and potential of the Oslo channel, and to conceptualize the agreement. He provided key elements such as "Gaza Plus" and mutual recognition to overcome impasses, but lacked the political credibility to be the principal salesman of the plan to the Israeli public. Rabin lacked Peres' grand design for Oslo, but had the intellectual honesty to recognize its potential benefits once it materialized as a viable option. He kept the process going by making critical decisions at important junctures and provided the political credibility needed for success.

After joining the Palmach in 1940, the *sabra* (native born) Rabin embarked on a military career that included serving as the commanding officer in the bloody battle of Harel in the Jerusalem corridor in 1948, head of the IDF Northern Command from 1956-59, and IDF chief of staff from 1964-68, during which he commanded Israeli forces in the Six Day War. Upon retirement from the military, Rabin served as Israel's ambassador to the United States. During that period, he formed a protégé-mentor relationship with then National Security Adviser Henry Kissinger, who added strategic and historical dimensions to Rabin's own self-taught penchant for analytical thinking. Rabin was attracted to Kissinger's concept of the balance-of-power, which focused on the propensity of states to act in their perceived national interests to promote order and stability.

The Polish-born Peres was a protégé of David Ben-Gurion and the architect of Israel's nascent military-industrial complex in the 1950s and 1960s. In 1947, he was appointed head of manpower (and shortly thereafter naval services) on the general staff of the Haganah, Israel's pre-state army and precursor to the IDF. Peres spent the 1948 War of Independence as a private in the IDF, but his requests to join a combat unit were denied on the grounds that his work for the general staff was more important. After the war, he was sent to the United States ostensibly to study, but he ended up replacing Teddy Kollek as the head of Israel's arms purchasing mission.[11] As a result, Peres lacked the military credentials that are highly regarded in a country where the army is considered the paramount national institution.

Yet Peres undoubtedly made a more important contribution to Israel's defense as a deal maker and diplomat than he could have as an infantry officer. In the 1950s, he developed Israel's first strategic relationship with a great power, France, which at that time was estranged from the Arab world due to its ongoing confrontation with Algeria. This relationship provided Israel with modern French weapons and was instrumental in the IDF's growth from a fledging independence force to a modern army. As director-general of the Defense Ministry, Peres also played a key role in the establishment of the Dimona nuclear reactor and other elements of Israel's defense.

Peres was not always considered as dovish as he is today. In his early political career, he was associated with a breakaway Labor party faction known as Rafi, whose views were more hawkish than those of the Ahdut Ha'avoda, the faction headed by Rabin mentor Allon. Peres sided with then Defense Minister Moshe Dayan, who was skeptical of Allon's idea of withdrawing from certain parts of the occupied territories and favored instead sharing control over certain governmental functions there with Jordan in an arrangement known as a "condominium." In the 1974 Rabin-Peres power struggle, Dayan (who had been forced to step down as defense minister due to Israel's lack of preparedness for the 1973 October War) backed Peres, while Allon backed Rabin. Despite Peres' devotion to maintaining and strengthening the IDF, his cosmopolitan style (in contrast to Rabin's prickly *sabra* temperament) and lack of combat experience created the perception of him as an outsider.

Neither Rabin nor Peres possessed an ideological view of the West Bank as a necessary part of Israel's biblical patrimony, and both saw themselves as intensely pragmatic. Rabin's taciturn demeanor lent itself to a more reactive and analytical form of governing, with a strong focus on detail, especially on security-related issues. Peres prides himself both on his expansiveness and sense of initiative, leading one of his aides to call him a "policy

---

[11] Matti Golan, *The Road To Peace* (New York: Warren Books, 1989), pp. 17-19.

entrepreneur" who assimilates information quickly through constant reading but does not allow details to obscure the larger picture.[12]

### Differing Strategic Visions

The differences between the two men were reinforced in the 1980s and early 1990s, particularly as their contrasting strategic visions became more pronounced. Although conceding that there are limits to the use of force to obtain political objectives, Rabin subscribed to the Kissingerian view that diplomacy not backed up by force could not produce results. Furthermore, even after the launching of Iraqi Scud missiles against Israel in the Gulf War, Rabin believed in the supreme importance of conventional military deterrence.

Peres agreed that Israel should have a strong military (backed by a non-conventional deterrent), but increasingly viewed security as the outgrowth of political understanding, with strength measured at least as much in economic terms as in military power. He emphasized the importance of regional economic and political cooperation and minimized the importance of territory in the age of missiles. In this, he saw himself in the mold of Jean Monnet, who after World War II believed in linking France and Germany in a web of economic relationships that would render another war unthinkable. Peres sought a similar solution for the Middle East.

The divergence of their views was most pronounced on the Palestinian issue. Until the *intifada*, Rabin was in no hurry to resolve the Palestinian dispute. In contrast, more than six months before the *intifada* broke out, Peres saw an opportunity to reach an agreement with Jordan that would break the impasse on the Palestinian issue. In a move that foreshadowed Oslo, then Foreign Minister Peres held secret talks and reached the so-called "London agreement" with King Hussein in April 1987. The agreement called for negotiations between Israel and a Jordanian-Palestinian delegation on the final disposition of the territories under the rubric of an international peace conference.

---

[12] A senior Peres adviser described a key difference between Peres' and Rabin's approaches to an issue: "Rabin takes the public position of the other side as being final, while Peres sees public pronouncements as an opening position to be modified in backroom negotiations."

Other aspects of Peres' behavior during the London negotiations would emerge as precursors to Oslo. For example, though he sometimes circumvented Rabin to push the Oslo process forward, Peres went even further during the London talks, notifying Prime Minister Shamir *after* he had reached a deal with King Hussein (although Peres insists he kept Shamir informed of his contacts with Jordan). He also tried to present the London agreement as an American proposal, in order to win broader support for it at home. Then, as more recently, the American secretary of state rejected the idea as a transparent ruse.

Although it is unclear whether Rabin, then serving as defense minister, knew about the London agreement in advance, he played a relatively passive role throughout Peres' negotiations with King Hussein, apparently concerned about potential Soviet influence in an international conference. Indeed, as was the case with Oslo, Rabin remained a skeptic rather than an immediate enthusiast; he refused to believe that Hussein would agree to such a conference until he saw the text of the agreement himself, after which he supported it. (Shamir ultimately quashed the plan.) Peres later claimed that the London agreement would have prevented the *intifada* and the high cost it exacted.

According to IDF statistics, some 2,000 Palestinians were killed and another 18,000 were injured by Israelis and fellow Palestinians during the *intifada*; roughly 120,000 Palestinians served time in Israeli prisons and detentions centers. By contrast, Israel suffered about 100 dead and 6,000 injured. Yet it was the *intifada* that led Rabin and Peres to agree that finding a political solution to the conflict was imperative. While serving in the national unity government with the Likud in 1989, the two developed the so-called "Shamir Plan," which called for elections in the territories as a precursor to Palestinian self-rule. Rabin saw elections as the vehicle to build an alternative Palestinian power base to the PLO leadership in Tunis.

## Rabin and Peres Cooperate on Oslo

The Oslo channel moved into high gear only after Peres became involved, particularly during the period of April-June 1993. He helped give conceptual shape to the negotiations, albeit sometimes by making controversial moves. No less significantly, he regularly held one-on-one meetings with Rabin throughout the process that are believed to have been important in convincing Rabin to move forward. In order for these meetings to occur, however, Peres had to return to Rabin's good graces. The lack of movement in the peace process, exacerbated by the surge in Hamas violence, may have pointed to the need for Rabin and Peres to work more closely together, but decades of personal enmity had created a layer of distrust between the two men that was difficult to overcome.

Peres and top aides Beilin, Savir, and Gil recognized this problem immediately after the election in 1992, and they decided that reconstructing the Rabin-Peres relationship was a *sine qua non* for ending their "internal exile" from the peace process. They knew they had to adopt a policy of restraint in order to convince prime minister that the "new" Peres was not the "indefatigable intriguant" Rabin had referred to in his memoirs fifteen years earlier. They abandoned the practice of using anonymous interviews with reporters to attack Rabin and refrained from responding to what they perceived as "provocations" by Rabin and his top aides.[13] All three had worked as Peres' spokesmen and were therefore aware of how press stories could inflame a situation.

This strategy started paying off for Peres around March 1993, when Rabin began taking him into his confidence on bilateral peace issues. (A dialogue on a range of other issues had existed prior to this, since Peres was the only other person in Rabin's cabinet who had any significant experience in international and security affairs.) Much of the content of the private Rabin-Peres meetings remains a mystery. They are believed to have been wide-ranging and more philosophical than the twelve to fifteen strategy sessions Rabin held to direct the Israeli negotiating team before and after each round in Oslo. High-level sources say that Rabin and Peres discussed how their advanced age required them to work together, as together they would either sink or swim. Peres apparently stressed that the survival of the Rabin government hinged on a breakthrough on peace, that Labor would not have a chance for reelection during their political lifetimes, and that the

---

[13] It was not always easy to ignore these slights. At one point, a top Peres aide told the foreign minister that "enough is enough" and that he must respond to attacks by Rabin supporters claiming that he was sabotaging electoral reform. Other top aides prevailed on Peres not to lose his temper and risk jeopardizing his entire "comeback"strategy.

intractable situation in Gaza could not be maintained indefinitely.[14]

To persuade Rabin to pursue the Oslo track, those close to Peres say he focused on security issues, used third-party assessments to bolster his own views, and played down the significance of controversial moves he himself had proposed. "Shimon would tell Rabin, 'I just talked to [then French President Francois] Mitterrand and Arafat told him moderate things,'" a former Peres aide said. "At the same time, Shimon may not say that the result of this down the road is a Palestinian state. Those conclusions he would leave for Rabin to make himself." A more senior Peres aide concurred. "Shimon played down the significance of talking with the PLO," he said. "Instead of talking about it as a revolutionary step, he would tell Rabin that it was something to try, and if it did not work, it did not work."

Although it is difficult to determine the actual effect of their conversations, Peres' claim that Rabin usually instinctively rejected his ideas is certainly plausible. Some ministers say Rabin involved Peres in the negotiations precisely to distance himself from the talks. Rabin ally and Agriculture Minister Yaacov Tsur recalls that when he confronted the prime minister in mid-1993 about rumored talks between Israel and the PLO, Rabin's terse response was, "I have given Peres some slack, under certain conditions."[15]

## Beilin: The True Believer

Without Rabin's support, analytical thinking, and decision making, the Oslo process would never have been significantly advanced or concluded. Without Beilin, however, Oslo would never have been attempted. Beilin was responsible for initiating Oslo; Peres subsequently lent his weight to the effort beginning in March before Rabin became deeply involved in the negotiations.

---

[14] Peres' public remarks about Gaza typically focused on demographics. In an interview in the Israeli newspaper *Davar* on April 13, 1994, he observed: "Gaza, for example, twenty years ago had 400,000 people. Now there are 800,000. In twenty years, there will be 1.6 million people. Can the Likud stop the flow of history? The flow of people? [With each passing day] there are more people in Gaza, more hate, more crowded [conditions] and more terror[ism]."

[15] Interview with Tsur, December 5, 1993. One could interpret Tsur's account as further evidence of Rabin's penchant for incremental decision making.

Beilin assisted the negotiators in formulating position papers before Rabin became involved in the talks, developed the ideas that sustained the process and percolated up to the decision-making level, and played a central role in decision making throughout the process.

Since the late 1970s, Beilin, a young journalist turned academic who wrote his Tel Aviv University dissertation on intergenerational conflict in Israel's three leading parties, believed that the PLO was the only possible partner for peace. For many years, he brought articles to that effect to Peres to try to prove that it was futile to talk to any Palestinian interlocutor who was not a member of the PLO. After the fall of the Likud-Labor government in 1990, Beilin signed the so-called "Notre Dame declaration" calling for Palestinian self-determination along with Palestinian activist Sari Nusseibeh.

Influenced by Barbara Tuchman's book *March of Folly*, Beilin believed that governments often passively slide down a road to disaster because they are blind to—or unwilling to see—the need to make tough decisions to reverse course. Undaunted by being in the minority, Beilin believed in clinging to one's views despite their unpopularity. Asked about the influence of the Tuchman book on his political thinking, Beilin replied that "people are the books they read, and I internalized that book. It was one of the most central books in my thinking. . . . Tuchman's book taught me that it is okay to go it alone. There is no wisdom in just following the crowd."[16]

Beilin's own road to Oslo was the shortest of any Israeli official because the backchannel coincided with and indeed reflected his own thinking. As one of his close associates remarked, Oslo marked a "fulfillment of ten years of [Beilin's] thinking. He always believed, even at the time of the London agreement, that the only partner [for negotiations] was the PLO. He would tell Peres at every instance why it won't work with others."

In addition to his ideological commitment to talks with the PLO Beilin added something that Peres often lacked—systematic staff work. Before and after virtually every round in Oslo, Beilin provided Peres with option papers on how to resolve impasses at the negotiating table. If Peres found the ideas acceptable, he

---

[16] Interview with Beilin, December 20, 1993.

brought them to the informal group led by Rabin. The option papers, which were usually the product of discussions with aides and the Oslo negotiators themselves, attempted to analyze the available alternatives for breaking the deadlock.

"The power of Yossi [Beilin] is to prepare the right paper at the right time," Hirschfeld later said. "He is thorough and he does his homework. He points out the problems and then he solves them."[17] Despite his boyish looks, Beilin was also a methodical political operator, having held senior government positions since 1984, when he served as an adviser to then Prime Minister Peres, and learned his way around the corridors of power. In 1986, he became co-director-general of the Foreign Ministry, and by 1988 he was deputy finance minister and attending all inner cabinet sessions in an *ex officio* capacity.

When Labor went into opposition in 1990, Beilin used Peres' control of the Labor party apparatus to ensure that the party took strong positions. Labor's November 1991 platform advocated several unprecedented and almost heretical positions, including calls to lift the ban on contacts with the PLO, enable Palestinians from East Jerusalem to serve as peace process interlocutors, and make territorial compromise on the Golan Heights the basis for peace with Syria. He was careful to nail down support for these ideas by dint of Peres' control of the party faithful, sometimes despite Rabin's wishes. His legwork ensured that they were translated into actual policy after the party won the next general election. He resumed attending inner cabinet meetings when he became deputy foreign minister in 1992. As a source close to Beilin said, "ten years ago, he would not have had the guts to pursue Oslo, but now, he feels at home in the system."

In a broader sense, Beilin saw himself as part of what he called the "third model" of Israeli politics. Neither aCincinnatus-like general who turned to politics late in life nor a party *apparatchik*, he believed academics could make the leap into politics because of their relative advantage as policy analysts. Using John F. Kennedy's "brain trust" as a paradigm, Beilin found a few like-minded colleagues serving as aides during Peres' 1984-86 stint as prime minister. (The group was nicknamed "The Blazers" due to their "yuppie" style of dress.) In the Oslo talks, his inner circle consisted of Hirschfeld, Pundik, Savir, Gur, and Gil.

---

[17] Interview with Hirschfeld, December 1, 1993.

## Rabin's Advisers

Rabin may have had misgivings about some of Beilin's ideas, but he lacked civilian advisers to advance his thinking or conceptualize a less ambitious vision. Rabin's advisers included government ministers, not policy analysts, who could not fill the vacuum because they were not as interested in the finer aspects of policy and, all too often, lacked the requisite intellectual depth. The only people Rabin could count on was the military. However, by dint of their profession, they were constrained in shaping the parameters of public debate inside the country.

Rabin did not rely completely on the military, however, as demonstrated by their exclusion from the Oslo process. He had supreme confidence in his own analytical and decision-making skills, and would often ask IDF intelligence to supply him with data bereft of their conclusions so that he could make up his own mind. Rabin's own staff focused on the elements that made his 1992 campaign successful: addressing domestic issues and maintaining his support within the party and among the public. As a result, Beilin and a few close aides dominated the intellectual side of foreign policy. One source close to Beilin later described the situation as "almost scary. We had no counterweight."

In his capacity as defense minister, Rabin sought advice on Arab-Israeli negotiations primarily from senior military officials with highly regarded analytical capabilities—Barak, his deputy Major General Amnon Shahak, and Saguy—and often relegated civilian advisers to a secondary role. Barak said that Rabin kept him informed about progress in Oslo and showed him drafts of the agreements being worked out there, but refuses to discuss the degree of consultation between him and Rabin about Oslo.[18] His negative remarks to the cabinet when the issue was brought to a vote suggest that if sought, his advice was not taken.

Barak publicly defended Rabin's exclusion of the military from Oslo, saying that "the real decision Rabin made, and I believe a justifiable one, was not to involve people in uniform at even the highest position in shaping the political decision that had to be made: whether to go into such a deal with the Palestinians or not." By excluding the military, he said, Rabin "avoided any stigma of

---

[18] Interview with Barak, December 11, 1994.

the politicization of the armed forces."[19] The IDF had provided Rabin in advance with a variety of scenarios on how to approach the political and security aspects of negotiations, Barak added, which allowed Rabin to "know exactly what we feel are the consequences and the meaning of every alternative."[20]

Peres said he believes that Rabin did not involve the military in decision making because he saw Oslo as a futile exercise.[21] A senior Peres aide agreed, but took a more nuanced view. "I think in the beginning Rabin didn't want to tell Barak and a couple others because he did not think Oslo was serious," he said, "but as things became serious, he did not consult them because he did not want them to slow him down." The generals "would have sought more time to try to nail down details, such as the level of security arrangements, control of the bridges, and the size of Jericho," said a senior Rabin aide. "Rabin did not believe that negotiations could go on too long in Oslo without leaking. He believed military people would just slow things down, and that details could be dealt with in the implementation."

This analysis is certainly plausible. Senior military officials later openly expressed their frustration with the security "holes" in the Oslo accord. Yet no evidence suggests that any of the top three generals would have opposed a PLO takeover of Gaza and Jericho. Yossi Ben-Aharon, director-general of the prime minister's bureau during the Shamir government, said that, together with the head of the Israel's domestic security service, Yaacov Peri, "there is not a Likudnik among them."[22]

Although their views on the Palestinian issue are not clear, the three senior military officials were known to favor progress on the Syrian front in order to alter the region's strategic equation. Saguy was the most pronounced advocate of a "Syria First" settlement, and began to say as early as 1990 that Israel had to make peace with Damascus. In September 1992, he told an interviewer that there was a "yearning" for peace among the Syrian people.[23] Saguy's annual intelligence assessments to the cabinet repeatedly described Damascus as serious about negotiating with Israel.

---

[19] Interview with Carson Tveit, Norwegian Television, September 11, 1994.
[20] Ibid.
[21] Interview with Peres, December 31, 1993.
[22] Interview with Ben-Aharon, November 30, 1993.
[23] *Yediot Aharonot*, September, 1992.

Shahak, for his part, told a group of foreign reporters traveling with Christopher in February 1993 that full withdrawal from the Golan would not necessarily put Israel in danger. Shahak's moderation extended to Palestinian talks as well. While serving as head of military intelligence in 1987, he also reportedly expressed the view in the Knesset Foreign Affairs and Defense committee that the PLO was the only representative of the Palestinians. He reportedly repeated this assertion during a verbal presentation of the March 1989 annual intelligence assessment to Shamir, Rabin, Peres, and Moshe Arens, who was foreign minister at the time.

Peri, who had the day-to-day responsibility for contending with Palestinian violence, was also known to favor accommodation over ideology. Though appointed by Shamir in April 1988 just after the outbreak of the *intifada*, Peri became close to Rabin, who was apparently impressed with his pragmatism, and remained so through the end of his tenure in early 1995. Around the time that Shamir led the Israeli delegation to the Madrid peace conference, Peri issued an internal directive ordering the Shin Bet to prepare for an impending new era: protecting Israeli security during Palestinian autonomy. Although there is no evidence that Rabin consulted Peri about Oslo, it seems clear that Peri supported the general thrust.

Barak, often rumored to be Rabin's preferred successor, also favored accommodation with the Arabs in return for security and peace. He has said repeatedly that Israel "must limit friction with the Arabs" in the years ahead to mitigate longer-term regional threats. Thus making peace with Israel's immediate neighbors fits into a broader regional strategy. "We have no control over whether Iran will have nonconventional nuclear capabilities in another ten years," he said. "Given this long-term uncertainty, it is not an exaggerated risk to attempt to relax the conflict in our immediate circle, including with Lebanon and Syria . . . as long as we do not waive our vital security interests."[24]

Resolving the Palestinian conflict also had regional implications. "On one hand, the Palestinians are weak," Barak said. "On the other hand, they are perceived by [Israeli] citizens to be the source of terror and day-to-day frictions, and they legitimize pan-Arab hostility toward Israel. As long as we reduce [Palestinian] terror without damaging any of Israel's vital interests

---

[24] *U.S. News and World Report*, December 26, 1994.

by smoothing relations with them, it will be more difficult to motivate hostile acts against us from Benghazi [Libya] to Teheran."[25]

The other members of the IDF General Staff favored Rabin's strategy of promoting secure and peaceful accommodation with neighboring Arabs in order to allow Israel to face future threats from Iran and Iraq. Rothschild, who had done a stint as deputy head of military intelligence, reported weekly to the cabinet on such issues as the poor economic conditions in the West Bank and Gaza. He, too, believed that negotiations with the Palestinians should be based on pragmatism rather than ideology.

Rabin's other civilian advisers—Neriah and Ambassador to the United States (and chief negotiator with Syria) Itamar Rabinovich—both favored accommodation with neighboring Arab states, but tended to focus on the Syrian track. Singer, who had caught Rabin's attention during eighteen years working in the IDF legal department, became Rabin's eyes and ears at Oslo. Singer translated the negotiating concepts with the PLO into legal language and worked closely with Rabin to ensure that the language of the DOP was agreeable to the prime minister.

Not surprisingly, the one Rabin adviser who unequivocally opposed the Oslo agreement was Rubinstein, a holdover from the Shamir government whom Rabin kept on after the election as head of Israel's delegation to the talks with the Palestinians in Washington in part to demonstrate that it was he and not Peres running the talks. Rabin ignored protests from Palestinian negotiators who charged that Rubinstein's continued presence signaled continuity with Shamir government policies. In addition, Rabin and Rubinstein agreed that Israel's guiding principle in negotiations should be to "keep options open"—in effect, that interim self-government should not preclude Israel from asserting sovereignty over the West Bank and Gaza in final status talks.

Rubinstein never recommended to Rabin that Israel seek to break the impasse in Washington by accepting PLO participation in the talks. In his view, Israel had conceded more at Oslo, including major principles such as territorial partition and probable Palestinian statehood, than even the Americans had sought when they proposed compromise language at the Washington talks in early May and late June 1993. Although

---

[25] Ibid.

senior IDF generals complained privately about not being informed about Oslo, Rubinstein resigned as chief negotiator with the Palestinians after news of the backchannel became public, although he remained chief negotiator on the Jordanian track and later became legal adviser to the Defense Ministry. For Rubinstein, the fact that all options were no longer open was worse than the personal insult of having been circumvented.

## The Israeli Decision-Making Apparatus

The Oslo process revolved around Rabin and Peres largely because Israel's decision-making process is highly personalized. There is neither an institutionalized, American-style National Security Council (NSC) staff nor a powerful "inner cabinet" forum. Israeli leaders, and Rabin in particular, eschewed an institutionalized staff. Because he also holds the defense portfolio, Rabin wields more authority than any prime minister in recent Israeli history.[26] Asked about the departure of four top aides in June 1994, Rabin commented dryly, "one more or less adviser does not change anything. I like the military way: a chain of command system."[27] Indeed, the scope of his authority is broad and the number of people who report directly to him is staggering.[28]

There are several reasons that an NSC-type staff structure has not caught on in Israel. Unlike U.S. presidents, who deal with many issues all over the globe as well as problems at home, Israeli prime ministers have traditionally focused on two areas of foreign policy, with which they have undoubtedly been dealing a good part of their lives: the Arab-Israeli conflict and U.S.-Israeli relations. As a result, they feel that their extensive personal experience in security and diplomacy vitiates the need for a professional NSC-style staff. Similarly, the members of Israel's fractious coalition government are often divided on policy questions, particularly those involving the occupied territories. In a deeper sense, technocracy is a dirty word to the older generation in Israel. There was a heavy emphasis on improvisation in the pre-

[26] Due to problems within the coalition, Rabin at one point held no less than five different portfolios during part of 1994.

[27] Interview on Israel Radio, June 13, 1994.

[28] See Appendix XX.

state era, and though Rabin and Peres are a generation younger, they retain a distrust of bureaucrats that seems to shape their antipathy toward interagency staffs and task forces of academic specialists. "There are no experts on the future, only the past," Peres is fond of saying. "Where were the Kremlinologists who predicted the fall of communism?"[29]

Since the IDF plays a dominant role in assessing national security issues, the interagency process remains relatively weak in Israel. The military surpasses other foreign policy bodies in intelligence collection capabilities, particularly since the Foreign Ministry does not have embassies in most Arab countries that could serve as an alternate source of information. In addition, the minister of defense wields great political power under Israel's coalition system, and a genuine NSC could cause considerable friction (although it might ensure that a prime minister who is not also minister of defense would retain control of security matters). And because the Arab-Israeli conflict has been the defining issue of domestic Israeli politics for the last twenty-five years, every premier has worried that a professional civilian staff would not adequately handle the political aspects of the issue.

A ministerial committee for national security consisting of the prime minister, a dozen senior ministers, and military advisers was convened every week, but other than approving military operations, it had little more actual influence than the cabinet at large. In the three major decisions made by the Rabin government during his first year—the Hamas expulsions, closure of the territories, and Operation Accountability—neither the inner cabinet nor the full cabinet exerted meaningful influence and merely approved plans submitted to them by Rabin. In the case of Oslo, both fora were kept in the dark and simply ratified an accord they had only glanced at during a brief cabinet discussion.[30]

Peace could have profound consequences for the Israeli decision-making process. Foreign policy issues would be less polarized than in the past, and the country's political spectrum

---

[29] Interview with Peres, December 30, 1993.

[30] There were two exceptions to this trend, however, both of which related to the peace process. In October 1992, the cabinet vetoed plans to stage deep-penetration bombing raids into Lebanon, fearing it could lead to a repeat of the 1982 Lebanon War, and in March 1994, the cabinet voted for a commission of inquiry into the Hebron massacre against the wishes of Rabin, who feared it could only sully the IDF's morale.

could realign along economic lines, as in the United States and Europe. As Israel establishes embassies in Arab nations, the Foreign Ministry's role in gathering information will increase, potentially shifting the bureaucratic balance of power away from the military.[31] Taken together, this would likely create a need for an interagency system coordinated by an NSC-style staff. Furthermore, the increasingly technical nature of issues will also create a more complex decision-making process. The technical nature of multilateral talks, for example, forced Israel to bring in a variety of new bureaucratic players from different ministries in order to develop its negotiating policies.

---

[31] Oslo was a rare departure from the Foreign Ministry's traditional subservient position in Israeli decision making. To protect its institutional gains and perhaps also to demonstrate that the balance of power has already begun to shift, Peres fought strenuously to prevent the deputy head of the Mossad, Ephraim Halevy, from being named Israel's first ambassador to Jordan.

# VI

## International and Regional Changes

Rabin's willingness to explore the Oslo channel derived in part from his analysis of international and regional changes resulting from the end of the Cold War and the political shifts caused by the Gulf War. Immediately upon taking office, he began to speak about a combination of short-term opportunities and long-term security considerations that made a resolution of the conflict with Israel's Arab neighbors by the end of the decade both possible and imperative. On the one hand, the end of the Cold War and the collapse of communism meant that there would no longer be a Soviet Union to bankroll radical Arab states or automatically supply them with weapons, or to provide the PLO with diplomatic support, paramilitary training in Eastern Europe, scholarships for Palestinian students, and other aid programs.[1]

On the other hand, the Gulf War drastically weakened Israel's most powerful foe, Iraq, and crippled its nascent nuclear capability; buried the myth of a united Arab political front and left the radical Arab camp in disarray; and demonstrated that the United States, Israel's patron and the world's only post-Cold War superpower, would intervene in the Middle East to protect its vital interests. Rabin's public remarks in the post-Gulf War years evinced his belief that the combination of these factors had

---

[1] The first sign of the significance of the post-Cold War shift in the Middle East came during Assad's visit to Moscow in 1987, when Mikhail Gorbachev told the Syrian leader that he should dismiss the idea of "strategic parity" with Israel and instead seek to resolve the conflict peacefully. Militant Arab states were not able to compensate for the loss of the Soviet Union with their own independent military force.

increased Israel's relative strength. Speaking at Tel Aviv University's Jaffee Center for Strategic Studies, Rabin said:

> I am convinced our deterrent capability has increased as a result of the crisis in the Gulf, if only indirectly and because the United States demonstrated its readiness to act resolutely. I am not saying that Washington will automatically do the same for Israel; nor has Israel ever asked the United States to do so. But the fact that this time the United States stood firm and was ready to become involved against an aggression in the Middle East adds somewhat to Israel's overall deterrence. It discourages initiation of war in the region, though I do not know for how long.[2]

The war also proved to be a catastrophe for the Palestinians. Financial and political support for the PLO from the Gulf states dried up after Arafat threw his support behind Saddam Hussein. The expulsion of 300,000 Palestinians from Kuwait meant an end to remittances to the West Bank and Gaza that Israeli officials calculated at no less than $400 million annually.[3] Saudi Arabia and Kuwait eliminated their payments to the PLO, including so-called "liberation taxes" paid by Palestinian expatriates working in the Gulf states, cutting the PLO annual budget virtually in half, to somewhere between $100 million and $120 million.[4]

Despite dipping into its reserves, the PLO had to close many of its offices and cut back on services. Most critically, support to the territories dropped from $120 million in 1989 to approximately $45 million in 1991 and 1992.[5] Hospitals, universities, community centers, and newspapers supported by the PLO were cut back or closed. Before the Gulf War, it is estimated that at least 90,000 Palestinian families in the occupied territories received small, monthly payments from the PLO Welfare Department's *intifada*

---

[2] Speech delivered at Tel Aviv University, May, 1991, excerpted in *Middle East Deterrence: The Convergence of Theory and Practice*, Aharon Kleiman, ed. (Tel Aviv: Jaffee Center for Strategic Studies, 1994).

[3] Rothschild testimony before the State Commission of Inquiry investigating the Hebron massacre, April 4, 1994.

[4] *U.S. News and World Report*, April 26, 1993, p. 49. From 1987 through 1990, the annual PLO budget stood at $199 million, of which Saudi Arabia contributed $85.7 million and Kuwait $47.1 million. During the same period, the Gulf states also contributed to a special *intifada* fund that totaled an additional $43 million.

[5] Ibid.

martyrs and widows fund in Amman, headed by Intisar al-Wazir, widow of the PLO's second-in-command, Khalil al-Wazir (known by his Arabic patronym as Abu Jihad).[6] After the war, those payments decreased dramatically.

Rabin initially believed that the PLO's political and financial weakness would make it more malleable and enable him to orchestrate the accord he had believed possible since 1988—a deal with Palestinians in the territories rather than with the PLO leadership in Tunis. Rabin rejected the PLO as a negotiating partner because of its insistence on a state encompassing all of the West Bank and Gaza, its involvement in terrorism (which also made it unacceptable to the Israeli public), and its claim to represent the millions of Palestinians in the *diaspora* whose dreams of return Israel could not accommodate. Rabin believed that a debilitated PLO would be forced to acquiesce to a deal made by local Palestinians to ease the occupation. The Democratic victory in the U.S. elections in November 1992 brightened the picture; the new Clinton administration would be far less likely to pressure Israel to make concessions to the Palestinians than a second-term Bush administration.

In a speech to newspaper editors in November 1992, Rabin likened the future of the PLO to the evolution of the World Zionist Organization, a quasi-governmental pre-state body that faded into oblivion after the formation of the official government of Israel.[7] Rabin believed that his predecessor, Yitzhak Shamir, could have hastened the decline of the PLO had he offered credible peace proposals in Washington and encouraged independent decision making by West Bank Palestinians. Toward that end, Rabin abolished the fiction that Israel opposed consultation between local Palestinians and the PLO—a policy that was already farcical under Shamir, who told aides that he did not object to such meetings as long as no photographs of the two groups together in Tunis were published.[8]

Moreover, during his first year in office, Rabin rarely criticized the PLO for engaging in violence. Rather, he accused Arafat of a lesser, political offense—preventing Palestinian negotiators from

---

[6] Ibid.

[7] Speech to annual editors luncheon in Beit Sokolov, November 2, 1992.

[8] In fact, the first public consultation (including photos) occurred three days before the Israeli election. Israeli police interrogated the Palestinians when they returned to the territories but took no further action.

moving forward at the peace table. Rabin hoped that the combination of a less strident approach to the PLO and the organization's acute political and financial crisis would encourage flexibility in Tunis that would lead Palestinians in the territories to move ahead at the peace table. In his speech at Tel Aviv University in November 1992, he said:

> I believe that among the leadership of the territories and outside of the territories, maybe even in [PLO headquarters in] Tunisia, there are today Palestinian leaders who have wised up, and they understand that they cannot repeat the mistakes of the past. . . . There are many among them who understand that it is better to establish the nucleus of a Palestinian entity, even if it is administrative.[9]

By eliminating the traditional emphasis on the PLO as a gang of brutal terrorists, however, Rabin eroded the moral base of Israel's anti-PLO stance and undermined the logic of refusing to talk to Arafat. And for all his hopes, he suspected that Arafat would not go along with a shift of authority from Tunis to the territories. In the same Tel Aviv speech, Rabin shared with the audience his belief "that he who stands at the head of the PLO fears, maybe justifiably from his personal perspective, that if [interim self-rule] is created, . . . such a body will become the source of Palestinian identity, and then what will the organization sitting in Tunis do?"[10]

Ultimately, however, the question was not whether Arafat would shift authority voluntarily to Palestinians in the territories—he would not—but rather whether the local Palestinians would face down their leader and force him to accept their leadership. By March 1993, Rabin and his top advisers had concluded they would not. That month, Saguy told a closed session of the Conference of Presidents of Major American Jewish Organizations that attempts to promote an independent Palestinian authority within the territories had failed. In his March meeting with Christopher, Rabin volunteered that he was dubious of progress in the Washington talks since the Palestinian negotiators refused to act independently of Arafat. When pressed

---

[9] Speech at inauguration of Steinmetz Center for Peace Research, Tel Aviv University, November 16, 1992.
[10] Ibid.

by Ross about the implications of such a conclusion, however, Rabin replied that Israel could not do business with the PLO.

## The Long-Term Threats

Rabin had long regarded Palestinian terrorism as a second-tier nuisance that posed no threat to Israel's existence and at worst inflicted suffering upon individual Israelis. However, Iraq's indiscriminate use of Scud missiles against Israel during the Gulf War—in an attempt to fragment the fragile coalition of moderate Arab states arrayed against it by inviting politically lethal Israeli retaliation—demonstrated that the Palestinian issue still resonated in intra-Arab strategic relations and that it needed to be resolved in order to prevent radical regimes such as Iran and Iraq from using it as a rallying cry for their own strategic purposes.

Rabin felt that the international and regional changes offered Israel a short-term "window of opportunity" to resolve the core conflict with Israel's Arab neighbors. Rabin believed it was important to minimize friction with the Arab world and reduce the prospects for a full-scale confrontation before the end of the decade, so that Israel could face the primary long-term strategic threats to Israel's very existence from an already-insurgent Iran and a rapidly recovering Iraq. In short, peace was more than an opportunity not to be missed—it was an imperative that Israel needed to seize to stave off threats down the road.

Rabin did not want an agreement for its own sake, however; an accord that sowed the seeds of the next war was not worth having. "When it comes to security," he said in his inaugural Knesset speech on July 13, 1992, "we will concede nothing. From our standpoint, security takes preference even over peace." At the same time, however, he stressed the need to explore the unparalleled window of opportunity in the peace process in order to avert long-term threats:

> It is our duty, to ourselves and to our children, to see the new world as it is now—to discern its dangers, explore its prospects and to do everything possible so the State of Israel will fit into this world whose face is changing. No longer are we necessarily a 'people that dwells alone,' and no longer is it true that 'the whole world is against us.' We must overcome the sense of isolation that has held us in its thrall for almost half a century.

We must join the international movement towards peace, reconciliation and cooperation that is spreading all over the entire globe these days—lest we be the last to remain, all alone, in the station. . . . A number of countries in our region have recently stepped up their efforts to develop and produce nuclear arms. . . . The possibility that nuclear weapons will be introduced in the Middle East in the coming years is a very grave and negative development from Israel's standpoint. . . . [T]his situation requires us to give further thought to the urgent need to end the Arab-Israeli conflict and live in peace with our Arab neighbors.

Rabin expanded on this theme in a speech two months later at the opening of Tel Aviv University's Steinmetz Peace Research Center. "I believe that we are on a path of no return . . . to reach peace, even if it takes another year or two years," he said. "I think that the reality of the international situation, the regional situation, the genuine need of nations and countries, is to arrive at a resolution of the dispute."[11] In a speech at the International Center for Peace in the Middle East in mid-December 1992, Rabin was more specific about the threat from Iran. Israel, he argued, had a seven-year "window of opportunity" to resolve the core conflict and make peace with its neighbors before the Iranian threat became real. "Today Iran is the leading disseminator of fundamentalist Islam in the region," he said. "Iran has replaced Iraq in its megalomaniacal ambitions in empire-building. . . . Within seven years from today, this will be the threat in the Middle East. We have this time to resolve problems. I believe we will succeed."[12]

Although in private discussions Rabin talked about the rise of Islamic movements in a variety of Middle Eastern countries—Iran, Algeria, Egypt, and Sudan—and the growing evidence that these groups inspired radical fundamentalism in the occupied territories, he realized that Gaza's appalling poverty and festering discontent fueled the trend and made it ripe territory for extremist agitation. Senior military and domestic intelligence officials hammered home the point that the withering of PLO-funded institutions in the West Bank and Gaza was creating a leadership

[11] Ibid.

[12] Speech delivered at the International Center for Peace in the Middle East, Jerusalem, December 17, 1992.

vacuum that was increasingly being filled by Hamas. This was a competition that Israel could no longer watch with indifference.[13]

One cannot overestimate the importance of the rise of Hamas in persuading Israel, and Rabin in particular, to pursue the opportunity that Oslo presented. Rabin feared that ascendant Islamic militants, whose absolutist approach would not permit political compromise with Israel, would emerge as the leading political force in the territories. Speaking to the Knesset shortly after attempting to weaken Hamas and the even more radical Islamic Jihad by deporting their leaders to Lebanon in December 1992, Rabin said:

> Our struggle against murderous Islamic terror is also meant to awaken the world which is lying [in] slumber. We call on all nations and all people to devote their attention to the great danger inherent in Islamic fundamentalism. That is the real and serious danger which threatens the peace of the world in the forthcoming years. The danger of death is at our doorstep. And just as the state of Israel was the first to perceive the Iraqi nuclear threat, so today we stand in the line of fire against the danger of fundamentalist Islam.[14]

Rabin's concern about the extremist threat continued throughout the Oslo process. In early August 1993, as Israeli representatives were secretly putting the finishing touches on the DOP with their PLO counterparts, he painted a gloomy picture of the territories as a cradle of growing Hamas radicalism at a meeting of the Knesset's Foreign Affairs and Defense Committee. And in testimony before the commission investigating the Hebron massacre, more than six months after the White House signing ceremony, Rothschild reiterated the long-standing Israeli view of the shifting political balance in the occupied territories. "By any standard, the PLO is financially bankrupt," he said. "Therefore, in any linear equation, when you compare the PLO to Hamas, Hamas wins. We have seen in the last two to three years, the group that is helping the [Palestinian] population is Hamas. The group that builds the orphanages, is concerned with education, builds schools, which has devoted itself to welfare—physical and

---

[13] Israel had initially supported the social welfare efforts of Hamas' predecessors in the early 1980s as a counterweight to the PLO.

[14] Speech to Knesset, January 1993.

spiritual—is Hamas. The whole [PLO] nationalist system has moved aside."[15]

## Choosing Between the Syrian and Palestinian Tracks

Rabin's view of the peace process fused two different perspectives: that of a politician, always conscious of what the political climate would allow, and that of a skilled analyst of Arab politics, focused on the region's strategic equation. As a politician, Rabin believed that major concessions on too many fronts would overload Israel's political circuits. He therefore sought a bilateral agreement that the Israeli public could more easily digest than a comprehensive settlement requiring painful concessions on several fronts simultaneously.

Moreover, as an analyst Rabin knew that focusing on bilateral agreements would allow Israel to play one Arab negotiating partner off against the others and thereby create a kind of "push-pull" diplomacy in which progress on one track promoted progress on the other, since each Arab party feared being left behind by the others.

Of the four Arab parties negotiating with Israel, Rabin viewed Syria and the Palestinians as primary interlocutors and Lebanon and Jordan as subsidiary actors. Lebanon was dominated by Syria and would not move ahead of Damascus; Jordan, with its large Palestinian population and fear of offending Syria, was unlikely to reach a separate accord with Israel.

As an analyst, Rabin believed that an agreement with Damascus was the key to resolving the core conflict, thereby reducing friction with the Arab world and allowing Israel to shift resources to prepare for the emerging threat from Iran and Iraq. Whereas a deal with the Palestinians would merely be "public relations," Rabin told Israel Television in January 1993, an accord with Syria would change the strategic equation of the region, bringing to an end the war of attrition against the Iranian-backed Hezbollah Islamic militants in the security zone along Israel's northern border with Lebanon. And, unlike the fragmented Palestinian camp, Syria had one leader who made decisions and could make them stick.

[15]Testimony before State Commission of Inquiry investigating the Hebron massacre, April 4, 1994.

A variety of political factors, however, including Syria's maximalist terms and the immediacy of the Palestinian problem, led Rabin to pursue the Palestinian track instead. Assad wanted the same deal that Sadat had extracted from Israel—full withdrawal from captured lands—yet gave no indication that he was willing to pay the same political price as Egypt: a formal peace treaty with Israel including recognition, full diplomatic relations, and a commitment to broad normalization.

A Syrian position paper put forward at the Washington peace talks a month after Rabin assumed power offered mere non-belligerency, essentially codifying the *de facto* truce between the two sides. In addition, there was widespread opposition in Israel to ceding control of the strategically crucial Golan Heights. Full withdrawal would require Rabin to dismantle all of the settlements on the Golan, a demand that would be politically difficult to implement, given the large number of Labor party supporters urged to settle on the Heights by previous Labor governments. "We did not have the [political] strength to dismantle the Golan settlements," Peres later recalled.[16]

Although Rabin saw Syria as the strategic core of Israel's conflict with the Arab world, the *intifada* had focused the Israeli public on the need to address the Palestinian issue. The deaths of Israeli civilians and soldiers in Gaza, an area without any strategic value to Israel in the post-Camp David era, also helped shape the public's view of the area as an unnecessary burden to be jettisoned. Rabin's own center-left coalition was much more energized about the Palestinian issue than about Syria, and both Labor and left-wing Meretz ministers agreed with Beilin's frequent declaration that "the Palestinian issue is the heart of the Arab-Israeli conflict." In response to popular sentiment, Rabin had publicly committed himself during his 1992 election campaign to reach an interim accord with the Palestinians within six to nine months of assuming office, and according to Peres, felt pressure to fulfill his campaign promise.[17]

Despite the potential long-term advantages of a deal with Syria, complete withdrawal from the Golan Heights was strategically and politically riskier (and less easily reversed by

---

[16] Interview with Peres, December 31, 1993. In January 1994, Rabin announced that Israel would hold a national referendum on any Israel-Syria agreement.

[17] Ibid. According to Peres, "Rabin promised the public that in six to nine months there would be a deal and nothing happened."

Israeli military power) than the agreement Rabin envisioned reaching with the Palestinians—an interim self-rule accord that would not require immediate territorial concessions or the dismantling of Jewish settlements, thus averting a clash with the 120,000 settlers in the territories. (As it turned out, the second phase of the Oslo deal requires significant IDF redeployment.)

Thus, for both political and analytical reasons Rabin decided to focus Israel's efforts on achieving a deal with the Palestinians. On at least two occasions, however, the lack of progress on that track led him to revisit the possibility of a reaching deal with Syria prior to the Oslo breakthrough. Rabin believed that the Palestinian boycott of the Washington peace talks in response to the Hamas deportations was only a bluff, and he decided to put pressure on the Palestinians by playing up prospects for a deal with Syria.

Any hopes for a "Syria First" strategy were quickly dashed, however, when Damascus tied resumption of the Washington talks to the PLO's return. For the first time since the Madrid conference, the Palestinians demonstrated that they had a *de facto* veto over Syrian movement in the peace process. At least partly in recognition of this, the Clinton administration quietly nudged Rabin to refocus on the Palestinian issue. At U.S. prodding, Israel made several gestures that coaxed the Palestinians back to the negotiating table in Washington in April. Rabin's attention then remained focused on the Palestinians, and a month later he upgraded the level of Israel's participation in the Oslo talks.

In early August the Oslo track was still bogged down, and the Americans—unaware that Israel and the PLO had advanced toward a deal in Oslo—were disappointed by the lack of progress on the Palestinian track in Washington and began to favor shifting the focus to Syria. Rabin awaited the outcome of Christopher's meeting that month in Syria before making his final moves at Oslo, and the lack of movement from Damascus factored into his decision to finalize Oslo. "When I decided to go all the way with [the Palestinians, it was because the Syrians] still demanded total withdrawal [from the Golan Heights], uprooting of the Israeli settlements [there], and were not even ready for full-fledged peace," he said.[18] Peres confirms that a major factor in Rabin's decision to clinch the deal with the PLO was the realization after Christopher's trip in August that there was no "Syrian option."

---

[18] Interview with Rabin, October 4, 1993.

# VII

## Rabin's Personal Road to Oslo

To understand Rabin's decision-making process, one needs to understand his style and self-image. He eschews the politics of inspiration and sees himself as a superior analyst who weighs options without emotional baggage. Rabin won a scholarship to Berkeley in 1940 to study hydraulic engineering but had to withdraw when he joined the Palmach. However, he continues to bring the detachment of an engineer to his role as a military officer and statesman, and believes he is uniquely capable of prioritizing Israel's pressing strategic concerns.

Rabin is not intellectually animated by the intricacies of public policy but rather is motivated by an old-fashioned sense of duty. Having led Israel's victory in the Six Day War, he seems to feel an obligation to resolve its consequences. Rabin has little regard for politicians, and dismisses much of Israel's political class for lacking the capacity for rigorous thinking and for preferring instead to engage in petty political intrigues and "headline hunting." According to one aide, if "you leak the contents of a meeting with the prime minister, you have just had your last meeting." Though he has been in politics for many years, he does not view himself as a politician. His ineptitude in dealing with party and coalition issues and general lack of charisma ironically give him a certain "anti-slick" public appeal.

Rabin refers to himself by the nickname given to him by others: "Lone Wolf." He is most comfortable with a select number of military officials and ultra-loyal staffers. He has no all-purpose adviser and likes to compartmentalize on an issue-by-issue basis. Like spokes radiating from the hub of a wheel, Rabin's staff circles around him and reports directly to him on specific issues. He uses members individually to carry out his orders rather than collectively to generate policies.

For a variety of reasons, Rabin probably would never have initiated the Oslo process on his own. To begin with, he is often bolder as an analyst dissecting a situation than as a political leader who must develop a policy and marshal support for it. Although he had come to the conclusion that there was little alternative to dealing with Arafat, he had not reached the stage where he could make the decision to do so, and probably never would have had the Oslo backchannel not been initiated and nurtured by Beilin and Peres. Once he became convinced of its viability, however, Rabin took charge of the Oslo decision-making process and saw it through, demonstrating that he is capable of bold action once he is convinced that the policy and the timing are right.

Though he lacked a grand design or comprehensive plan for a breakthrough with the PLO, Rabin's willingness to explore the Oslo option—however tentative—was crucial. It did not, as some critics charged, represent a 180-degree change in his thinking. Rabin's remarks in the year following his election stressed the need for compromises in making peace with the Palestinians and the Arab world. Moreover, after his analysis changed and he accepted the idea that Arafat was the key to a deal, Rabin was open to the suggestions of Beilin and Peres.

On a personal level, Rabin's receptivity to Oslo reflected his anti-ideological pragmatism and intellectual honesty. Perhaps as a result of his military background, Rabin's vaunted sense of pragmatism was repelled by Shamir's ideologically charged approach to the West Bank as the land of Jewish biblical patrimony. He also took a realistic approach to his treatment of political rival Peres, alternating between personal antipathy and political practicality. Although he had initially intended to exclude Peres from the peace process, the deportation crisis forced him to give his foreign minister a greater role, and he similarly relied on Peres to help guide the negotiations on the DOP.[1]

---

[1] A similar pattern emerged after the DOP was completed. Amid public criticism of Peres' role in Oslo after the White House signing ceremony, Rabin took exclusive control for himself and his generals. Although on paper Peres was head of the "liaison committee," in reality Rabin locked him out of the talks for two months. However, after the December 1993 Rabin-Arafat summit meeting in Cairo proved a fiasco, Rabin agreed that Peres should not only rejoin the talks but lead the sessions.

Rabin's intellectual honesty was reflected in his ability to reverse his own long-held views, most obviously in acquiescing to direct negotiations with the PLO. Senior Peres aide Nimrod Novik said that "Rabin observes what he considers reality [and] builds a foundation [for his views] brick by brick. But then he gets stuck in those views. . . . To change, he needs indisputable evidence that he is wrong. However, if there is a brick missing from the wall, he can tear down the whole thing."[2]

When, for example, the UN Security Council unanimously condemned the December 1992 Hamas deportations and demanded that Rabin return the deportees, he initially rebuffed them, saying that the entire affair would be forgotten once Clinton took office. But when the Arabs boycotted the peace talks and calls for sanctions against Israel mounted, Rabin reversed course and reached an agreement with Secretary of State Christopher on the immediate return of some deportees and shortened the period of expulsion for the rest.

## The Consistency of Rabin's Strategic Vision

Rabin's personal road to Oslo was both consistent with and a departure from his strategic vision. Although critics complained that his decision to negotiate directly with the PLO was a betrayal of his previous thinking, it actually stemmed largely from currents within his strategic approach.

Rabin inherited from his predecessor a negotiating framework that required Israel to deal simultaneously with four different Arab parties, and he never made a secret of his distaste for multiple, simultaneous peace negotiations, which he viewed as a strait-jacket holding Israel hostage to the maximalist demands of the most intransigent Arab negotiating partner.[3] Though publicly supportive of the Madrid framework, Rabin observed that the history of the Arab-Israeli conflict had demonstrated that successful agreements—the 1974 Egyptian and Syrian

---

[2] Interview with Novik, November 7, 1993.

[3] Although Rabin complained bitterly about the Madrid structure when the simultaneous talks deadlocked, subsequent events demonstrated that the format was not inherently incompatible with separate negotiations, and certain substantive aspects—particularly negotiating with the Palestinians about an interim period rather than final status issues—actually appealed to Rabin.

disengagements, the 1975 Sinai II disengagement, and the 1978 Camp David accords—were reached bilaterally and discretely. A rare display of Arab unity effectively precluded altering the procedural framework, however, and Israel acquiesced to Arab demands to maintain the simultaneous talks format.[4]

Critics of the Oslo negotiations who claimed that Rabin could have agreed to negotiate directly with the PLO at the Washington peace talks ignored the heavy pressure Syria would have exerted on the Palestinians not to move ahead of Damascus, as well as fact that such talks would have undermined Israel's key card in the negotiations, the very fact of mutual recognition. Focusing on bilateral instead of multiple and simultaneous agreements allowed Rabin to play one Arab negotiating partner off against the other, and met his domestic political needs as well: The Israeli public would find a single bilateral agreement much easier to digest than a comprehensive agreement requiring painful concessions on several fronts simultaneously.

Apart from the structure of negotiations, Rabin has consistently believed that any deal with the Arabs should yield third-party benefits to Israel. The annex to the U.S.-brokered 1975 Sinai II accord, negotiated by a Rabin-led Israeli government, included tremendous political and military benefits to Israel. On the political level, the accord went far beyond a disengagement of forces by establishing a virtual U.S.-Israel alliance and the principle that Washington would not force Israel to talk to the PLO—a concept for which successive Israeli governments were grateful.[5] On the military level, Sinai II enabled Israel to make a qualitative leap forward in the mid-1970s in the type of U.S. aircraft it received, moving from Phantoms and Skyhawks to F-15s and F-16s—and, more important, in its developing strategic relationship with the United States.

---

[4] Previous efforts by the Likud government of Yitzhak Shamir to keep the Arab delegations separate reached absurd dimensions, including staggering the sessions and even having the delegates enter the State Department through different doors. In the heady days following the historic Madrid conference, Shamir devoted the better part of his semi-annual meeting with President Bush not to the subject of bilateral cooperation or U.S. loan guarantees, but rather to a discussion of minor details of separating the Arab delegations, much to the annoyance of Bush and ultimately to no avail.

[5] Among them was the second Rabin administration in 1993. The absence of U.S. pressure led Arafat to authorize the Oslo channel, after it became apparent that the United States would refrain from delivering Israeli concessions in the Washington talks.

Rabin expected a similar "arms for peace" military assistance package from the United States to offset the security risks Israel had incurred in the Oslo accord. During his first visit to the United States after the historic handshake with Arafat on the White House lawn, he secured President Clinton's support for Israel's acquisition of an advanced export model of the F-15 fighter-bomber capable of reaching Tehran, as well as sophisticated technology such as Cray supercomputers that had previously been blocked by the Pentagon. He also won permission for Israel to sell commercial satellite launchers in the United States, which had been denied in the past out of fear that it would boost Israel's noncommercial (i.e., military) satellite program.

In addition, Israel won some key diplomatic benefits from other parties as a result of Oslo. Jerusalem established or renewed ties with some thirty countries and the Vatican. The most important of these was the formal peace treaty signed with Jordan in the Arava desert on October 26, 1994. Also important for both their symbolism and actual access in the Arab world, are the exchange of liaison offices between Israel and Morocco, and an agreement in principle with Tunisia to do the same. After a visit by Rabin in December 1994, Oman—a member of the Gulf Cooperation Council (GCC)—signaled its willingness to establish low-level diplomatic relations in the form of liaison offices.

After North Africa, the Gulf states seem most willing to improve relations with Israel. Bahrain and Qatar hosted Israeli officials at multilateral talks on the environment and arms control. Perhaps most importantly, the GCC announced that its members would suspend enforcement of the secondary and tertiary economic boycotts imposed by the Arab League on Israel for more than forty years.[6] Kuwait announced it would allow foreigners with Israeli stamps in their passports into the country, and Beilin met with an official of Saudi Arabia's Washington embassy to discuss Saudi participation in industrial development in the Gaza Strip. In an interview with a French reporter, Iraqi Foreign Minister Tariq Aziz said that in the aftermath of the peace process, Iraq no longer considers Israel its enemy.[7]

---

[6] This ban remained significant not only because it hampered intra-regional trade, but because it scared away American, European, and Asian investors and made it difficult for Israel to be the Middle East distribution center for multinational companies.

[7] *Mideast Mirror*, November 7, 1994, pp.17-18.

## The Functionalist-Territorialist Debate

Ever since his mentor, Yigal Allon, proposed the "Allon Plan" for territorial compromise in 1968, Rabin has advocated partitioning the West Bank. The Allon Plan called for Israel to withdraw from the densely populated Palestinian areas that comprise roughly two-thirds of the West Bank but retain strategic positions around Jerusalem and in the Jordan Valley for security. It was designed to protect Israel's eastern flank from infiltrations by PLO forces based in Jordan and create defensible borders without annexing substantial portions of the Palestinian population. The plan would have left about 700 of the roughly 2,100 square miles of the West Bank under Israeli control: the Jordan Rift Valley and eastern slopes of the West Bank ridge that includes the main east-west routes to the heart of Israel, the northern Dead Sea, and the Judean Desert up to the city of Hebron, with minor modifications along the Green Line and substantial changes in the "greater Jerusalem" area.

The so-called "territorialist-functionalist debate" has been a defining issue of Israeli politics for a quarter century. In essence, territorialists believe that the basis for a settlement with the Palestinians lies in defining the area within which the inhabitants would have autonomy. Functionalists, on the other hand, worry that any kind of boundaries might become permanent, and therefore they believe that the Palestinians should be given authority over various governmental *functions* (e.g., taxation, education) rather than specific territory.

Few Israeli leaders have been as consistent in their commitment to the territorialist position as Yitzhak Rabin. He has always sided against Labor party leaders such as Dayan who favored a functional solution and has little use for Israelis who oppose yielding any land in the West Bank because they believe it is Jewish biblical patrimony. Yet Rabin did not reject the Dayan approach completely. Rather, he saw the functionalist approach, as codified by the Camp David accords, as a *short-term* measure that would ultimately lead to a long-term territorial solution. Accordingly, the 1992 Labor campaign platform stipulated that any interim agreement leave security and border control in the hands of Israel, and not address settlements or Jerusalem.[8]

---

[8] In an interview on June 19, 1994, Singer noted that Rabin's concern was "places the Labor party wanted to keep" such as security zones and settlement blocs.

The notion of an interim period also appealed to Rabin as an opportunity to test the willingness and ability of Palestinian leadership to control Palestinian extremists, while allowing him to defer venturing into such major political minefields as dismantling settlements and the permanent boundaries of Jerusalem. Moreover, the notion of an interim accord with Palestinians had a bipartisan legacy derived from the Camp David accords and could therefore attract the support of a broad spectrum of the Israeli public. An interim, functional autonomy period might create a new pro-Labor political baseline in Israel that could in turn make subsequent territorial partition more achievable. As the current coalition agreement makes clear, partition remains the ultimate goal of the Rabin government.

## Retaining the Jordan Option

Yet Rabin is equally adamant that any future Palestinian entity should be linked to Jordan. The question remains whether the Oslo accord, which was a prerequisite for an Israel-Jordan treaty, either ensured a Palestinian-Jordanian federation or foreclosed that option once and for all. In a post-Oslo interview, Rabin insisted that the accord did not represent a betrayal of Jordan,[9] and reiterated his vision of final status as two states, Israel and Jordan, with a less-than-independent Palestinian entity sandwiched between them. Rabin emphasized this message in private as well. He reportedly met with King Hussein after Oslo on a yacht in the Gulf of Aqaba to assure him of Israel's continuing commitment to include Jordan in the final arrangements.

Rabin has publicly emphasized the importance of the Hashemite kingdom as a buffer state between Israel and one of its most truculent foes, Iraq. One of his greatest fears is that Jordan could be easily destabilized and that, should the Hashemite kingdom fall, it would be replaced by a militant Islamic government that would foment radicalism in the West Bank, perhaps even inviting Iraq to rule the area in order to further the cause of Arab enmity against Israel.[10]

---

[9] Interview with Rabin, October 4, 1993.

[10] As a result, Israel was relieved to hear of the setback that the Islamists suffered in the last Jordanian election, thanks to the new electoral rules set down by the

Though the Oslo accord did not foreclose a Palestinian federation or confederation with Jordan, it did not ensure one either, and thus in this sense deviated from Rabin's previous strategic thinking. The interim accord is not purely functional as originally conceived. Its territorial element—Israeli withdrawal from (rather than mere redeployment in) Gaza and Jericho—runs counter to Rubinstein's strategy of keeping all options open for final status talks because, in certain respects, it essentially created a Palestinian "mini-state" in Gaza and Jericho the ultimate size and degree of autonomy of which are to be determined in final status negotiations.

In Oslo, Rabin set in motion a dynamic that could foreseeably result in an independent Palestinian state not linked to Jordan. This possibility has always been anathema to him, because of his fear that such an entity would be a destabilizing force for Israel and for Jordan. Its economic viability notwithstanding, Rabin's traditional doubts and concerns about a prospective Palestinian state have not changed: that it might negotiate with neighboring Arab countries, deploy heavy weapons on the West Bank mountain ridges overlooking the narrow coastal strip where the bulk of Israel's population and industrial base are located, and allow the return of hundreds of thousand of Palestinian refugees from Lebanon and Jordan who could form an irredentist core that would foment continued violence. No doubt issues such as these will be at the core of final status negotiations.

Rabin's willingness to incur these risks in the Oslo agreement represents the most significant element of change in his strategic thinking. Although his public statements prior to Oslo reflected an *a priori* opposition to a Palestinian state, in private conversations after the accord was unveiled Rabin spoke as if he were reconciling himself to such an outcome. He now seems willing to wait and see whether the interim evolves in a manner compatible with Israel's security interests, and has even said that he would not oppose a Palestinian state in Gaza.[11]

At the same time, however, his aides say that the prime minister is aware that Israel is not exactly powerless when it

---

monarch. Rabin's hope was that the Oslo accord would push the international community to provide more assistance to Jordan as an integral partner in Middle East peace, and that the United States would broker a post-Gulf War reconciliation between Saudi Arabia and Jordan to further bolster King Hussein's position.

[11] Interview with Rabin, April 12, 1995.

comes to curbing possible Palestinian adventurism. Rabin has made clear that Israel's primary coercive lever in the post-Oslo period is likely to be economic, particularly the threat of closing off the territories and thereby denying Palestinian day-laborers access to jobs in Israel, which are a vital source of revenue for the Palestinian economy.[12]

On a political level, should the self-rule experiment fail, Israel could effectively freeze discussions on the final disposition of the occupied territories. In the event that the PLO is either incapable or unwilling to arrest deteriorating conditions affecting Israeli security, the IDF could resort to conducting militarily raids. It seems unlikely that Rabin would actually "roll back" PLO control over Gaza and Jericho, since Israel is relieved to be rid of the Gaza quagmire and would be loathe to reacquire it.

The decision to limit the IDF's freedom of movement by acquiescing to a territorial component in the accord also represents a significant departure from Israeli deterrence doctrine, which puts a premium on retaliation and preemption, and thus a sharp shift in Rabin's thinking. During his election campaign, Rabin often asserted that Israel would be in charge of security throughout the territories. Yet it is precisely the idea of IDF withdrawal that made Gaza-Jericho so appealing to the PLO. Talks would not have succeeded, Nabil Shaath said, had Israel not finally uttered the "W-word."[13]

In the post-Oslo negotiations on implementation that led to the Cairo agreement in May 1994, Rabin sought to win back some security-related concessions that seemingly could have been made in Oslo. He did win full Israeli control over settlement blocs rather than individual settlements, though it took months of haggling in Taba and Cairo to reach a conclusion that could easily have been reached earlier. The same is true for the principle of joint patrols, which are designed to protect Israelis during the interim period. For Rabin, these gains represented precedents to be used in future negotiations over the remainder of the West Bank.

---

[12] Briefing for reporters at Defense Ministry, May 25, 1994.
[13] Interview with Shaath, September 3, 1994.

## The Role of the United States

Rabin's decision not to coordinate with Washington on the Oslo channel represented another important shift in his strategic vision. Whereas the Norwegians updated American officials about the Oslo channel (even when Washington displayed little interest), Rabin himself never did. This ran counter to a long record of Rabin's statements that peace with the Arabs could be achieved only through prior coordination with Washington, as exemplified by his own support for the negotiations of the U.S.-brokered Sinai II accord. The Clinton administration, for its part, liked the Rabin government and happily eschewed the arm-twisting that had characterized Washington's approach to the Shamir government on the issues of the peace process and loan guarantees.

U.S. officials say the lack of coordination regarding Oslo was part of a broader pattern. Rabin did not give Washington advance notice of two other key decisions made over the course of his first year in office: the Hamas deportations and Operation Accountability. Samuel Lewis, former ambassador to Israel and head of policy planning in the State Department during the first year of the Clinton administration, explained that "no Israeli government will give prior warning on security-related issues, because they think we will try to prevent them from acting. They may be right. The Israelis say they don't inform us because they don't want to complicate our relations with the Arabs, but I think that is just a rationalization."[14]

Yet Oslo did not fit into the strict category of military/security issues. And though it is possible that Rabin did not consult with the United States out of concern about potential leaks, it seems more likely that it was due to his own incremental decision-making approach. Skeptical of the chances for success, Rabin probably either saw no purpose in bringing Washington into the deal, or skirted U.S. involvement because he feared the Americans would push Israel to accept terms it would otherwise reject.

In fact, he had little to fear; the Clinton administration's record is one of extraordinary cooperation with Israel. During the Hamas deportation crisis, for example, Christopher rebuffed Arab pressure to impose UN sanctions on Israel and instead quietly sought to coordinate a compromise with Rabin. Similarly, when

---

[14] Interview with Lewis, February 2, 1994.

Israel presented Washington with the *fait accompli* of Operation Accountability, U.S. officials accepted Israel's strategy and successfully brokered a ceasefire. On two occasions during the Washington peace talks, the United States proposed "bridging" language entirely acceptable to Israel. Indeed, the Palestinians consistently complained that U.S.-Israeli cooperation was too strong.

Perhaps ironically, close coordination between Israel and the United States in these other areas made Oslo possible. The PLO's inability to drive a wedge between the two governments forced Arafat to realize that the Palestinians could not impose a solution on Israel. According to Nabil Shaath, the organization realized that "the U.S. could not deliver Israel, but rather Israel would have to deliver the U.S."[15] Senior U.S. officials concur with this assessment. "Given the sensitivity of what negotiating with the PLO means, this is a decision that we could have never forced Israel to take," said Ross. "It had to make that choice on its own."[16]

---

[15] *Jerusalem Post*, September 3, 1993.
[16] Interview with Ross, January 31, 1994.

# VIII

## The Lessons of Oslo

### The Importance of Secrecy

The Oslo accord, though an important breakthrough, is but one part of the ongoing saga of the Arab-Israeli peace process. Its special character, however, offers a number of important lessons for putative peacemakers charged with taking those next tentative yet crucial steps down the road to a comprehensive regional settlement.

Some Israeli negotiators in Washington, upset that their own government circumvented them by conducting secret talks in Oslo, privately believe that Israel could have achieved a better deal by negotiating directly with the PLO in the framework of the formal Washington talks. That argument, however, fails to take into account the likely Syrian reaction to such a development: Damascus would have exerted heavy pressure on the Palestinians not to make a deal until Syria's demands had been met. More important, since one of Israel's main cards in the negotiations with the PLO was mutual recognition, conducting formal talks with the organization before obtaining a declaration of principles would have precluded Israel from obtaining the benefit of that concession.

The importance of a secret backchannel was first demonstrated to Israel in 1977, when Dayan held clandestine exploratory talks in Morocco with his Egyptian counterpart, Hassan Tuhami. According to Egyptian officials, the Dayan-Tuhami meeting laid the groundwork for the core agreement in the Camp David accord—full return of the Sinai in return for full peace—and Sadat's historic trip to Jerusalem. Similar preparation preceded the Washington Declaration ending the state of war between Israel and Jordan in July 1994.

One element that is critical to the success of secret, preparatory discussions is informality. Informal sessions enable both sides to explore the parameters of a deal without making irrevocable concessions. Instead, they can consider a wide range of different possibilities. This advantage would be particularly useful in the case of the Golan, where there are an array of issues to be worked out simultaneously. The more than three years of negotiations between Israel and Syria since the Madrid peace conference seem more like an "Alphonse-Gaston" routine, in which each side wants the other to reveal its proposal for the extent of withdrawal and the extent of peace. In fact, there are more variables at work in what Rabin calls the "the package of peace." Ideally, informal diplomacy should resolve the most difficult issues and then allow the formal negotiations to handle the details.

Informal sessions offer the important additional advantage of avoiding media scrutiny—and thus public wrangling—during the course of negotiations. In overt negotiations, the progress of which is generally reported by the press, both sides thrive on ambiguity and deferring difficult problems. Negotiators therefore tend to play to the home crowd by spouting uncompromising opening positions. The result does not serve the negotiations well, although it does provide sure-sell copy for journalists.

## No U.S. Pressure

The opposing parties came together in Oslo without political pressure from Washington. This puts to rest the notion that there can be no movement toward Middle East peace in the absence of sustained U.S. pressure on Israel. Arafat went to Oslo precisely because he knew he could not obtain a better deal by relying on Washington to "deliver" Israel. This does not mean that U.S. pressure was never a factor; the Bush administration's decision to withhold loan guarantees for immigrant absorption no doubt contributed to the Likud's loss in the Israeli election in 1992. Labor's victory, however, was largely the result of conditions prevailing in Israel at the time. Shamir was perceived by many Israelis as reluctant to move toward a peaceful accommodation with the Palestinians for ideological reasons, which provided the

United States with some leeway to pressure Shamir on the issue of settlement expansion in the West Bank and Gaza.

The domestic perception of Rabin as more eager for a negotiated settlement than Shamir was counterbalanced by his credibility in safeguarding Israeli security interests, and so the more appropriate U.S. role is the one outlined by Clinton himself after his first White House meeting with the new prime minister: "minimizing the risks of peace" to Israel.[1] This means offering resources, hardware, intelligence and perhaps even personnel as third-party assurances to assuage Israeli (and potentially Syrian) security concerns that could impede an otherwise mutually satisfactory deal.

There are limits, however, in extrapolating from the Oslo experience when it comes to the U.S. role in future Israeli-Syrian negotiations. Washington was excluded from Oslo, but it is unlikely that the Americans can be kept out of any deal with Syria. Damascus views negotiations with Israel as a means of improving its relations with the United States, and therefore will want Washington involved as much as possible. Assad also hopes that, as a "full partner," the United States will use its influence to press Israel on Golan withdrawal. Senior U.S. officials recognize that it is precisely this prospect that worries Rabin, and therefore Jerusalem is believed to be more reluctant about heavy U.S. involvement than Damascus.

At the same time, Rabin has already made clear Israel's need for a compensation package to offset the risks of Golan withdrawal. This—and any Israeli expectation of American participation in Israeli-Syrian security arrangements—will require Washington to play a greater role in the actual diplomacy than simply footing the costs of peace. Should Rabin conclude that something approximating full Israeli withdrawal from the Golan is necessary to achieve peace, he may tacitly or explicitly invite greater U.S. involvement to overcome domestic constraints. If Rabin perceives that U.S. involvement is helping him to achieve a settlement he wants—as opposed to imposing positions on Israel that he does not want to accept—he may decide that a U.S. proposal would be politically beneficial. It may be easier for Rabin to accept a U.S. plan calling for an Israeli withdrawal from Golan in return for normalization, security arrangements, and offsetting

---

[1] White House press conference, March 11, 1993.

American military aid than for the prime minister to propose such a deal himself. The same may be true of Assad.

## Limiting the Role of Unofficial Negotiators

There is little doubt that Hirschfeld and Pundik played a vital role in establishing the Oslo channel. It is difficult to conceive how the transition from Israel's perception of the PLO as demons into suitable partners for negotiations could have occurred without the two academics, with their long-standing contacts with Palestinians, serving as a bridge between the two sides. At the same time, however, their role proved to be more extensive than warranted.

The Sarpsborg DOP, which Hirschfeld and Pundik drafted at the start of the talks, ultimately served as a basis for the Oslo accord. Yet it contained elements that were contrary to Israeli policy, forcing official Israeli negotiators Savir and Singer to expend limited political capital and make concessions in the ensuing four months just to retract some of the unacceptable elements to which the academics had agreed. Among these were unqualified Palestinian jurisdiction, the inclusion of Jerusalem in Palestinian self-rule (and allowing the city to serve as its headquarters), a UN trusteeship in Gaza, and acceptance of binding third-party arbitration.

Although other key Israeli concessions made in Sarpsborg were probably unavoidable if a deal were ultimately to be achieved, the issue is more a question of timing. Fairly early on in the Oslo talks, for example, the academics agreed that Israel would negotiate the status of Jerusalem at some future date, thus depriving official Israeli negotiators of bargaining chips after negotiations were upgraded. One Oslo negotiator said privately that the two academics "should not have been [involved in] drafting a DOP." Singer likened them to non-surgeons who realize only in the middle of an operation that they are not qualified.

It is unfair to blame only Hirschfeld and Pundik for this situation, however. They operated on the basis of precious little guidance from superiors such as Beilin and Peres, who themselves had no way of knowing in advance that the Oslo channel would develop the way it did, and thought the academics' most important role would be to help discern the position of the other side. The bottom line, however, is that people nominally representing the Israeli government advanced proposals that were at variance with official policy.

Approximately 62 percent of the Israeli public supported the Oslo accord after it was signed. Before Oslo, support for talks with the PLO rarely exceeded 40 percent. The Israeli public trusted Rabin to safeguard national security; hard-nosed policies such as the deportation of Islamic activists, closure of the occupied territories, and Operation Accountability—regardless of their actual efficacy—won the prime minister the credibility on security that he needed to take risks for peace.

Polls conducted by Rabin's staff during the secret Oslo talks showed that the public would support him if he reached a deal with Arafat. According to pollster Kalman Geyer, public support for such risks began building during the Gulf War, when Iraq's use of Scud missiles against Israel made Israelis realize that radical regimes such as Iraq could exploit the unresolved Palestinian issue as a rallying cry for their own regional hegemonic purposes. "After the Gulf War," Geyer said, "there was a turning point in the Israeli public's attitude toward the peace process. For the first time, Israelis saw the peace process as a component of security."[2]

This realization did not amount to a "blank check" for the Rabin government, however. Although the public was not naive enough to believe that the Oslo accord represented the end of terror, it did expect that violence would be confined largely to the occupied territories beyond the Green Line. Popular support for the Oslo accord remained steady at around 60 percent for the next year, although it tended to dip just after terrorist attacks and then return to its previous level shortly thereafter. In the wake of a series of suicide bombings inside the Green Line, however, culminating in the incineration of a bus in the heart of Tel Aviv, support dropped to around 52 percent and as of February 1995 had not recovered.[3]

---

[2] Interview with Geyer, February 28, 1995.
[3] Ibid.

## Importance of Psychological Breakthroughs

Oslo demonstrated that diplomatic achievements often require psychological breakthroughs. As important as the DOP was in establishing a blueprint for an Israel-PLO accord, mutual recognition was a *sine qua non* for creating a climate among the Israeli and Palestinian populations within which a peace process was possible. Psychological breakthroughs became a direct part of the bargaining process as well. For example, though there was no formal link between negotiations on mutual recognition and the DOP, they clearly influenced each other in practice. The PLO viewed mutual recognition as a prerequisite to its agreement to an interim accord.

This pattern of trading substance for symbolism could reappear during the Syrian negotiations as Israel seeks dramatic gestures from a very untheatrical Assad. Beyond concrete acts of normalization such as establishing a Syrian embassy in Tel Aviv, Israel will insist upon a summit between Rabin and Assad as a means of persuading its own public that Syria is sincere about peace.

The importance of symbolism should not be dismissed. For Palestinians, the idea that Israel no longer regarded the PLO as a terrorist organization amounted to a genuine breakthrough marking a new level of respect from a once contemptuous foe. For Israelis, Arafat's pledge to renounce terrorism and annul the section of the 1964 Palestine National Charter calling for Israel's destruction was seen as a highly significant indicator of a serious commitment to peace, and thus his subsequent failure to deliver on the promise hurt Arafat's credibility as a negotiating partner.

The handshake between Rabin and Arafat on September 13, 1993 is evidence of the importance of symbolism. According to a CNN poll, a high-water mark 62 percent of Israelis supported the DOP that day. Yet both men have at other times failed to fully understand the importance of symbolism. As of early 1995, for example, Israeli officials have not succeeded in pressing Arafat to convene the PNC in order to amend the charter, accepting instead his explanation that he lacks a two-thirds majority supporting his position, and that he will seek to reshape the body once he has a handle on the situation in Gaza-Jericho.

Symbolism will play an even more important role in negotiations with Syria. Rabin realizes that there is broader public support for retaining the Golan than for keeping the entire West

Bank. Domestic pressure in the form of polling data, political rallies and demonstrations, ubiquitous bumper-stickers, and signs hanging from apartments buildings are unmistakable. Officials in the prime minister's office admit that concern about public attitudes led Rabin to declare his intention to hold either a referendum on a draft Israel-Syria agreement or early elections.

Handled adroitly, however, the referendum could defuse mounting pressure from the public, the religious Shas party and hawkish Labor MKs, and even improve Rabin's position in negotiations with Assad. It is not insignificant that Rabin's first mention of possible evacuation of the Golan settlements coincided with his declaration on holding the referendum. Unlike the Oslo accord, an agreement with Syria will be subjected to close public scrutiny before it is approved.

Assad must convince not only Rabin of his sincerity, but also sway a majority of the Israeli public. This will require a campaign of public diplomacy that runs against the grain of Assad's prickly and incremental style of negotiating. A combination of symbolic actions and meticulous security arrangements will be the key to convincing Israelis that a Syrian-controlled Golan will not be the launching pad for the next war. Israelis need to know that peace is every bit as tangible as the territorial asset they will be yielding.

Clear, unambiguous statements from Assad on his vision of peace with Israel, visits by Israeli journalists to Damascus,[4] and perhaps even a summit meeting between Rabin and Assad would be essential to change the political climate and create a constituency for concessions on Golan. In 1976, for example, public opinion clearly opposed returning all of the Sinai in exchange for peace with Egypt. After Sadat visited Jerusalem, public opinion reversed itself.

Peace with Egypt was more broadly accepted by the Israeli body politic than will be a final settlement with Syria or the Palestinians. The entire Labor opposition backed Begin's decision to return the Sinai; any final disposition of the Golan or West Bank is highly unlikely to win the backing of the Likud opposition, and therefore makes public support all the more critical for Rabin. Leadership is obviously necessary to achieve peace, but is not sufficient; no Israeli government can ratify a peace agreement that is unsupported by public opinion.

---

[4] See *New York Times*, October 28, 1994, p. A1.

## Impartial Analysis

Rabin was highly dependent for information regarding the Oslo negotiations upon the two men who were most intimately involved in the evolution of the Oslo process and therefore had the greatest stake in its success: Peres and Beilin. He had no aides who could independently analyze developments from afar. Although his understandable desire to preserve secrecy led him to restrict the number of aides involved in the Oslo talks, impartial advisers could have given him a dispassionate sounding board upon which to test ideas. As it was, he had no security personnel, intelligence aides, or experts on Palestinian affairs advising him on Oslo. Though he possesses extensive experience in security affairs, Rabin would have benefited from the involvement and advice of top experts, including the IDF chief of staff.

Input from the military might even have modified the Oslo accord, perhaps preventing protracted discussions in the implementation phase. For example, the wording of the agreement seemed to give the Palestinians control of the area surrounding the Gush Katif settlements. Had these arrangements been implemented, each settlement would have been isolated in a sea of Palestinian jurisdiction that would have threatened Israeli lines of communication and reinforcement.

After six months of implementation talks, Israel and the Palestinians finally agreed that Israeli control of settlements required authority over entire settlement "blocs" and not just the settlements themselves. This will be an important precedent when Israel seeks to retain control of certain zones of the West Bank in final status talks. Earlier input from the military might have resolved this issue in the original Oslo talks, thereby obviating the need to deal with it in the post-Oslo implementation negotiations.

Rabin demonstrated that he had learned this lesson when he named senior IDF officers as the primary (and virtually only) negotiators during the implementation talks. There is some justifiable criticism that this decision went too far in the other direction, but it did improve decision making and create a forum for discussion on implementation;[5] unlike his informal and

---

[5] This should not be understood to mean that Israel achieved all of its substantive goals in those talks. As one participant said later: "We did not think we would extend Jericho the way the Palestinians wanted . . . to Karantal, Marutas, and Nebi Musa. We also did not plan to give them a passport."

sometimes even haphazard style during the Oslo talks, Rabin included a notetaker in his post-Oslo meetings with the IDF general staff to discuss security strategy.[6] Rabin is unlikely to exclude the military from negotiations with Syria that, to a far greater degree than Oslo, revolve around security. Rabin has made clear that Israel will not sign a declaration of principles with Syria without a prior outline on security issues.

## The Political Clock and Implementation Deadlines

The fragility of Rabin's governing coalition appears to have played a strong role in propelling Oslo forward, even as it precluded progress on issues such as settlements. Rabin's aides say the premier spoke often of the need to deliver on his campaign promise to reach an accord within six to nine months of taking office. Rabin liked to emphasize the window of opportunity for peace in the Arab world, but he was also aware of the political winds blowing within his own country. The Labor-Meretz alignment was not something Rabin could rely on, particularly since 1992 marked the first time in fifteen years that the Likud was totally excluded from government.

The swing vote in Israeli elections is traditionally very narrow. Had the right-wing bloc taken only one Knesset seat from the left in the elections in 1992, this would have enabled the Likud to join the Rabin government as a junior coalition partner. In the two "national unity governments" that existed between 1984-90, neither party could enact its own platform and left the country with indecisive leadership on several important matters. This was a more serious problem for Labor than Likud, which generally favored the pre-Oslo *status quo*.

The direct election of the prime minister planned for 1996 will not end Israel's parliamentary system of government. It will still take sixty-one votes in the Knesset to obtain approval for the naming of a government and to pass legislation or a budget. Labor certainly cannot dismiss the possibility of a different political configuration in the aftermath of the elections in 1996, perhaps a

---

[6] Rabin's weekly meetings with the heads of the Mossad and Shin Bet have always included a notetaker, in keeping with the recommendations of the Agranat Commission, which investigated the reasons for Israel's lack of warning and preparation before the 1973 Yom Kippur War.

center-right instead of center-left government. This has led Beilin to call for accelerating negotiations with the Palestinians by skipping over the interim agreement that he helped draft, and is likely to prompt some in Labor to press for concluding negotiations with all of the various Arab parties before the elections. Arafat is likely to be equally keen to conclude the final disposition of territories before the elections, fearing that delay could mean a Likud government in one form or another. Used properly, the specter of the Likud "waiting in the wings" could even help Rabin in negotiations with the Palestinians and other Arab parties.

Implementation of the Oslo accord was delayed because the DOP did not address several basic issues—e.g., control of crossing points, the size of Jericho, and nature of security arrangements. William Quandt, National Security Council staff member for the Near East during the Nixon and Carter administrations and a participant in the Camp David negotiations, recalls a similar problem during those talks. The political echelon was more intent on reaching a deal, he said, than addressing technical difficulties that threatened stalemate. Senior Israeli officials suggest that it was precisely for this reason that Rabin did not involve his closest military aides in Oslo decision making.

Yet the advantage of dealing with technical issues in the early phase is that resolution can be sought in the context of broader principles, where tradeoffs should be easier to make. Although this may involve making more difficult decisions up front, it would prevent a later loss of momentum when issues are more likely to be viewed in isolation from the bigger picture. If thorny issues are intentionally deferred, implementation deadlines should be realistically extended to take into account the technical complexity of resolving them at a later date.

In the case of both Camp David and Oslo, the implementation deadlines were not met. Negotiations on implementation of the Oslo accord took seven months instead of the prescribed two. At the same time, negotiators *over*estimated the period of actual withdrawal, allotting four months for a process that ultimately took only two weeks, albeit partly because the IDF had begun removing infrastructure during the negotiations themselves. As it turned out, the timing worked out well in the end. The IDF completed its withdrawal only a month behind schedule, which in fact correlated to the amount of time the PLO boycotted negotiations in the aftermath of the Hebron massacre.

No less critical for the Palestinians will be IDF redeployment from Palestinian population centers in the West Bank and the holding of elections during the second phase of self-rule, which is running far behind schedule. Israelis note that the Oslo accord talks about "aims" and "goals" as opposed to hard and fast deadlines. This is little consolation to the Palestinians, however, who chafe at the fact that Israel has effectively linked progress in negotiations on IDF redeployment and subsequent elections to the Palestinian Authority's taking more effective measures to ensure Israeli security.

This is not to say there should be *no* deadlines; timetables are needed to preserve momentum, especially in the case of Oslo, where both Israel and the PLO feared that rejectionists on both sides would seek to torpedo the dramatic accord. Setting unrealistic deadlines, however, even for tactical reasons, runs the risk of building unrealizable expectations that could ultimately undermine the agreement.

## Creating Unrealistic Expectations

The aim of the Oslo accord was to bridge the competing demands of Israelis and Palestinians to a small strip of land by shaping a *modus vivendi* that would lead to lasting coexistence between the two peoples. If the Labor party had its druthers, it would have favored an immediate territorial partition in a bid to disentangle Israelis and Palestinians. Rabin and Peres, however, had to settle for what they thought was feasible rather than what they deemed desirable. The political climate among both Israelis and Palestinians precluded a "no-fault" divorce, so they were forced to accept a kind of "shotgun wedding."

Rabin and Peres believed that the interim agreement would be the first step toward what Rabin often refers to as "separation," but both men knew it would not produce an outbreak of idyllic harmony between Israelis and Palestinians. The Oslo accord was marketed to the Israeli public, however, as the attainment of an historic reconciliation between the two peoples. Soaring expectations merely increased the level of disappointment that accompanied post-Oslo terror attacks.

During the Oslo negotiations, PLO officials assured their Israeli counterparts that, in return for mutual recognition, Arafat—as the 'sole, legitimate representative' of the Palestinian people—would be able to enforce the deal, control terrorism, and otherwise ensure Israeli security. On that basis, Rabin persuaded Israelis that one of the virtues of the Oslo accord was that Arafat would crack down on Hamas. There is no evidence, however, that this premise was tested in advance to determine whether Arafat had either the ability or the will to curb attacks by Islamic extremists against Israelis. On the contrary, Arafat may even believe that his negotiating position is enhanced by his opponents' resort to violence, without which Israel might never have exited Gaza.

This is not to suggest that there was an alternative to the Oslo accord, or to Arafat as a Palestinian interlocutor, particularly since Israel's original goal was withdrawal and not reconciliation. Had this premise been tested in advance, however, the Oslo accord and Gaza-Jericho implementation agreement would have been structured somewhat differently. For example, Israel might not have forsworn all rights of preemption and hot pursuit had it known that there are limits to Palestinian security cooperation.

The Gaza-Jericho agreement considerably constrains Israel's flexibility in dealing with terrorism. Rabin's domestic credibility was enhanced before the Oslo accord by three decisions—the Hamas expulsions, closure of territories, and Operation Accountability—that signaled to the Israeli public that flexibility in peace negotiations would not mean a lax posture on security issues. Although none of these initiatives succeeded in completely ending violence, they enhanced Rabin's domestic popularity and enabled him to move forward in talks with the Palestinians. Similar steps are much tougher to take in the wake of the Oslo accord, which has reduced considerably Rabin's ability to pursue independent peace and security policies with the Palestinians.

Specifically, the Oslo accord and subsequent implementation agreement limited Israel's ability to engage in hot pursuit, preemption, and retaliation in the event of violence. Deporting suspected Hamas militants or chasing armed fugitives in Gaza is no longer politically viable, because such actions will be seen at best as coming at Arafat's expense, and at worst as a derogation of both the letter and spirit of the agreement. Thus, though in the past Rabin's firm response to threats of terrorism and violence increased his domestic support, he is now forced to find other means of achieving the same end. In the absence of Palestinian cooperation, Rabin will be seen as powerless to deal with the security issues that have been his strongest suit.

Rabin has increasingly referred to the idea of "separation" as both a temporary and long-term solution to Israeli security concerns and Palestinian demands for greater autonomy. Although physical barriers such as fences are considered impractical and politically undesirable before final status talks, the government has increased the number of foreign workers to minimize the dependence on the estimated 50,000 Palestinian day laborers who rely on work in Israel. The lack of a Palestinian industrial base causes living conditions in the West Bank and Gaza to plummet whenever extended security closures are imposed in the aftermath of terrorism against Israelis. Although the idea of Palestinian industrial enterprise zones is being discussed to help create employment opportunities and foster economic growth in the self-governing areas, the process of economic separation could take a couple of years. A more immediate remedy may involve Israeli transfer payments to the Palestinians in the form of unemployment compensation.

Oslo demonstrated that settlements are perhaps Rabin's most sensitive domestic political issue. Arafat's willingness to postpone negotiations on the status of settlements until talks on the final disposition of the territories ensured that Israel could defer an internal showdown over this issue. Peres later explained that the government "wanted to push through an agreement with minimum opposition. That is one of the reasons why we insisted the settlements remain where they are. We thought that any different approach would split the nation beyond recognition. I was very happy that we were able to avoid this split."[7]

The limited agenda of the Oslo process is largely responsible for its relative success. Israel and the PLO agreed to defer the most difficult issues, including Jerusalem, refugees, and settlements, until negotiations on the final status of the occupied territories, in the hope that the experience of the interim phase itself would soften attitudes toward final status issues and make compromise more likely. Each side viewed this as a major concession on its part—for the Israelis, that they would even agree to discuss those three issues; for the PLO, that they would be willing to defer them

---

[7] Press conference with foreign correspondents, March 8, 1994. The foreign minister also claimed that the decision to postpone movement on the Syrian track was in large part tied to Damascus' insistence that any deal on the Golan be linked to dismantling the settlements that are home to some 11,000 Israeli citizens, many of whom were Labor voters in 1992.

for several years. The increasing level of violence, however, may make it impossible to avoid a showdown over some settlements even before final status talks, and ironically may accelerate the timetable leading to final status negotiations themselves.[8]

A series of domestic political confrontations over settlements could be no less (and perhaps even more) difficult for Rabin than negotiations with the PLO over final status. Should Rabin decide that some withdrawal of settlements is necessary, he will focus on the more isolated outposts, in order to avoid provoking a substantial segment of the Israeli population. As a security analyst, he would prefer to limit the points of friction between settlers and a hostile Palestinian population in the territories. As a politician, however, Rabin will be wary of provoking passive support for settlers among the public or within his coalition.

If the settlers take up arms against the IDF, they will lose credibility with the public. If, however, Rabin appears trigger-happy and uses force without provocation, it could profoundly widen the political chasm in Israeli society. Rabin's early attempts to isolate the settlers politically backfired by denigrating and delegitimizing the majority of law-abiding settlers while treating the hardcore radicals with kid gloves. In fact, Rabin needs to pursue the opposite policy if he is to succeed in isolating the extremists and win public support for uprooting certain settlements. His predicament is complicated by the fact that some of the most problematic settlers, such as those in Hebron, are also the most ideologically committed.

---

[8] Public pressure in Israel and among the Palestinians could prevent the attainment of a final agreement, particularly in regard to the volatile issue of Jerusalem. Even as Rabin insists that Israel will not cede any territory in Jerusalem, Arafat speaks of East Jerusalem as the capital of a Palestinian state. While academics and others have spoken about creative, non-territorial solutions to determining the final status of the city, it is possible and maybe even probable that this issue could block a final Israel-Palestinian peace treaty. Under such circumstances, negotiators on both sides may even have to consider a *second* interim agreement, which will deal with disposition of territory in the West Bank and defer the status of Jerusalem for some future negotiation.

According to a map of final status contained in a report written by Joseph Alpher, then director of Tel Aviv University's Jaffee Center for Strategic Studies, and endorsed by Environment Minister Yossi Sarid, Israel is likely to insist on retaining control over 70 percent of the Jewish settlers, who currently occupy approximately 11 percent of the West Bank.

# Epilogue

By early 1995, the euphoria of the White House signing ceremony had faded and been replaced by the sobering reality of mounting terrorism and the steep political obstacles that still lie ahead. Although 1994 witnessed a series of notable achievements—from the Cairo agreement on implementing the Oslo accord to Arafat's triumphant return to Gaza and the establishment of the Palestinian Authority (PA) to the breakthrough in peace making with Jordan—new problems seemed to arise faster than past issues could be resolved. Perhaps most worrisome is the continuing instability in the Israel-PLO relationship, which must develop into a cooperative partnership if the peace process is to ultimately succeed.

Israeli and Palestinian leaders both wanted to demonstrate that Oslo will benefit their respective publics, but this is proving difficult. For the PA, that meant raising the standard of living in Gaza and Jericho, but the slow pace of institution-building and relative dearth of international funding for investment and infrastructure have frustrated efforts to achieve quick results. For the Rabin government, it meant reducing violence, and Arafat's failure to prevent terrorist attacks against Israelis resulted in friction with the PA and widespread Israeli dissatisfaction with the peace deal that increases with every attack.

For Israel, the most important by-product of the Oslo accord thus far is its peace treaty with Jordan, the first such agreement between Israel and an Arab state since the 1979 peace treaty with Egypt. The Oslo accord cracked the facade of Arab unity that had prevented King Hussein from formalizing his long-standing clandestine relationship with Israel, and the fear that Syria might cut a separate deal with Israel and deprive Jordan of the benefits of peace (and the fact that Damascus would not risk its improving relationship with Washington by attempting to wreck the peace process) prompted Amman to reach a deal with Israel first.

Although Israel's separate peace agreements with the PLO and Jordan deprived Syria of some of its political leverage, they did not precipitate a breakthrough between Jerusalem and Damascus, whose negotiations continue to move glacially. And though few observers seriously expected something of the magnitude of Sadat's visit to Jerusalem, Assad seemed incapable of reaching out to his adversaries and demonstrating his commitment to peace.

In addition to its effects on other bilateral negotiations, the Oslo accord stimulated progress in the various multilateral negotiations that resulted from the Madrid peace conference and improved Israel's relations with several Arab, Muslim, and other developing nations. Another outgrowth was the economic summit held in Casablanca in October 1994, which brought together leaders from throughout the Middle East and North Africa as well as representatives of 900 companies interested in investment opportunities in the region, laying the groundwork for potentially beneficial economic cooperation. The event was a vindication of sorts for Peres, who had pressed the idea a year earlier in a secret meeting in Jordan with King Hussein. Not surprisingly, Syria and Lebanon refused to send representatives to the summit, which they considered an inappropriate step toward "normalization" with Israel in the absence of a comprehensive peace in the region.

## Implementing the DOP

Less than two weeks after the Rabin-Arafat handshake on the White House lawn, the Knesset registered its support for the Labor government by approving the DOP by a vote of 61-50 with nine abstentions. But the DOP was just the beginning. The next step was to negotiate an agreement with the PLO on how to implement the agreement. "There are more than a hundred issues I did not think of" while negotiating the DOP, Rabin told his cabinet in late September.

Stung by criticism that he had allowed the dovish Peres to play too prominent a role in Oslo while excluding the IDF, Rabin turned negotiations on implementing the DOP over to senior officers whom he trusted more than Foreign Ministry officials and whose involvement was reassuring to the public. Shahak was named chief negotiator, planning chief Major General Uzi Dayan was named head of the security subcommittee, and Rothschild was put in charge of transferring civilian authority to the PLO.

Arafat named Nabil Shaath as his chief negotiator, and appointed Ramallah businessman Jamil Tarifi to negotiate with Rothschild on civilian affairs.

The implementation talks, held initially at the tiny Egyptian resort area of Taba near Eilat, quickly bogged down. Media attention encouraged negotiators to stake out tough positions and play to public opinion, and the two sides were divided conceptually on the level of cooperation that would exist between them during the interim period. Israeli officials made clear that there could not be adequate security unless Israeli and Palestinian troops worked together, but the Palestinians' immediate concern was establishing their administration. "They said essentially, 'Give us the keys,' " said one Israeli negotiator.

The deadline in the Oslo agreement for completing the first phase of implementation negotiations was December 13, but the two sides were nowhere near agreement and it soon became clear that it would not be ready by that date. Rabin and Arafat sparred publicly over whether they had to adhere to the "holy dates" in the DOP. A meeting between the two at Mubarak's Cairo palace on December 12 proved a fiasco and (as was the case in the aftermath of the December deportation crisis) Rabin was forced to turn to Peres to overcome the impasse.

But it took more than the foreign minister to put the talks back on track. The venue was changed from Taba to an unknown location in Cairo, which took the negotiations out of the view of the media. In addition, each side started making conceptual changes. The Palestinians agreed to various forms of security cooperation (such as joint patrols with the IDF) and allowed Israel to define clusters of individual settlements as single cohesive blocs, making it easier for the IDF to defend them.

In return, Israel dropped its insistence that the IDF be allowed to go anywhere to protect Israelis—yielding on the concepts of "hot pursuit" and preemption that have been key elements of Israeli military doctrine since the pre-state era—and accepted a role in Gaza limited to protecting the estimated 4,500 Israelis in the Katif bloc and isolated settlements.[1] To achieve this, the two sides created a so-called "yellow zone" around Katif and Rafah

---

[1] In his remarks to the Knesset prior to the vote on the DOP, Rabin said the IDF would have free reign. Only after being pressed by parliamentarians in a closed-door session of the Foreign Affairs and Defense Committee two months later did he admit that Israel would not have hot pursuit rights.

within which the IDF would exercise security authority and the PA would have civilian control.

Peres managed to resolve the more delicate issue of control over crossing points between the autonomous areas and Jordan and Egypt. Arafat insisted that the PA have complete control over the borders, charging that otherwise Gaza and Jericho would amount to little more than Palestinian *"Bantustans."* Rabin, however, feared that this would result in unfettered arms smuggling and Palestinian immigration. The two sides ultimately reached an agreement whereby Israeli border officials would remain behind mirrored glass largely out of sight but retain a veto over the entry of individuals and other security matters.

## The Hebron Massacre

Negotiations on the size of Jericho, the number of Palestinian prisoners to be released, and the details of economic relations between Israel and the PA were still underway when disaster struck. On February 25, 1994, extremist Jewish settler Baruch Goldstein opened fire on Muslims praying in Hebron's Tomb of the Patriarchs, a site holy to both faiths, killing twenty-nine Palestinians before being beaten to death by enraged survivors. Riots ensued across the territories and, facing intense domestic pressure, Arafat suspended the implementation talks and called for the dismantling of the Jewish settlement in Hebron housing some 400 Israelis. Rabin refused, citing an agreement in the DOP that the disposition of settlements would be discussed only in final status negotiations slated to begin no later than two years after the completion of Gaza-Jericho implementation talks.

Rabin did agree, however, to the deployment of an unarmed "temporary international presence in Hebron" (TIPH), a step Israel had assiduously avoided since gaining control of the territories in 1967—out of fear that even something as seemingly benign as the TIPH would set a precedent that could ultimately lead to a UN trusteeship of the territories. But Rabin felt it was the only way to revive the negotiations and maintain the momentum of the peace process. Although it allowed the negotiations to succeed, the TIPH itself proved a failure. Lacking the authority to intercede in violent confrontations between the IDF and Palestinians, its members were mocked as powerless by the residents of Hebron and withdrawn after three months.

When the implementation talks resumed a month later, Israel agreed to release approximately 5,000 Palestinian prisoners and detainees held in Israeli installations, including members of Hamas not charged with capital offenses (but only if they pledged to desist from violence and support the peace process) and prisoners accused of killing Palestinians who had collaborated with Israel. No one accused of killing an Israeli—whether the victim was a Jew or an Arab—was released. As of this writing, only 4,000 of the prisoners had been freed, the release of the others having been delayed by public outrage in Israel following subsequent terrorist attacks.

In contast, the two sides reached an economic agreement relatively quickly and amicably. They established free trade between Israel and the Palestinian autonomous areas (except on five basic agricultural commodities to protect Israeli farmers), allowed the PA to import limited quantities of goods from the Arab world, and set roughly equal quotas and customs duties on imports from all other sources. The PA also agreed to postpone the establishment of a central bank in favor of a lesser monetary authority and retain the Jordanian *dinar* and the Israeli *shekel* instead of creating its own currency; Israel agreed to allow the PA to adopt a value-added tax slightly lower than its own and to transfer to the PA most of the income tax collected from Palestinians working in Israel, though it reserved the right to suspend the movement of labor for security reasons.

The last issue to be resolved was defining the size of the Jericho area. In a late night meeting (part of which was attended by Christopher) at Mubarak's palace, Rabin agreed to an area of sixty-two square kilometers. The implementation agreement's May 4 signing ceremony in Cairo was disrupted, however, when Arafat—believing that the two sides had agreed to expand the Jericho area within three months—suddenly refused to sign maps delineating the smaller area in an appendix to the 186-page document. A dispute broke out in the middle of the ceremony, which was broadcast live. After a brief intermission, during which aides on both side scrambled to assuage Arafat's misgivings, the PLO chairman relented and once again Middle East diplomacy ended in exhaustion instead of elation.

The mistrust demonstrated at the Cairo signing ceremony increased dramatically several days later when a tape of a speech Arafat made in a mosque in Johannesburg became public. In the speech, the PLO leader called upon Muslims to wage a *jihad* ("holy struggle") for Jerusalem and likened the Oslo accord to a truce that the Prophet Muhammad had reached with the Quraysh tribe and then abrogated ten years later. Although Arafat explained his use of the word *jihad* as a struggle for peace, many Israelis pointed to the statement as evidence of PLO perfidy.

In addition to the political damage caused by the *jihad* remark, Arafat dropped a second bombshell in the Johannesburg speech by alluding to the letter that Peres had written on maintaining the status of Palestinian institutions in Jerusalem. Unwitting Israeli officials initially denied the existence of the letter before Peres was forced to reveal the truth—though he insisted that since the letter had been addressed to Norwegian Foreign Minister Holst rather than Arafat, he technically had not lied when he said he had made no secret promises to the Palestinians.

## Security and Economic Development

After his return to the occupied territories on July 1, Arafat confounded predictions by setting up his headquarters in gritty Gaza instead of more serene Jericho or (as Israeli intelligence had expected) returning quickly to Tunis and running the PA from a distance. Two intertwined themes have dominated efforts to implement the Oslo accord: security and economic development.

The PA needs capital to finance development and thereby create an atmosphere of greater stability. Immediately after the DOP was signed, more than thirty-five countries pledged a total of $2.2 billion to be disbursed to the autonomous areas over five years. The donors did not deliver all of the funds they pledged, however, initially because of what they said was insufficient Palestinian planning and accounting. According to Rabin, at least $65 million due from the Arab countries alone in 1994 never arrived. To ensure that their donations finance development projects and not mismanagement and corruption, the donors delegated oversight authority to the World Bank. Arafat resisted these efforts, which he considered a humiliating threat to his control over the PLO's financial largesse, which has traditionally been one of the keys to his power.

After months of haggling, the World Bank agreed to monthly disbursements of some $13 million for recurrent administrative costs such as salaries, but the large-scale development projects needed to generate much-needed jobs and improve living standards remain stalled. The slow pace of change eroded Arafat's standing among the population and increased support for radical groups that perpetrate terrorist attacks against Israelis. This initiated a self-perpetuating cycle in which violence prompted the Rabin government to seal off the territories, thereby depriving Palestinians of their chief source of employment and exacerbating the economic conditions that lead to increased support for further extremism. American officials privately estimate that the roughly 50 percent reduction in the number of Palestinian workers allowed into Israel resulted in a daily loss of revenue in Gaza of approximately $1 million. Thus, by the spring of 1995, a key premise of Oslo—that economic development equals security— had proven difficult to realize.

Meanwhile, the provisions in the DOP that require the PA to maintain security within the autonomous areas effectively placed Arafat in the middle of a "zero-sum" equation between Israel on one side and Hamas and Palestinian Islamic Jihad on the other. If he cracked down too hard on peace process opponents, he risked further eroding his support among Palestinians by increasing the perception that he is essentially an agent of the Israelis; if he did not create at least the appearance of observing the DOP, however, he risked losing his credibility among the Israelis and thus their willingness to continue further negotiations.

Rabin had persuaded the Israeli public of the wisdom of the Oslo accord in part by claiming that Arafat could combat terrorism more effectively than the IDF because he does not have to worry (as the prime minister does) about the legality of his methods. What he and other Israelis failed to recognize, however, is that the PA lacked the political will to confront Hamas directly. Arafat reached a tacit agreement with Islamist leaders to avoid violence among the various Palestinian factions and against Israelis in PA-administered territory, but he did not get them to forswear attacks against Israelis in territories still under Israeli control.

In response to Israel's demands that he act to curtail the fundamentalist violence that claimed the lives of more than 100 Israelis since the signing of the Oslo agreement, Arafat has ordered the arrests of hundreds of Hamas suspects, only to release them shortly thereafter when the media spotlight passed. His commitment to security was put to its first major test in October 1994 when Hamas kidnapped Israeli soldier Nachshon Waxman. Rabin suspended peace talks, sealed off the occupied territories, and enlisted Mubarak and Christopher to secure Arafat's cooperation in finding Waxman. Under heavy pressure, Arafat initiated a manhunt in Gaza and imprisoned scores of Hamas activists before Israel tracked Waxman to an Israeli-controlled area of the West Bank, where he was ultimately killed by his captors during a failed Israeli rescue attempt.

Two subsequent suicide bombings within Israel—one on a bus in the heart of Tel Aviv that killed twenty-two civilians and another at a crossing point near the city of Netanya that killed twenty-one people (mostly young IDF conscripts)—further enraged Israelis. Terrorism cut into support for both the Oslo accord and Rabin himself, who many felt had betrayed the promise implicit in his criticism of Likud settlement policy during the election in 1992: that a peace agreement with the Palestinians would insulate voters inside the Green Line from violence.

Israel's Oslo negotiators seem to have assumed that, as the "sole legitimate representative" of the Palestinian people, Arafat would be willing and able to control terrorism, assure the security of Israelis in the self-rule areas, and otherwise maintain his side of the deal. There is no evidence that they tested this premise in advance by seeking explicit guarantees from Arafat on how he would respond to terrorism or by conducting a rigorous internal assessment of his capability to do so—steps that would have allowed them to craft more precise language in the DOP on issues such as preemption and hot pursuit. Had the Oslo agreement been based on the strictly territorial division the Labor party had historically envisioned, Arafat's security commitments would not have been so critical. But domestic political constraints forced Rabin to accept an interim deal whose point of departure was an uneasy coexistence between Israelis and Palestinians.

Both sides have charged the other with violations of the accord. The Israelis are upset by what they see as the Palestinian Authority's lack of effort in combating terrorism, ranging from weak intelligence cooperation to the fact that terrorist leaders have neither been tried nor punished to their failure to enforce a stated policy of confiscating unlicensed weapons, particularly from members of radical groups opposed to the peace process. Peres is fond of saying that although Israel does not expect the PA to produce 100 percent success, it would like to see 100 percent effort. Strong Israeli, U.S., and Egyptian pressure in early 1995 forced Arafat to finally establish secret "state security courts" in which a relatively small number of low-level Islamist radicals were convicted of terrorist attacks. At the same time, Israel did not appreciate the fact that the PA unilaterally increased the number of its security personnel from 9,000 to 16,000 in contravention of the Oslo accord.

The Palestinians respond with their own countercharges, arguing that Israeli construction around Jerusalem violates the accord, which said the status of the city is to be determined in final status talks. (Israel disputes the assertion, noting that it pointedly refused to commit itself to freeze expansion in the city or even in the West Bank.) The Palestinians also complain that, as of mid-1995, safe passage between the West Bank and Gaza had not been implemented due to Israeli security concerns in the aftermath of terror attacks. More critically, the Palestinians are upset that the entire second phase of the interim agreement, including elections and IDF redeployment, is running far behind schedule. Israelis counter that progress on the second phase is linked to Palestinian security measures.

By June 1995, these thorny issues seemed close to resolution. Violence subsided after Arafat took stronger measures against terrorism and reached an informal agreement with Islamic militants to temporarily suspend terrorist attacks that he argued had delayed increased Palestinian autonomy. In response and despite continuing antagonism on security issues, Israeli officials agreed to extend Palestinian jurisdiction to thirty-three areas of civilian affairs (rather than eight areas as originally envisioned) throughout the West Bank during the interim period, even though the PA would not have a corresponding deployment of security personnel in those areas.

The following month, the two sides reached a tentative agreement to expand Palestinian self-rule by withdrawing Israeli troops in stages from virtually all Arab cities in the West Bank and redeploying them in rural areas and around Jewish settlements, where they would retain responsibility for security. In advance of Palestinian elections for a self-rule council, the IDF would withdraw from Jenin, Nablus, Tulkarm, Qalqilya, and parts of Ramallah and Bethlehem (complete withdrawal from these two cities awaits the construction of bypass roads). A second phase of redeployment from the Palestinian countryside—simply termed in the Oslo accord as "further redeployments"—would be completed no later than mid-1997.

Israel insisted on redeploying in phases for two reasons. First, to allow for the construction of roads that would enable Israeli settlers to bypass Palestinian cities. Though these alternate routes will not prevent attacks by determined terrorists, Rabin stressed their importance in reducing daily friction between settlers and Palestinians. The prime minister hopes to postpone a politically risky confrontation with the settlers, particularly the more ideological factions living in outlying areas near Palestinian cities, until after the 1996 Israeli elections. This will also give all of the settlers—from those who pin their hopes on a Likud victory and resultant redeployment "freeze" to those who have already pledged defiance and instigated clashes with Palestinians—more time to adapt to the evolving geopolitical landscape.

Second, the phases create a kind of interim period *within* the interim period—a protracted testing period during which Israel would retain leverage based on the PA's security performance. If the evacuated cities prove to be havens for terrorists, Rabin would feel compelled to respond forcefully or risk being labelled as soft on security, particularly in advance of pending Israeli elections. As Arafat and the PA have an interest in expanding and consolidating their authority in the West Bank (and thus, indirectly, in keeping Rabin in power), in theory they will take steps to prevent terrorism.

Despite these conditions, the negotiations on redeployment highlighted what some critics of the Oslo accord consider its central flaw: although the DOP specifically states that the interim agreement will not determine the ultimate disposition of the occupied territories, withdrawal from certain areas of the West Bank during the interim period will be practically irreversible later on. Israeli officials privately acknowledged that the agreement would likely emerge as the *de facto* blueprint for a final status agreement, in that they agreed to allow greater Palestinian autonomy in areas they expected to relinquish in the final negotiations—in part to lock in these concessions in the event that the 1996 elections result in a Likud-controlled government.

As a result, redeployment not only represents yet another historic turning point in relations between Israelis and Palestinians, but sets in motion political and geographic dynamics that, though evolving at different speeds, will have potentially far-reaching consequences.

The political dynamic is the more immediate of the two. In addition to withdrawal from the cities, Israel agreed to give the PA administrative control over the 600,000-700,000 Palestinians living in the roughly 450 villages outside the cities—including the deployment of blue-uniformed municipal policemen (as opposed to green-fatigued paramilitary border policemen) in many of those villages. Thus, although Israel would still occupy the vast majority of the territory in the West Bank, its nearly three decades of control over the daily lives of the inhabitants would effectively end.

Moreover, leaving places in the West Bank like Bethlehem, Ramallah, and Nablus—places which hold a certain historical and biblical resonance for Israelis and Jews throughout the world—is qualitatively different from abandoning the quagmire that was the Gaza Strip. In a sense, the interim agreement begins transforming Israel's relationship to the West Bank from a religious/ideological question laden with emotion and symbolism to a strictly security-based issue similar to that involving the Golan Heights.

Conversely, the elections tentatively scheduled to be held throughout the West Bank and Gaza at the end of 1995 will give the Palestinians a renewed sense of independence and empowerment while providing Arafat and the PLO-based PA with a mantle of legitimacy (both internally and externally) that they had previously lacked. This could remove Arafat's excuse for his lack of deliberate action and also allow him to make politically risky concessions on final borders.

In contrast, the territorial component of redeployment would involve a more gradual transfer of authority—from Palestinian cities as "islands" in a "sea" of Israeli sovereignty to Jewish settlements as islands in a sea of Palestinian authority—but one with potentially far-greater significance; the transition process will result in the effective partition of what was Mandatory Palestine.

At the same time, the interim agreement could still allow Israel to maintain and even consolidate its control over the roughly 11 percent of the West Bank (particularly the areas surrounding and west of Jerusalem) where some 70 percent of the settlers live and which even liberal Israelis believe should be retained for security reasons in a final peace agreement. That leaves more remote Jewish settlements, the Jordan Valley, the eastern sector of Jerusalem, the status of Palestinian refugees from the 1948 war, and the issue of Palestinian statehood to be resolved in final status talks.

## Completing the Triangle: Peace with Jordan

Prior to Oslo, King Hussein had managed to become the region's longest-reigning monarch by avoiding open peace with Israel while maintaining a clandestine (albeit widely known) relationship with Israel. The PLO's overt agreement with Israel not only rendered Jordan's *sub rosa* relationship unnecessary, but threatened to eclipse Amman's political and economic interests unless the king rapidly broadened Jordan's ties with Israel and secured a role for the kingdom in shaping the development of the new Palestinian entity.

There was also a personal factor in Hussein's desire to reach a more formal peace. He had witnessed the assassination of his grandfather, King Abdullah, in Jerusalem in 1951 by a Palestinian who opposed his efforts to reconcile with Israel. Hussein, who was recovering from a cancer operation, reportedly wrote to President Clinton in 1994 that he was determined to fulfill that part of his grandfather's legacy and leave his own.

To their credit, Rabin and Peres quickly recognized and seized the opportunity to make peace with Jordan. In two separate meetings with American officials shortly after Oslo, Peres hammered home the need to pursue a rapid breakthrough with Jordan. He called this a "storming strategy" that would complete a "natural triangle" with the Palestinians. Though not opposed to the idea, U.S. officials were skeptical that it was possible and concerned that Syria's Assad would feel isolated and attempt to sabotage both the Palestinian and Jordanian tracks. There was also an unstated fear that Israel might get sidetracked and forgo a strategic peace with Syria in favor of a separate deal with Jordan.

With Rabin's blessing, Peres asked Ephraim Halevy, deputy head of the Mossad and the long-time liaison between the two countries, to arrange a meeting with King Hussein a few days before Jordan's November elections. In nine hours of talks that ended near dawn on November 3, the two sides drafted a four-page document in which Jordan agreed to sign a peace treaty with Israel in exchange for an Israeli commitment to negotiate border demarcation and re-allocation of water from the Yarmuk and Jordan Rivers. It also called for linking the two countries' electricity grids and raised the idea of Israeli help in winning Jordanian debt relief from the United States.

The document was doomed before the ink had even dried, however. Due perhaps to his rivalry with Rabin, Peres was unable to resist dropping a hint to the Israeli media about the progress with Jordan. "Remember November 3," he remarked off-handedly to reporters, setting off a wave of heightened attention and speculation about the normally inconspicuous Israel-Jordan relationship. The leak infuriated the Jordanians, particularly because the timing—just days before national elections—would allow Islamic opposition parties to exploit rumors of secret peace talks with Israel.

Moreover, having dealt with Arafat himself for over twenty-five years, Hussein was skeptical that the Oslo accord would last very long. Knowing that there would be no need to improve relations with Israel if Oslo collapsed, Hussein decided not to pursue the November 3 agreement. Although the talks between Israel and Jordan eventually resumed, Rabin refused to negotiate border and water issues outside the context of a comprehensive peace, and the two sides were reduced to discussing banking in the occupied territories and joint efforts to control insects.

Yet the king also realized that he could not risk further economic and political isolation. The United States and Persian Gulf countries had sharply reduced their aid to Amman in response to Jordanian support for Iraq during the Gulf War. Iraq itself, a major market for Jordanian exports before the war, is now an economic cripple and political pariah. Saudi officials rebuffed Hussein's request for a meeting during a private pilgrimage to Mecca in April and, when he failed to respond to a letter from Clinton urging a resumption of peace talks with Israel, Christopher deliberately snubbed the king by not visiting Amman during two trips to the region in May.

Perhaps more importantly, Israel and Syria had exchanged peace proposals through the United States for the first time. The prospect of an agreement between the two adversaries threatened to minimalize the importance of (and thus the potential benefits from) an Israel-Jordan agreement. But it took the Israel-PLO economic agreement on May 4 to finally convince Hussein to resume high-level talks with Israel. Jordanian officials say the king was stunned by a provision known as "List B" in the agreement which limited Jordanian exports to the territories and would, he believed, effectively preclude an economic role for Jordan there.

On May 19, Hussein and Crown Prince Hassan met with Rabin and several of his aides at the London home of Lord Victor Mishcon, a Jewish politician with ties to Peres. After another meeting two weeks later, Hussein agreed to move the talks back to Jordan and Israel and announce the move at a trilateral (U.S.-Israel-Jordan) economic meeting in Washington on June 7.[2]

Both sides knew that the announcement would test the *de facto* Syrian veto on public Israeli-Jordanian negotiations and neither was certain how the Syrians would react. Although Hussein had met with Assad in Damascus in May, sources say he did not discuss the ongoing negotiations with Israel. When news of the impending announcement leaked out, the Syrian prime and foreign ministers canceled a trip to Amman for talks on economic cooperation. Assad's other options were limited, however. Using terrorism to sabotage the Israel-Jordan peace process would only exacerbate Damascus' isolation and undercut its goal of being removed from the U.S. State Deparment's list of states supporting international terrorism.

In an attempt to convince Syria not to react strongly to the upgraded Israel-Jordan talks, Clinton phoned Assad twice the following month and committed Christopher to pursue progress in Israel-Syria talks. Washington also made sure that Assad took notice of Rabin's statement in June that another war was inevitable unless Israel concluded a peace treaty with Damascus. Sources say Syria saw this as a favorable signal that Rabin was not trying to exclude Syria by making a separate peace with Amman.

Meanwhile, Halevy traveled to Washington to urge U.S. officials to grant Jordan's plea for debt forgiveness and other requests. In a meeting at the White House on June 22, Clinton told Hussein he would urge Congress to forgive Jordan's $700 million debt and that he would favorably consider requests for agricultural credits, financing for Boeing jets, and U.S. weapons (including F-16 fighters) to modernize the Jordanian military, but that Congress needed to be convinced of Jordan's willingness to make peace with Israel. A public meeting with Rabin, Clinton suggested, would be a visible symbol of that commitment.

The monarch was noncommittal, saying that progress first had to be made on bilateral issues between Israel and Jordan and thus implying that a meeting with Rabin would be possible a few months later. On July 9, Hussein told his parliament that such a

---

2 Any lingering doubts Hussein may have had about the prospects for a stable peace with Israel were laid to rest during a meeting earlier that month between Crown Prince Hassan and Israeli opposition leader Benjamin Netanyahu in which the latter renounced Likud's long-held view that Jordan is Palestine and assured Hassan that they shared a common enemy—a Palestinian state.

meeting was essential for obtaining American assistance. Three days later, he wrote Clinton that he was ready for a public meeting with the Israeli prime minister. Senior U.S. officials speculate that Hussein had crossed a "psychological threshold" and wanted to move quickly before opposition to the meeting coalesced; Israeli officials offer another explanation for the king's sudden urgency—concern that Jordan might miss the annual Congressional budgeting cycle.

## Crossing the Rubicon

Hussein agreed to meet Rabin near the two countries' narrow Read Sea coasts in Eilat-Aqaba, but he would not sign a peace treaty until they began negotiations over border demarcation and water redistribution. Israeli officials agreed but along with U.S. officials suggested moving the ceremony to Washington in order to highlight the American sponsorship of the peace process and ensure that Congress would not overlook the gravity of the event. Rabin dispatched Halevy to Amman to finalize the negotiations, which were completed July 20. Although Christopher got a brief look at agreement (which would come to be known as the Washington Declaration) the next day in Rabin's office, stunned U.S. officials—who were amazed that the deal had been completed without their assistance—received the exact text the night before the White House signing ceremony, the second such event in less than a year.

Although media coverage of the ceremony focused on the fact that the agreement ended the technical state of war between Israel and Jordan, more significant was the already evident warmth between the two states, particularly in contrast to the "cold" peace that has marked Israeli-Egyptian ties since Camp David. In addition to economic cooperation, Rabin and Hussein announced agreements on tourism, telecommunications, electric power, and air corridors, as well as their intention to open border crossings near the Aqaba-Eilat area and along their northern border. They also pledged joint efforts to combat security threats and terrorism.

Perhaps the most controversial aspect of the Washington Declaration was Israel's official recognition of Jordan's "special role" in Jerusalem. Although King Hussein formally renounced legal ties to the West Bank in 1988, he studiously maintained Jordanian administration of Muslim holy sites in Jerusalem—

including paying the salaries of the *waqf* (Islamic trust) watchmen—that endured after Israel captured the eastern half of the city in 1967. Following talks in June between Peres and Morocco's King Hassan (who headed the Arab League's committee on Jerusalem), Rabin and Peres began to differentiate between Jerusalem's political and religious dimensions. They adopted King Hussein's them that sovereignty over Muslim holy places in Jerusalem belongs only to God and began to use the Talmudic terms "celestial" and "earthly" Jerusalem in conversations with reporters to emphasize the distinction.

The idea was to satisfy Muslim religious aspirations by alluding to a kind of extraterritorial status for the Dome of the Rock and al Aqsa Mosques while maintaining Israel's political control over the city. In the Declaration, Israel said it would give Jordan's religious role in Jerusalem special consideration in final status negotiations with the Palestinians scheduled to begin in two years. This elicited an angry reaction from the Palestinians and other Arabs and contributed to Jordan's small but vocal opposition—including the sixteen Islamist deputies in the eighty-member parliament—to any deal with Israel. Sources say that, having crossed the psychological Rubicon by defying Syria, Hussein wanted to complete the peace treaty with Israel before the autumn session of parliament. Once the deal was signed, any criticism would have to be directed at the king himself rather than at the vague notion of cooperation with Israel.

## Closing the Deal

Following the signing of the Washington Declaration, working-level teams led on one side by Rubinstein and Bentsur and on the other by Jordanian Ambassador to Washington Fayiz Tarawneh began to meet alternately in Jordan and Israel to resolve the sensitive issues of water allocation, border demarcation, and mutual security. The Jordanians were adamant that there could be no peace treaty until these issues were resolved, and on several occasions the leaders of the two countries had to become personally involved to overcome impasses.

After decades of clandestine meetings, Rabin now traveled openly to Hussein's Aqaba palace and the two elder statesmen developed an excellent rapport. The prime minister could not refrain from comparing the trust he had in Hussein to the testiness of his relationship with Arafat. "Now, *this* is a country. Everything is organized," aides recount Rabin saying, contrasting the Jordanian regime to the nascent Palestinian Authority. Moreover, Rabin and Hussein shared what they believed was a realistic view of Palestinian political aspirations, the threat from growing Islamic militancy, and the role of Israeli-Jordanian cooperation as a bulwark against both.

Several key concessions on both sides enabled them to achieve a breakthrough relatively quickly. When Jordan complained that Israel was violating a formula for allocating water from the Jordan and Yarmuk Rivers which had been brokered by the United States in the mid-1950s, Rabin agreed to return 50 million cubic meters of water to Jordanian control. The two sides also discussed projects such as dams that might yield Jordan an additional 50 million cubic meters of water and Israel agreed to solicit international support to finance them.

The most creative solutions involved border demarcation. After surveying the border area in an unpublicized tour in an IDF helicopter, Rabin did not contest Jordan's claim that Israel had expanded its eastern frontier in 1969 by an estimated 360 square kilometers, some of which had since become farmland. Jordan demanded every inch of its former territory but agreed to allow Israel to retain about thirty kilometers of the farmland in exchange for territory in the Arava border area that had never been under Jordanian sovereignty. In addition, Jordan agreed to "lease" some 2.8 square kilometers of land under cultivation near the Yarmuk in the north and in Kibbutz Zofar along the Arava border to Israeli farmers for twenty-five years with an option to renew.

The compromise allowed Jordan to regain sovereignty over its territory without forcing Israel to uproot farmland. More important to Rabin, it established a precedent for retaining some Golan settlements after a peace agreement with Syria. Within twenty-four hours of the deal's announcement, however, Assad declared that he would never agree to any such arrangement. Rabin remained hopeful that another aspect of normalization—the king's agreement to establish a Jordanian embassy in Israel within a month of the peace treaty's ratification by both countries' parliaments—might serve as a precedent for the Syrian track.

From Israel's standpoint, the most important element of the treaty was Hussein's undertaking not to allow a third country to deploy forces in Jordan in a way that could threaten Israel. This would greatly diminish the chance of an attack along Israel's long and narrow "eastern front." Addressing this threat in the Israel-Jordan peace treaty was also seen as an advantage in Labor's future political battles over the West Bank; in a sense, a non-belligerent Jordan offered Israel greater strategic depth than that provided by the West Bank.

With President Clinton in attendance, the Israel-Jordan peace treaty was signed near the border crossing just north of Aqaba-Eilat on October 26, 1994. Rabin's face showed none of the angst that was evident when he shook Arafat's hand just over a year earlier at the White House. In fact, he appeared to enjoy the carnival-like setting in Arava as thousands of balloons were released into the air and senior Israeli and Jordanian officers exchanged gifts. Reflecting the Israeli consensus on peace with Jordan, the Likud joined Labor in approving the treaty in the Knesset by a margin of 105-3 with six abstentions.

## Reviving the Syria Track

As the focus of the Oslo process and the Israel-Jordan peace treaty shifted to implementation, the last major diplomatic objective for Rabin is negotiating peace with Syria. Although the formal negotiations between the two sides which began in Madrid were suspended in February 1994 following the Hebron massacre, potentially more fruitful talks began that summer between their respective ambassadors to Washington—Syria's Walid Moualem and Israel's Itamar Rabinovich—with U.S. officials in the room.

The two sides remain separated by substantive gaps on the four key elements of an agreement: the extent of Israel's withdrawal from Golan, the degree of peace and normalization (e.g., diplomatic relations, trade, tourism, etc.) that Syria will offer in return, the timetable for and connection between these two elements, and the security arrangements that will be needed to maintain the peace.

Although Rabin refuses to state explicitly that Israel will withdraw completely from the Golan until Assad defines the term of peace and normalization, he has come close by saying that the depth of withdrawal is linked to the depth of peace. After meetings with President Clinton in Geneva and Damascus in January and October 1994, Assad declared that Syria had made a "strategic choice" to pursue peace, but he refuses to elaborate on the terms of peace until Rabin commits himself to full withdrawal.

The United States, which is more directly involved in the Israel-Syria track than it was in Oslo, is trying to break the stalemate. Direct talks between Israeli and Syrian negotiators in Washington have been supplemented and at times supplanted by U.S. mediators and particularly Secretary of State Christopher, who made eight trips to the region in 1994 alone. The Syrian president apparently favors U.S. involvement because he believes that only Washington can deliver Jerusalem and the important third-party benefits of any deal with Israel.

One of the key factors behind the stalemate in these talks is that neither Syria nor Israel have demonstrated the sense of urgency that made Oslo possible, although the gaps between their positions have narrowed. In May 1994, Christopher convinced both sides to exchange proposals on the four areas of contention. Assad finally accepted the principle of a phased withdrawal and subsequently agreed to extend the timetable from a few months to one year—though preferably before Israel's 1996 elections so that a Likud government could not halt the process before completion.

By the time Clinton visited Damascus in late October 1994, Assad's timetable for withdrawal had been stretched to eighteen months, though he reportedly joked to U.S. officials that he couldn't understand the need for such a drawn-out process when Israel had managed to seize the Golan in only six days. Rabin, however, insisted on a gradual and partial evacuation of Golan over a four-year period in order to test Syrian compliance with normalization and security arrangements. Israel wanted Damascus to establish an embassy in Tel Aviv after a token withdrawal in the initial phase, as Egypt did in the Camp David accords, while Assad insisted on only minor aspects of normalization until full withdrawal has been completed.

Talks entered a new phase in December 1994 when Assad agreed to send Syrian army Chief of Staff General Hikmat Shihabi to Washington to discuss security arrangements with his Israeli counterpart, Ehud Barak. Syria evidently expected Shihabi's mere presence to elicit fundamental compromises from Israel, but Barak merely outlined the detailed security arrangements that Israel believes it needs in any peace agreement: early warning stations on the Golan's Mt. Hermon and disproportionately deeper demilitarized zones on the Syrian side of the border to reflect the fact that Israel will be giving up the strategically superior plateau.

Upset that Barak did not bring new concessions, Assad suspended the talks for the next three months. During a visit to

Damascus and Jerusalem in March 1995, Christopher won Assad's consent to resume the negotiations between the ambassadors but not the talks between senior military officers. Over the next month, Rabinovich and Moualem remained deadlocked on Syria's demand that security arrangements such as limited troop and armor zones be equal on both sides of the Golan. Rabin rejected that principle, noting that Israel would be taking a greater military risk than Syria by withdrawing from the strategic heights. The goal of the security arrangements is not symmetry, he observed, but to prevent either side from launching a surprise attack.

Rabin did yield, however, on his prior insistence that each side cut its standing forces.[3] He also called for the deployment of a multinational force of military observers—including U.S. troops—on the Golan to monitor compliance with the security terms, akin to the force that monitors the terms of the Israel-Egypt peace in the Sinai. Rabin asserted that the observer force should not be large or have a fighting capability (he has hinted that Israel would request fewer than 1,000 U.S. personnel for the Golan force, roughly equal to the number currently stationed in the Sinai) as this would only limit Israel's options in a crisis.

By June 1995, the United States had brokered a set of security principles, the first agreement between the two countries since the Madrid peace process began, in which Syria no longer insisted on strictly symmetrical demilitarized and limited-force zones. This paved the way for the renewal of talks between the chiefs of staff, in which Lt-Gen. Amnon Shahak succeeded Ehud Barak, who retired from the IDF and joined the Rabin government as minister of the interior. These talks were to be followed by further discussions between lower-ranking officers.

Israel and Syria have both indicated that a settlement between them would be linked to an Israeli peace treaty with Lebanon that would include security arrangements along Israel's northern border. Israel insists that Beirut disarm the Hezbollah, an extremist Shi'a militia engaged in a war of attrition against Israel and its Christian allies in the so-called "security zone" in southern

---

[3] According to the London-based International Institute for Strategic Studies, Syria has twelve standing divisions. In contrast, the IDF has only three and relies primarily on reserves, making it vulnerable to a Syrian surprise attack. Rabin reportedly backed away from the idea of mutual force reductions when the Syrians suggested cuts in Israel's air force and alleged nuclear weapons, two areas in which it has a decisive advantage. He rebuffed Likud criticism by noting that the Camp David accords did not reduce Egypt's armed forces.

Lebanon. Though Hezbollah is financed by Iran, its flow of arms and base of operations in Lebanon's Bekaa Valley are controlled by Syria. Israel believes that Damascus could prevent Hezbollah's activities in the security zone but prefers to use it as a lever to force Israel to negotiate over the Golan.

Rabin has said that the IDF would withdraw from the security zone after Beirut deploys its army in the south and demonstrates its willingness and ability to prevent Hezbollah violence for a six-month period. Furthermore, Israel wants its proxy, the South Lebanon Army, integrated into the regular Lebanese armed forces. Rabin no longer insists on the withdrawal of Syria's 35,000 troops from Lebanon, which marks a deviation from the Likud government's position linking IDF withdrawal to the departure of "all foreign forces." Rabin criticized this as unrealistic and said in subsequent meetings of the Knesset Foreign Affairs and Defense Committee that Israel would not object if some Syrian troops are diverted from missions in Syria for deployment in Lebanon.

Taken together, the obstacles ahead in the peace process—implementing the interim agreement with the Palestinians, achieving peace with Syria, building real economic relationships with a still-reluctant Arab world—are no less daunting than those the Rabin government faced when it first came to office in 1992. But the decision to pursue the Oslo channel and make peace with the PLO was the key to transforming these hypothetical possibilities into genuine options. For Yitzhak Rabin and Israel itself, the challenge ahead is to see whether the promise of Oslo can be fully realized, bringing Israel and its neighbors the full, comprehensive, and lasting peace their peoples deserve.

# Appendixes

# APPENDIX I

## SECURITY COUNCIL RESOLUTION 242
*November 22, 1967*

The Security Council,

Expressing its continuing concern with the grave situation in the Middle East,

Emphasizing the inadmissibility of the acquisition of territory by war and the need to work for a just and lasting peace in which every State in the area can live in security,

Emphasizing further that all Member States in their acceptance of the Charter of the United Nations have undertaken a commitment to act in accordance with Article 2 of the Charter,

1. Affirms that the fulfillment of Charter principles requires the establishment of a just and lasting peace in the Middle East which should include the application of both the following principles:

(I) Withdrawal of Israeli armed forces from territories occupied in the recent conflict;

(ii) Termination of all claims or states of belligerency and respect for and acknowledgment of the sovereignty, territorial integrity and political independence of every State in the area and their right to live in peace within secure and recognized boundaries free from threats or acts of force;

2. Affirms further the necessity

(a) For guaranteeing freedom of navigation through international waterways in the area;

(b) For achieving a just settlement of the refugee problem;

(c) For guaranteeing the territorial inviolability and political independence of every State in the area, through measures including the establishment of demilitarized zones;

3. Requests the Secretary-General to designate a Special Representative to proceed to the Middle East to establish and maintain contacts with the States concerned in order to promote agreement and assist efforts to achieve a peaceful and accepted settlement in accordance with the provisions and principles in this resolution;

4. Requests the Secretary-General to report to the Security Council of the progress of the efforts of the Special Representative as soon as possible.

## THE CAMP DAVID ACCORDS
*September 17, 1978*

### A FRAMEWORK FOR PEACE IN THE MIDDLE EAST
### AGREED AT CAMP DAVID

Muhammad Anwar al-Sadat, President of the Arab Republic of Egypt, and Menachem Begin, Prime Minister of Israel, met with Jimmy Carter, President of the United States of America, at Camp David from September 5 to September 17, 1978, and have agreed on the following framework for peace in the Middle East. They invite other parties to the Arab-Israeli conflict to adhere to it.

PREAMBLE

The search for peace in the Middle East must be guided by the following:

The agreed basis for a peaceful settlement of the conflict between Israel and its neighbors is United Nations Security Council Resolution 242, in all its parts.

After four wars during thirty years, despite intensive human efforts, the Middle East, which is the cradle of civilization and the birthplace of three great religions, does not yet enjoy the blessings of peace. The people of the Middle East yearn for peace so that the vast human and natural resources of the region can be turned to the pursuits of peace and so that this area can become a model for coexistence and cooperation among nations.

The historic initiative of President Sadat in visiting Jerusalem and the reception accorded to him by the Parliament, government and people of Israel, and the reciprocal visit of Prime Minister Begin to Ismailia, the peace proposals made by both leaders, as well as the warm reception of these missions by the peoples of both countries, have created an unprecedented opportunity for peace which must not be lost if this generation and future generations are to be spared the tragedies of war.

The provisions of the Charter of the United Nations and the other accepted norms of international law and legitimacy now provide accepted standards for the conduct of relations among all states.

To achieve a relationship of peace, in the spirit of Article 2 of the United Nations Charter, future negotiations between Israel and any neighbor prepared to negotiate peace and security with it, are necessary for the purpose of carrying out all the provisions and principles of Resolutions 242 and 338.

Peace requires respect for the sovereignty, territorial integrity and political independence of every state in the area and their right to live in peace within secure and recognized boundaries free from threats or acts of force. Progress toward that goal can accelerate movement toward a new era of reconciliation in the Middle East marked by cooperation in promoting economic development, in maintaining stability, and in assuring security.

Security is enhanced by a relationship of peace and by cooperation between nations which enjoy normal relations. In addition, under the terms of peace treaties, the parties can, on the basis of reciprocity, agree to special security arrangements such as demilitarized zones, limited armaments areas, early warning stations, the presence of international forces, liaison, agreed measures for monitoring, and other arrangements that they agree are useful.

## FRAMEWORK

Taking these factors into account, the parties are determined to reach a just, comprehensive, and durable settlement of the Middle East conflict through the conclusion of peace treaties based on Security Council Resolutions 242 and 338 in all their parts. Their purpose is to achieve peace and good neighborly relations. They recognize that, for peace to endure, it must involve all those who have been most deeply affected by the conflict. They therefore agree that this framework as appropriate is intended by them to constitute a basis for peace not only between Egypt and Israel, but also between Israel and each of its other neighbors which is prepared to negotiate peace with Israel on this basis.

With that objective in mind, they have agreed to proceed as follows:

A.) West Bank and Gaza

1. Egypt, Israel, Jordan and the representatives of the Palestinian people should participate in negotiations on the resolution of the Palestinian problem in all its aspects. To achieve that objective, negotiations relating to the West Bank and Gaza should proceed in three stages:

(a) Egypt and Israel agree that, in order to ensure a peaceful and orderly transfer of authority, and taking into account the security concerns of all the parties, there should be transitional arrangements for the West Bank and Gaza for a period not exceeding five years. In order to provide full autonomy to the inhabitants, under these arrangements the Israeli military government and its civilian administration will be withdrawn as soon as a self-governing authority has been freely elected by the inhabitants of these areas to replace the existing military government. To negotiate the details of a transitional arrangement, the Government of Jordan will be invited to join the negotiations on the basis of this framework. These new arrangements should give due consideration both to the principle of self-government by the inhabitants of these territories and to the legitimate security concerns of the parties involved.

(b) Egypt, Israel, and Jordan will agree on the modalities for establishing the elected self-governing authority in the West Bank and Gaza. The delegations of Egypt and Jordan may include Palestinians from the West Bank and Gaza or other Palestinians as mutually agreed. The parties will negotiate an agreement which will define the powers and responsibilities of the self-governing authority to be exercised in the West Bank and Gaza. A withdrawal of Israeli armed forces will take place and there will be a redeployment of the remaining Israeli forces into specified security locations. The agreement will also include arrangements for assuring internal and external security and public order. A strong local police force will be established, which may include Jordanian citizens. In addition, Israeli and Jordanian forces will participate in joint patrols and in the manning of control posts to assure the security of the borders.

(c) When the self-governing authority (administrative council) in the West Bank and Gaza is established and inaugurated, the transitional period of five years will begin. As soon as possible, but not later than the third year after the beginning of the transitional period, negotiations will take place to determine the final status of the West Bank and Gaza and its relationship with its neighbors, and to conclude a peace treaty between Israel and Jordan by the end of the transitional period. These negotiations will be conducted among Egypt, Israel, Jordan, and the elected representatives of the inhabitants of the West Bank and Gaza. Two separate but related committees will be convened, one committee, consisting of representatives of the four parties which will negotiate and agree on the final status of the West Bank and Gaza, and its relationship with its neighbors, and the second committee, consisting of representatives of Israel and representatives of Jordan to be joined by the elected representatives of the inhabitants of the West Bank and Gaza, to negotiate the peace treaty between Israel and Jordan, taking into account the agreement reached on the final status of the West Bank and Gaza. The negotiations shall be based on all the provisions and principles of UN Security Council Resolution 242. The negotiations will resolve, among other matters, the location of the boundaries and the nature of the security arrangements.

The solution from the negotiations must also recognize the legitimate rights of the Palestinian people and their just requirements. In this way, the Palestinians will participate in the determination of their own future through:

(1) The negotiations among Egypt, Israel, Jordan and the representatives of the inhabitants of the West Bank and Gaza to agree on the final status of the West Bank and Gaza and other outstanding issues by the end of the transitional period.

(2) Submitting their agreement to a vote by the elected representatives of the inhabitants of the West Bank and Gaza.

(3) Providing for the elected representatives of the inhabitants of the West Bank and Gaza to decide how they shall govern themselves consistent with the provisions of their agreement.

(4) Participating as stated above in the work of the committee negotiating the peace treaty between Israel and Jordan.

2. All necessary measures will be taken and provisions made to assure the security of Israel and its neighbors during the transitional

period and beyond. To assist in providing such security, a strong local police force will be constituted by the self-governing authority. It will be composed of inhabitants of the West Bank and Gaza. The police will maintain continuing liaison on internal security matters with the designated Israeli, Jordanian and Egyptian officers.

3.   During the transitional period, representatives of Egypt, Israel, Jordan, and the self-governing authority will constitute a continuing committee to decide by agreement on the modalities of admission of persons displaced from the West Bank and Gaza in 1967, together with necessary measures to prevent disruption and disorder. Other matters of common concern may also be dealt with by this committee.

4.   Egypt and Israel will work with each other and with other interested parties to establish agreed procedures for a prompt, just and permanent implementation of the resolution of the refugee problem.

B.) Egypt-Israel

1.   Egypt and Israel undertake not to resort to the threat or the use of force to settle disputes. Any disputes shall be settled by peaceful means in accordance with the provisions of Article 33 of the Charter of the United Nations.

2.   In order to achieve peace between them, the parties agree to negotiate in good faith with a goal of concluding within three months from the signing of the Framework a peace treaty between them while inviting the other parties to the conflict to proceed simultaneously to negotiate and conclude similar peace treaties with a view to achieving a comprehensive peace in the area. The Framework for the Conclusion of a Peace Treaty between Egypt and Israel will govern the peace negotiations between them. The parties will agree on the modalities and the timetable for the implementation of their obligations under the treaty.

C.) Associated Principles

1.   Egypt and Israel state that the principles and provisions described below should apply to peace treaties between Israel and each of its neighbors—Egypt, Jordan, Syria and Lebanon.

2.   Signatories shall establish among themselves relationships normal to states at peace with one another. To this end, they should undertake to abide by all the provisions of the charter of the United Nations. Steps to be taken in this respect include:

(a) full recognition;

(b) abolishing economic boycotts;

(c) guaranteeing that under their jurisdiction the citizens of the other parties shall enjoy the protection of the due process of law.

3.   Signatories should explore possibilities for economic development in the context of final peace treaties, with the objective of contributing to the atmosphere of peace, cooperation and friendship which is their common goal.

4.   Claims Commissions may be established for the mutual settlement of all financial claims.

5.   The United States shall be invited to participate in the talks on matters related to the modalities of the implementation of the agreements and working out the timetable for the carrying out of the obligation of the parties.

6.   The United Nations Security Council shall be requested to endorse the peace treaties and ensure that their provisions shall not be violated. The permanent members of the Security Council shall be requested to underwrite the peace treaties and ensure respect for their provisions. They shall also be requested to conform their policies and actions with the undertakings contained in this Framework.

For the Government of the Arab Republic of Egypt:                A. Sadat

For the Government of the Israel:                                M. Begin

Witnessed by:                                              Jimmy Carter
                                    President of the United States of America

# THE REAGAN PEACE INITIATIVE[1]
### *September 1, 1982*

First, as outlined in the Camp David accords, there must be a period of time during which the Palestinian inhabitants of the West Bank and Gaza will have full autonomy over their own affairs. Due consideration must be given to the principle of self-government by the inhabitants of the territories and to the legitimate security concerns of the parties involved.

The purpose of the 5-year period of transition, which would begin after free elections for a self-governing Palestinian authority, is to prove to the Palestinians that they can run their own affairs and that such Palestinian autonomy poses no threat to Israel's security.

The United States will not support the use of any additional land for the purpose of settlements during the transition period. Indeed, the immediate adoption of a settlement freeze by Israel, more than any other action, could create the confidence needed for wider participation in these talks. Further settlement activity is in no way necessary for the security of Israel and only diminishes the confidence of the Arabs that a final outcome can be freely and fairly negotiated.

I want to make the American position well understood: The purpose of this transition period is the peaceful and orderly transfer of authority from Israel to the Palestinian inhabitants of the West Bank and Gaza. At the same time, such a transfer must not interfere with Israel's security requirements.

Beyond the transition period, as we look to the future of the West Bank and Gaza, it is clear to me that peace cannot be achieved by the formation of an independent Palestinian state in those territories. Nor is it achievable on the basis of Israeli sovereignty or permanent control over the West Bank and Gaza. So the United States will not support the establishment of an independent Palestinian state in the West Bank and we will not support annexation or permanent control by Israel.

There is, however, another way to peace. The final status of these lands must, of course, be reached through the give-and-take of negotiations. But it is the firm view of the United States that self-government by the

---

[1] Following Israel's invasion of Lebanon in June 1982, the United States attempted to revive the Camp David peace process by presenting this proposal.

Palestinians of the West Bank and Gaza in association with Jordan offers the best chance for a durable, just and lasting peace.

We base our approach squarely on the principle that the Arab-Israeli conflict should be resolved through negotiation involving an exchange of territory for peace. This exchange is enshrined in UN Security Council Resolution 242, which is, in turn, incorporated in all its parts in the Camp David agreements. UN Resolution 242 remains wholly valid as the foundation stone of America's Middle East peace effort.

It is the United States' position that—in return for peace—the withdrawal provision of Resolution 242 applies to all fronts, including the West Bank and Gaza.

When the border is negotiated between Jordan and Israel, our view on the extent to which Israel should be asked to give up territory will be heavily affected by the extent of true peace and normalization and the security arrangements offered in return.

Finally, we remain convinced that Jerusalem must remain undivided, but its final status should be decided through negotiations.

In the course of the negotiations to come, the United States will support positions that seem to us fair and reasonable compromises and likely to promote a sound agreement. We will also put forward our own detailed proposals when we believe they can be helpful. And, make no mistake, the United States will oppose any proposal—from any party and at any point in the negotiating process—that threatens the security of Israel. America's commitment to the security of Israel is ironclad.

## APPENDIX IV

## REAGAN'S TALKING POINTS[2]
*September 1, 1982*

A.) We will maintain our commitment to Camp David.

B.) We will maintain our commitment to the conditions we require for recognition of and negotiation with the PLO.

C.) We can offer guarantees on the position we will adopt in negotiations. We will not be able, however, to guarantee in advance the results of these negotiations.

## TRANSITIONAL MEASURES

A.) Our position is that the objective of the transitional period is the peaceful and orderly transfer of authority from Israel to the Palestinian inhabitants.

B.) We will support:

• The decision of full autonomy as giving the Palestinian inhabitants real authority over themselves, the land and its resources, subject to fair safeguards on water.

• Economic, commercial, social and cultural ties between the West Bank, Gaza and Jordan.

• Participation by the Palestinian inhabitants of East Jerusalem in the election of the West Bank-Gaza authority.

• Real settlements freeze.

• Progressive Palestinian responsibility for internal security based on capability and performance.

---

[2] These "talking points" accompanied and were intended to clarify the basis for the U.S. peace initiative. See *New York Times*, September 9, 1982.

C.) We will oppose:

• Dismantlement of the existing settlements.

• Provisions which represent a legitimate threat to Israel's security, reasonably defined.

• Isolation of the West Bank and Gaza from Israel.

• Measures which accord either the Palestinians or the Israelis generally recognized sovereign rights with the exception of external security, which must remain in Israel's hands during the transitional period.


FINAL STATUS ISSUES

A.) UNSC Resolution 242

It is our position that Resolution 242 applies to the West Bank and Gaza and requires Israeli withdrawal in return for peace. Negotiations must determine the borders. The U.S. position in these negotiations on the extent of the withdrawal will be significantly influenced by the extent and nature of the peace and security arrangements offered in return.

B.) Israeli sovereignty

It is our belief that the Palestinian problem cannot be resolved (through) Israeli sovereignty or control over the West Bank and Gaza. Accordingly, we will not support such a solution.

C.) Palestinian state

The preference we will pursue in the final status negotiation is association of the West Bank and Gaza with Jordan. We will not support the formation of a Palestinian state in those negotiations. There is no foundation of political support in Israel or the United States for such a solution. The outcome, however, must be determined by negotiations.

D.) Self-determination

In the Middle East context the term self-determination has been identified exclusively with the formation of a Palestinian state. We will not support this definition of self-determination. We believe that the Palestinians must take the leading role in determining their own future and fully support the provision in Camp David providing for the elected representatives of the inhabitants of the West Bank and Gaza to decide how they shall govern themselves consistent with the provision of their agreement in the final status negotiations.

E.) Jerusalem

We will fully support the position that the status of Jerusalem must be determined through negotiations.

F.) Settlements

The status of Israeli settlements must be determined in the course of the final status negotiations. We will not support their continuation as extraterritorial outposts.

## ADDITIONAL TALKING POINTS

1. The approach to Hussein

• The President has approached Hussein to determine the extent to which he may be interested in participating.

• King Hussein received the same U.S. positions as you.

• Hussein considers our proposal and gives them serious attention.

• Hussein understands that Camp David is the only base that we will accept for negotiations.

• We are also discussing these proposals with the Saudis.

2.   Public Commitment

• Whatever the support from these or other Arab states, this is what the President has concluded must be done.

• The President is convinced his positions are fair and balanced and fully protective of Israel's security. Beyond that, they offer the practical opportunity of eventually achieving the peace treaties Israel must have with its neighbors.

• He will be making a speech announcing these positions, probably within a week.

3.   Next Procedural Steps

• Should the response to the President's proposal be positive, the United States would take immediate steps to relaunch the autonomy negotiations with the broadest possible participation as envisaged under the Camp David agreements.

• We also contemplate an early visit by Secretary Shultz in the area.

• Should there be a positive response, the President, as he has said in his letter to you, will nonetheless stand by his position with proper dedication.

## THE LONDON AGREEMENT[3]
*April 11, 1987*

(Accord between the Government of Jordan, which has confirmed it to the Government of the United States, and the Foreign Minister of Israel, pending the approval of the Government of Israel. Parts "A" and "B," which will be made public upon agreement of the parties, will be treated as proposals of the United States to which Jordan and Israel have agreed. Part "C" is to be treated with great confidentiality, as commitments to the United States from the Government of Jordan to be transmitted to the Government of Israel.)

A THREE-PART UNDERSTANDING BETWEEN JORDAN AND ISRAEL

A.) Invitation by the UN secretary general: the UN secretary general will send invitations to the five permanent members of the Security Council and to the parties involved in the Israeli-Arab conflict to negotiate an agreement by peaceful means based on UN Resolutions 242 and 338 with the purpose of attaining comprehensive peace in the region and security for the countries in the area, and granting the Palestinian people their legitimate rights.

B.) Decisions of the international conference: The participants in the conference agree that the purpose of the negotiations is to attain by peaceful means an agreement about all the aspects of the Palestinian problem. The conference invites the sides to set up regional bilateral committees to negotiate bilateral issues.

C.) Nature of the agreement between Jordan and Israel: Israel and Jordan agree that:

1. The international conference will not impose a solution and will not veto any agreement reached by the sides;

---

[3] This document resulted from a secret meeting between Israeli Foreign Minister Shimon Peres and King Hussein of Jordan in London in April 1987. See *Ma'ariv*, January 1, 1988, in Foreign Broadcast Information Service (FBIS) *Daily Report*, Near East and South Asia, January 4, 1988, pp. 30-31.

2. The negotiations will be conducted in bilateral committees in a direct manner;

3. The Palestinian issue will be discussed in a meeting of the Jordanian, Palestinian, and Israeli delegations;

4. The representatives of the Palestinians will be included in the Jordanian-Palestinian delegation;

5. Participation in the conference will be based on acceptance of UN Resolutions 242 and 338 by the sides and the renunciation of violence and terror;

6. Each committee will conduct negotiations independently;

7. Other issues will be resolved through mutual agreement between Jordan and Israel.

This document of understanding is pending approval of the incumbent governments of Israel and Jordan. The content of this document will be presented and proposed to the United States.

# APPENDIX VI

## THE SHULTZ INITIATIVE[4]
*March 4, 1988*

I set forth below the statement of understandings which I am convinced is necessary to achieve the prompt opening of negotiations on a comprehensive peace. This statement of understandings emerges from discussions held with you and other regional leaders. I look forward to the letter of reply of the Government of Israel in confirmation of this statement.

The agreed objective is a comprehensive peace providing for the security of all the states in the region and for the legitimate rights of the Palestinian people.

Negotiations will start on an early date certain between Israel and each of its neighbors which is willing to do so. These negotiations could begin by May 1, 1988. Each of these negotiations will be based on the United Nations Security Council Resolutions 242 and 338, in all their parts. The parties to each bilateral negotiation will determine the procedure and agenda at their negotiation. All participants in the negotiations must state their willingness to negotiate with one another.

As concerns negotiations between the Israeli delegation and the Jordanian-Palestinian delegation, negotiations will begin on arrangements for a transitional period, with the objective of completing them within six months. Seven months after transitional negotiations begin, final status negotiations will begin, with the objective of completing them within one year. These negotiations will be based on all the provisions and principles of United Nations Security Council Resolution 242. Final status talks will start before the transitional period begins. The transitional period will begin three months after the conclusion of the transitional agreement and will last for three years. The United States will participate in both Negotiations and will promote their rapid conclusion. In particular, the United States will submit a draft agreement for the parties' consideration at the outset of the negotiations on transitional arrangements.

Two weeks before the opening of negotiations, an international conference will be held. The Secretary General of the United Nations will

---

[4] Text of the letter that Secretary of State George P. Shultz wrote to Israeli Prime Minister Yitzhak Shamir outlining the American peace proposal. A similar letter was sent to King Hussein of Jordan. See *New York Times*, March 10, 1988.

be asked to issue invitations to the parties involved in the Arab-Israeli conflict and the five permanent members of the United Nations Security Council. All participants in the conference must accept United Nations Security Council Resolutions 242 and 338, and renounce violence and terrorism. The parties to each bilateral negotiation may refer reports on the status of their negotiations to the conference, in a manner to be agreed. The conference will not be able to impose solutions or veto agreements reached.

Palestinian representation will be within the Jordanian-Palestinian delegation. The Palestinian issue will be addressed in the negotiations between the Jordanian-Palestinian and Israeli delegations. Negotiations between the Israeli delegation and the Jordanian-Palestinian delegation will proceed independently of any other negotiations.

This statement of understanding is an integral whole. The United States understands that your acceptance is dependent on the implementation of each element in good faith.

Sincerely yours,

George P. Shultz

## ISRAELI GOVERNMENT PEACE INITIATIVE[5]
*May 14, 1989*

GENERAL:

1. This document presents the principles of a political initiative of the government of Israel which deals with the continuation of the peace process; the termination of the state of war with the Arab states; a solution for the Judea, Samaria and the Gaza District; peace with Jordan; and a resolution of the problem of the residents of the refugee camps in Judea, Samaria and the Gaza District.

2. The document includes:

A.) The principles upon which the initiative is based.

B.) Details of the processes for its implementation.

C.) Reference to the subject of the elections under consideration. Further details relating to the elections as well as other objects of the initiative will be dealt with separately.

BASIC PREMISES:

3. The initiative is founded upon the assumption that there is a national consensus for it on the basis of the basic guidelines of the government of Israel, including the following points:

A.) Israel yearns for peace and the continuation of the political process by means of direct negotiations based on the principles of the Camp David accords.

B.) Israel opposes the establishment of an additional Palestinian state in the Gaza District and in the area between Israel and Jordan.

---

[5] After the 1988 election gave the Likud the upper hand in a second National Unity Government, pressure from the newly elected Bush administration, the *intifada*, and the Labor party prompted Shamir to propose this peace intiative.

C.) Israel will not conduct negotiations with the PLO.

D.) There will be no change in the status of Judea, Samaria and Gaza other than in accordance with the basic guidelines of the government.

## SUBJECTS TO BE DEALT WITH IN THE PEACE PROCESS:

A.) Israel views as important that the peace between Israel and Egypt, based on the Camp David accords, will serve as a cornerstone for enlarging the circle of peace in the region, and calls for a common endeavor for the strengthening of the peace and its extension, through continued consultation.

B.) Israel calls for the establishment of peaceful relations between it and those Arab states which still maintain a state of war with it, for the purpose of promoting a comprehensive settlement for the Arab-Israel conflict, including recognition, direct negotiations, ending the boycott, diplomatic relations, cessation of hostile activity in international institutions or forums and regional and bilateral cooperation.

C.) Israel calls for an international endeavor to resolve the problem of the residents of the Arab refugee camps in Judea, Samaria and the Gaza District in order to improve their living conditions and to rehabilitate them. Israel is prepared to be a partner in this endeavor.

D.) In order to advance the political negotiation process leading to peace, Israel proposes free and democratic elections among the Palestinian Arab inhabitants of Judea, Samaria and the Gaza District in an atmosphere devoid of violence, threats and terror. In these elections a representation will be chosen to conduct negotiations for a transitional period of self-rule. This period will constitute a test for coexistence and cooperation. At a later stage, negotiations will be conducted for a permanent solution, during which all the proposed options for an agreed settlement will be examined, and peace between Israel and Jordan will be achieved.

E.) All above mentioned steps should be dealt with simultaneously.

F.) The details of what has been mentioned in (D) above will be given below.

## THE PRINCIPLES CONSTITUTING THE INITIATIVE STAGES:

5. The initiative is based on two stages:

A.) Stage A—a transitional period for an interim agreement.

B.) Stage B—permanent solution.

6. The interlock between the stages is a timetable on which the plan is built; the peace process delineated by the initiative is based on resolutions 242 and 338, upon which the Camp David accords are founded.

TIMETABLE:

7. The transitional period will continue for five years.

8. As soon as possible, but not later than the third year after the beginning of the transitional period, negotiations for achieving a permanent solution will begin.

Parties Participating in the Negotiations in Both Stages:

9. The parties participating in the negotiations for the first stage (the interim agreement) shall include Israel and the elected representation of the Palestinian Arab inhabitants of Judea, Samaria and the Gaza District. Jordan and Egypt will be invited to participate in these negotiations if they so desire.

10. The parties participating in the negotiations for the second stage (permanent solution) shall include Israel and the elected representation of the Palestinian Arab inhabitants of Judea, Samaria and the Gaza District, as well as Jordan; furthermore, Egypt may participate in these negotiations. In negotiations between Israel and Jordan, in which the elected representation of the Palestinian Arab inhabitants of Judea, Samaria and the Gaza District will participate, the peace treaty between Israel and Jordan will be concluded.

SUBSTANCE OF THE TRANSITIONAL PERIOD:

11. During the transitional period the Palestinian Arab inhabitants of Judea, Samaria and the Gaza District will be accorded self-rule, by means of which they will, themselves, conduct their affairs of daily life. Israel will continue to be responsible for security, foreign affairs and all matters concerning Israeli citizens in Judea, Samaria and the Gaza District. Topics involving the implementation of the plan for self-rule will be considered and decided within the framework of the negotiations for an interim agreement.

SUBSTANCE OF THE PERMANENT SOLUTION:

12. In the negotiations for a permanent solution, every party shall be entitled to present for discussion all the subjects it may wish to raise.

13. The arrangements for peace and borders between Israel and Jordan.

DETAILS OF THE PROCESS FOR THE IMPLEMENTATION OF THE INITIATIVE:

14. First and foremost, dialogue and basic agreement by the Palestinian Arab inhabitants of Judea, Samaria and the Gaza District, as well as Egypt and Jordan if they wish to take part, as above mentioned, in the negotiations on the principles constituting the initiative.

15. Immediately afterwards will follow the stage of preparations and implementation of the election process in which a representation of the Palestinian Arab inhabitants of Judea, Samaria and Gaza will be elected. This representation:

   A.) Shall be a partner to the conduct of negotiations for the transitional period (interim agreement).

   B.) Shall constitute the self-governing authority in the course of the transitional period.

   C.) Shall be the central Palestinian component, subject to agreement after three years, in the negotiations for the permanent solution.

In the period of the preparations and implementation there shall be a calming of the violence in Judea, Samaria and the Gaza District.

16. As to the substance of the elections, it is recommended that a proposal of regional elections be adopted, the details of which shall be determined in further discussions.

17. Every Palestinian Arab residing in Judea, Samaria and the Gaza District, who shall be elected by the inhabitants to represent them—after having submitted his candidacy in accordance with the detailed document which shall determine the subject of the elections—may be a legitimate participant in the conduct of negotiations with Israel.

18. The elections shall be free, democratic and secret.

19. Immediately after the election of the Palestinian representation, negotiations shall be conducted with it on an interim agreement for a transitional period which shall continue for five years, as mentioned above. In these negotiations, the parties shall determine all the subjects relating to the substance of the self-rule and the arrangements necessary for its implementation.

20. As soon as possible, but not later than the third year after the establishment of the self-rule, negotiations for a permanent solution shall begin. During the whole period of these negotiations until the signing of the agreement for a permanent solution, the self-rule shall continue in effect as determined in the negotiations for an interim agreement.

## U.S.-SOVIET LETTER OF INVITATION
## TO THE MADRID PEACE CONFERENCE
*October 18, 1991*

After extensive consultations with Arab states, Israel, and the Palestinians, the United States and the Soviet Union believe that an historic opportunity exists to advance the prospects for genuine peace throughout the region. The United States and the Soviet Union are prepared to assist the parties to achieve a just, lasting, and comprehensive peace settlement, through direct negotiations along two tracks, between Israel and the Arab states, and between Israel and the Palestinians, based on United Nations Security Council Resolutions 242 and 338. The objective of this process is real peace.

Toward that end, the president of the United States and the president of the USSR invite you to a peace conference, which their countries will co-sponsor, followed immediately by direct negotiations. The conference will be convened in Madrid on 30 October 1991.

President Bush and President Gorbachev request your acceptance of this invitation no later than 6:00 PM Washington time, 23 October 1991, in order to ensure proper organization and preparation of the conference.

Direct bilateral negotiations will begin four days after the opening of the conference. Those parties who wish to attend multilateral negotiations will convene two weeks after the opening of the conference to organize those negotiations. The co-sponsors believe that those negotiations should focus on region-wide issues such as arms control and regional security, water, refugee issues, environment, economic development, and other subjects of mutual interest.

The co-sponsors will chair the conference which will be held at ministerial level. Governments to be invited include Israel, Syria, Lebanon, and Jordan. Palestinians will be invited to attend as part of a joint Jordanian-Palestinian delegation. Egypt will be invited to the conference as a participant. The European Community will be a participant in the conference, alongside the United States and the Soviet Union and will be represented by its presidency. The Gulf Cooperation

Council will be invited to send its secretary-general to the conference as an observer, and GCC member states will be invited to participate the negotiations on multilateral issues. The United Nations will be invited to send an observer, representing the secretary-general.

The conference will have no power to impose solutions on the parties or veto agreements reached by them. It will have no authority to make decisions for the parties and no ability to vote on issues or results. The conference can reconvene only with the consent of all the parties.

With respect to negotiations between Israel and Palestinians who are part of the joint Jordanian-Palestinian delegation, negotiations will be conducted in phases, beginning with talks on interim self-government arrangements. These talks will be conducted with the objective of reaching agreement within one year. Once the agreed interim self-government arrangements will last for a period of five years. Beginning in the third year of the period of interim self-government arrangements, negotiations will take place on permanent status. These permanent status negotiations, and the negotiations between Israel and the Arab states, will take place on the basis of resolutions 242 and 338.

It is understood that the co-sponsors are committed to making this process succeed. It is their intention to convene the conference and negotiations with those parties that agree to attend.

The co-sponsors believe that this process offers the promise of ending decades of confrontation and conflict and the hope of a lasting peace. Thus, the co-sponsors hope that the parties will approach these negotiations in a spirit of good will and mutual respect. In this way, the peace process can begin to break down the mutual suspicions and mistrust that perpetuate the conflict and allow the parties to begin to resolve their differences. Indeed, only through such a process can real peace and reconciliation among the Arab states, Israel, and the Palestinians be achieved. And only through this process can the peoples of the Middle East attain the peace and security they richly deserve.

## APPENDIX IX

## ISRAELI LABOR PARTY PLATFORM
*November 1991*

### SECURITY/FOREIGN AFFAIRS

• In favor of immediate talks with the Palestinians on the autonomy plan as an interim solution. Talks will be held with Palestinians from the territories, including from East Jerusalem, but not directly with the PLO. The permanent settlement with the Palestinians and the various Arab states will be worked out in bilateral talks. Regional problems can be dealt with in an international conference.

• Jerusalem is to remain united, under Israeli sovereignty, as the capital of Israel.

• A permanent solution will be based on territorial compromise.

• There will be no return to the 1967 borders, but Israel will be willing to give up, in return for peace, those territories which have a dense Palestinian population in the West Bank and Gaza Strip. Territorial compromise is also possible on the Golan Heights. Territories from which Israel will withdraw will be demilitarized.

• There will be no additional state between Israel and the Jordan River (no Palestinian mini-state). Labor favors the establishment of a Palestinian-Jordanian political entity, whose constitutional structure will be determined by the Jordanians and the Palestinians themselves.

• The special relationship with the United States is invaluable. Israel should not accept American dictates on issues involving its vital interests. Differences of opinion should be ironed out by means of talks, and every effort should be made to avoid situations of loss of confidence.

### GOVERNMENT AND ELECTORAL REFORM

• Strongly supported the law for the direct election of the prime minister.

• Favors ranking the qualifying threshold to 2.5 percent. Supports electoral reform under which half the MKs will be elected in multi-member constituencies and the other half by proportional representation.

• Aspires to conclude the drafting of a constitution.

## SOCIAL AND ECONOMIC POLICY

• Aspires to a society based on social justice and equal opportunities.
• A good economic policy must be based on a mixture of private initiative and government direction. The government must also be responsible for infrastructure. There should be privatization of government-owned enterprises, though the government should maintain a controlling interest in enterprises dealing with raw materials and military production.
• The Histadrut is a vital tool in the realization of the desired goals, and must keep up with the times in terms of its structure and modus operandi.

## IMMIGRANT ABSORPTION

• The successful absorption of the new immigrants is a top-priority goal.
• The absorption of new immigrants cannot be left exclusively to market forces. The government must be directly involved in housing, social absorption, and job creation.
• The successful absorption of the immigrants requires massive investment in infrastructure, industrial development, and services. This task can only be achieved if all the possible financial means are mobilized inside Israel, from world Jewry, and from the international community.

## RELIGION AND STATE

• Advocates the separation of religion and politics. The relationship between religion and state must be defined in a constitution.
• There should be no religious and no anti-religious coercion.
• The mass exemption of yeshiva students from military service, and religious girls from national service, must end.
• There should be no change in the definition of a Jew as it currently appears in the Law of Return.

## APPENDIX X

## U.S. PROPOSAL FOR ISRAELI-PALESTINIAN STATEMENT[6]
*May 12, 1993*

Israel and the Palestinians agree that it is time to put an end to the conflict between them. Reaffirming their commitment to the peace process launched at Madrid, they seek to negotiate their differences and create a peaceful future in which Israelis and Palestinians will live side-by-side, in peace, for generations to come.

The goal of the current Arab-Israeli peace process is real and comprehensive peace, based on United Nations Security Council Resolutions 242 and 338. Toward this goal, in line with the invitation to the Madrid peace conference, the two sides want to reach agreement as soon as possible on interim self-government arrangements for the Palestinians in the territories.

The negotiating process is being conducted in phases: The first phase of the negotiations is directed toward reaching agreement on interim self-government arrangements for five years; and the second phase of the negotiations will be directed toward reaching agreement on permanent status based on United Nations Security Council Resolutions 242 and 338. The two sides concur that the agreement reached between them on permanent status will constitute the implementation of Resolutions 242 and 338.

The two sides agree that this process is one, and its two phases are interlocked in the agreed time-frame. They further agree that the outcome of the permanent status negotiations should not be prejudiced or preempted by agreements reached for the interim phase. They further agree that all options within the framework of the agreed basis of negotiations should remain open.

During the interim period, a major change will occur in the existing situation in the territories. Functions of the Israeli Civil Administration will be transferred to the Palestinians, and the Civil Administration will be dissolved. The two sides agree that an important outcome of this first phase is the empowerment of Palestinians through the negotiation of

---

[6] This first U.S. effort to "bridge" Israeli and Palestinian ideas for a declaration of principles was not warmly received by either party. The Palestinians considered it too close to the Israeli position, and the Israelis criticized the timing of its release at the end of the ninth round of Washington talks. See *Mideast Mirror*, May 14, 1993.

interim self-government, which should give Palestinians greater control over the decisions that affect their lives and fate.

It should also put an end to the confrontation between Israel and the Palestinians, and create a new relationship between them. It is Israel's view that the security needs of both sides should be taken into consideration, while overall security responsibility, as well as the responsibility for Israelis in the territories, will remain under Israel during the interim period. It is the Palestinian view that the objective of security arrangements is to achieve regional stability and respond to mutual needs, as well as to create the conditions of real peace.

Over the past three weeks, Israel and the Palestinians have taken an important step toward these objectives. They have created working groups on key issues, including land and water, the concept of interim self-government, and humanitarian affairs and human rights. The two sides have engaged in substantive discussions, and have narrowed some of the key differences between them, although there are many issues discussed in the Israeli-Palestinian track and in the Israeli-joint-Jordanian-Palestinian plenary that have not been included in this statement and that remain to be resolved. The omission of these issues in this statement is without prejudice to the positions of the two sides.

The two sides have agreed that a Palestinian elected interim self-government authority (whose name will be determined) will be established through free, fair, general, and direct elections. These elections will be held in accordance with agreed modalities to be negotiated, including agreed supervision and international observers. Detailed negotiations will take place concerning the modalities for the elections.

The Palestinian authority will assume all of the powers and responsibilities agreed during the negotiations. This will include executive and judicial powers (by independent judicial organs), as well as those legislative powers within the responsibilities transferred to it, subject to agreed principles to be negotiated. Due consideration will be given to the need to review legislation in force in remaining areas, as appropriate.

The two sides have agreed that the territories are viewed as a single territorial unit. They agree that issues related to sovereignty will be negotiated during talks on permanent status, and that negotiations on the land issue during the interim period will take place without prejudice to territorial integrity; that is, the territories will be treated as a whole, even while they negotiate the difficult issues of land management, usage, and planning. They have different views on land and jurisdiction, which they will continue to discuss.

This joint statement represents an important first step toward reaching agreement on interim arrangements.

The two sides will direct their efforts to bridging remaining substantive differences. They have committed themselves to work toward creating a positive climate for these negotiations. They agree that there is no acceptable alternative to making these negotiations succeed, and it is the only realistic pathway to achieving a just and enduring peace.

# APPENDIX XI

## RABIN'S LETTER TO ARAFAT RECOGNIZING THE PLO
*September 9, 1993*

Yasser Arafat
Chairman
The Palestinian Liberation Organization

Mr. Chairman,

In response to your letter of September 9, 1993, I wish to confirm to you that, in light of the PLO commitments included in your letter, the Government of Israel has decided to recognize the PLO as the representative of the Palestinian people and commence negotiations with the PLO within the Middle East peace process.

Sincerely,

Yitzhak Rabin
Prime Minister of Israel

# APPENDIX XII

## ARAFAT'S LETTER TO RABIN RECOGNIZING
## ISRAEL'S RIGHT TO EXIST IN PEACE
*September 9, 1993*

Mr. Prime Minister,

The signing of the Declaration of Principles marks a new era in the history of the Middle East. In firm conviction thereof, I would like to confirm the following PLO commitments:

The PLO recognizes the right of the State of Israel to exist in peace and security.

The PLO accepts UN Security Council Resolutions 242 and 338.

The PLO commits itself to the Middle East peace process, and to a peaceful resolution of the conflict between the two sides and declares that all outstanding issues relating to permanent status will be resolved through negotiations.

The PLO considers that the signing of the Declaration of Principles constitutes a historic event, inaugurating a new epoch of peaceful coexistence, free from violence and all other acts which endanger peace and stability. Accordingly, the PLO renounces the use of terrorism and other acts of violence and will assume responsibility over all PLO elements and personnel in order to assure their compliance, prevent violations and discipline violators.

In view of the promise of a new era and the signing of the Declaration of Principles and based on Palestinian acceptance of Security Council Resolutions 242 and 338, the PLO affirms that those articles of the Palestinian Covenant which deny Israel's right to exist, and the provisions of the Covenant which are inconsistent with the commitments of this letter are now inoperative and no longer valid. Consequently, the PLO undertakes to submit to the Palestinian National Council for formal approval the necessary changes in regard to the Palestinian Covenant.

Sincerely,

Yasser Arafat
Chairman, The Palestine Liberation Organization

## ARAFAT'S LETTER TO NORWEGIAN FOREIGN MINISTER
## JOHAN JORGEN HOLST ON THE INTIFADA
*September 9, 1993*

Dear Minister Holst,

I would like to confirm to you that, upon the signing of the Declaration of Principles, I will include the following positions in my public statements.

In light of the new era marked by the signing of the Declaration of Principles, the PLO encourages and calls upon the Palestinian people in the West Bank and Gaza Strip to take part in the steps leading to the normalization of life, rejecting violence and terrorism, contributing to peace and stability and participating actively in shaping reconstruction, economic development and cooperation.

Sincerely,

Yasser Arafat
Chairman
The Palestine Liberation Organization

## THE ISRAEL-PLO DECLARATION OF PRINCIPLES
*September 13, 1993*

The Government of the State of Israel and the P.L.O. team (the "Palestinian Delegation"), representing the Palestinian people, agree that it is time to put an end to decades of confrontation and conflict, recognize their mutual legitimate and political rights, and strive to live in peaceful coexistence and mutual dignity and security and achieve a just, lasting and comprehensive peace settlement and historic reconciliation through the agreed political process. Accordingly, the two sides agree to the following principles:

ARTICLE I—Aim of the Negotiations

The aim of the Israeli-Palestinian negotiations within the current Middle East peace process is, among other things, to establish a Palestinian Interim Self-Government Authority, the elected Council (the "Council"), for the Palestinian people in the West Bank and the Gaza Strip, for a transitional period not exceeding five years, leading to a permanent settlement based on Security Council Resolutions 242 and 338.

It is understood that the interim arrangements are an integral part of the whole peace process and that the negotiations on the permanent status will lead to the implementation of Security Council Resolutions 242 and 338.

ARTICLE II—Framework for the Interim Period

The agreed framework for the interim period is set forth in this Declaration of Principles.

ARTICLE III—Elections

1.  In order that the Palestinian people in the West Bank and Gaza Strip may govern themselves according to democratic principles, direct free and general political elections will be held for the Council under agreed supervision and international observation, while the Palestinian police will ensure public order.

2.   An agreement will be concluded on the exact mode and conditions of the elections in accordance with the protocol attached as Annex 1, with the goal of holding the elections not later than nine months after the entry into force of this Declaration of Principles.

3.   These elections will constitute a significant interim preparatory step toward the realization of the legitimate rights of the Palestinian people and their just requirements.

ARTICLE IV—Jurisdiction

Jurisdiction of the Council will cover West Bank and Gaza Strip territory, except for issues that will be negotiated in the permanent status negotiations. The two sides view the West Bank and the Gaza Strip as a single territorial unit, whose integrity will be preserved during the interim period.

ARTICLE V—Transitional Period and Permanent Status Negotiations

1.   The five-year transitional period will begin upon the withdrawal from the Gaza Strip and Jericho area.

2.   Permanent status negotiations will commence as soon as possible, but not later than the beginning of the third year of the interim period, between the Government of Israel and the Palestinian people's representatives.

3.   It is understood that these negotiations shall cover remaining issues, including: Jerusalem, refugees, settlements, security arrangements, borders, relations and cooperation with other neighbors, and other issues of common interest.

4.   The two parties agree that the outcome of the permanent status negotiations should not be prejudiced or preempted by agreements reached for the interim period.

ARTICLE VI—Prepatory Transfer of Powers and Responsibilities

1.   Upon the entry into force of this Declaration of Principles and the withdrawal from the Gaza Strip and the Jericho area, a transfer of authority from the Israeli military government and its Civil Administration to the authorized Palestinians for this task, as detailed

herein, will commence. This transfer of authority will be of a preparatory nature until the inauguration of the Council.

2. Immediately after the entry into force of this Declaration of Principles and the withdrawal from the Gaza Strip and Jericho area, with the view to promoting economic development in the West Bank and Gaza Strip, authority will be transferred to the Palestinians on the following spheres: education and culture, health, social welfare, direct taxation, and tourism. The Palestinian side will commence in building the Palestinian police force, as agreed upon. Pending the inauguration of the Council, the two parties may negotiate the transfer of additional powers and responsibilities, as agreed upon.

ARTICLE VII—Interim Agreement

1. The Israeli and Palestinian delegations will negotiate an agreement on the interim period (the "Interim Agreement").

2. The Interim Agreement shall specify, among other things, the structure of the Council, the number of its members, and the transfer of powers and responsibilities from the Israeli military government and its Civil Administration to the Council. The Interim Agreement shall also specify the Council's executive authority, legislative authority in accordance with Article IX below, and the independent Palestinian judicial organs.

3. The Interim Agreement shall include arrangements, to be implemented upon the inauguration of the Council, for the assumption by the Council of all of the powers and responsibilities transferred previously in accordance with Article VI above.

4. In order to enable the Council to promote economic growth, upon its inauguration, the Council will establish, among other things, a Palestinian Electricity Authority, a Gaza Sea Port Authority, a Palestinian Development Bank, a Palestinian Export Promotion Board, a Palestinian Environmental Authority, a Palestinian Land Authority and a Palestinian Water Administration Authority, and any other Authorities agreed upon, in accordance with the Interim Agreement that will specify their powers and responsibilities.

5. After the inauguration of the Council, the Civil Administration will be dissolved, and the Israeli military government will be withdrawn.

ARTICLE VIII—Public Order and Security

In order to guarantee public order and internal security for the Palestinians of the West Bank and the Gaza Strip, the Council will establish a strong police force, while Israel will continue to carry the responsibility for defending against external threats, as well as the responsibility for overall security of Israelis for the purpose of safeguarding their internal security and public order.

ARTICLE IX—Laws and Military Orders

1.   The Council will be empowered to legislate, in accordance with the Interim Agreement, within all authorities transferred to it.

2.   Both parties will review jointly laws and military orders presently in force in remaining spheres.

ARTICLE X—Joint Israeli-Palestinians Liaison Committee

In order to provide for a smooth implementation of this Declaration of Principles and any subsequent agreements pertaining to the interim period, upon the entry into force of this Declaration of Principles, a joint Israeli-Palestinian Liaison Committee will be established in order to deal with issues requiring coordination, other issues of common interest, and disputes.

ARTICLE XI—Israeli-Palestinian Cooperation in Economic Fields

Recognizing the mutual benefit of cooperation in promoting the development of the West Bank, the Gaza Strip and Israel, upon the entry into force of this Declaration of Principles, an Israeli-Palestinian Economic Cooperation Committee will be established in order to develop and implement in a cooperative manner the programs identified in the protocols attached as Annex III and Annex IV.

ARTICLE XII—Liaison and Cooperation with Jordan and Egypt

The two parties will invite the Governments of Jordan and Egypt to participate in establishing further liaison and cooperation arrangements between the Government of Israel and the Palestinian representatives, on the one hand, and the Governments of Jordan and Egypt, on the other hand, to promote cooperation between them. These arrangements will include the constitution of a Continuing Committee that will decide by agreement on the modalities of admission of persons displaced from the West Bank and Gaza Strip in 1967, together with necessary measures to prevent disruption and disorder. Other matters of common concern will be dealt with by this Committee.

ARTICLE XIII—Redeployment of Israeli Forces

1.   After the entry into force of this Declaration of Principles, and not later than the eve of elections for the Council, a redeployment of Israeli military forces in the West Bank and the Gaza Strip will take place, in addition to withdrawal of Israeli forces carried out in accordance with Article XIV.

2.   In redeploying its military forces, Israel will be guided by the principle that its military forces should be redeployed outside populated areas.

3.   Further redeployments to specified locations will be gradually implemented commensurate with the assumption of responsibility for public order and internal security by the Palestinian police force pursuant to Article VIII above.

ARTICLE XIV—Israeli Withdrawal from the Gaza Strip and Jericho Area

Israel will withdraw from the Gaza Strip and Jericho area, as detailed in the protocol attached as Annex II.

ARTICLE XV—Resolution of Disputes

1.   Disputes arising out of the application or interpretation of this Declaration of Principles, or any subsequent agreements pertaining to the interim period, shall be resolved by negotiations through the Joint Liaison Committee to be established pursuant to Article X above.

2.   Disputes which cannot be settled by negotiations may be resolved by a mechanism of conciliation to be agreed upon by the parties.

3.   The parties may agree to submit to arbitration disputes relating to the interim period, which cannot be settled through conciliation. To this end, upon the agreement of both parties, the parties will establish an Arbitration Committee.

ARTICLE XVI—Israeli-Palestinian Cooperation Concerning Regional Programs

Both parties view the multilateral working groups as an instrument for promoting a "Marshall Plan," the regional programs and other programs, including special programs for the West Bank and Gaza Strip, as indicated in the protocol attached as Annex IV.

ARTICLE XVII—Miscellaneous Provisions

1.  This Declaration of Principles will enter into force one month after its signing.

2.  All protocols annexed to this Declaration of Principles and Agreed Minutes pertaining thereto shall be regarded as an integral part hereof.

Done at Washington, D.C., this thirteenth day of September, 1993.

For the Government of Israel:                           Shimon Peres
For the PLO:                                           Mahmoud Abbas

Witnessed by:     Warren Christopher          Andrei Kozyrev
                  United States of America     Russian Federation

ANNEX I—Protocol on the Mode and Conditions of Elections

1.  Palestinians of Jerusalem who live there will have the right to participate in the election process, according to an agreement between the two sides.

2.  In addition, the election agreement should cover, among other things, the following issues:

  A.  The system of elections;

  B.  The mode of the agreed supervision and international observation and their personal composition; and

  C.  Rules and regulations regarding election campaign, agreed arrangements for the organizing of mass media, and the possibility of licensing a broadcasting and TV station.

3.  The future status of displaced Palestinians who were registered on 4th June 1967 will not be prejudiced because they are unable to participate in the election process due to practical reasons.


ANNEX II—Protocol on Withdrawal of Israeli Forces
from the Gaza Strip and Jericho Area

1.  The two sides will conclude and sign within two months from the date of entry into force of this Declaration of Principles, an agreement on the withdrawal of Israeli military forces from the Gaza Strip and Jericho area. This agreement will include comprehensive arrangements to apply in the Gaza Strip and the Jericho area subsequent to the Israeli withdrawal.

2.  Israel will implement an accelerated and scheduled withdrawal of Israeli military forces from the Gaza Strip and Jericho area, beginning immediately with the signing of the agreement on the Gaza Strip and Jericho area and to be completed within a period not exceeding four months after the signing of this agreement.

3.   The above agreement will include, among other things:

A.   Arrangements for a smooth and peaceful transfer of authority from the Israeli military government and its Civil Administration to the Palestinian representatives.

B.   Structure, powers and responsibilities of the Palestinian authority in these areas, except: external security, settlements, Israelis, foreign relations, and other mutually agreed matters.

C.   Arrangements for the assumption of internal security and public order by the Palestinian police force consisting of police officers recruited locally and from abroad (holding Jordanian passports and Palestinian documents issued by Egypt). Those who will participate in the Palestinian police force coming from abroad should be trained as police and police officers.

D.   A temporary international or foreign presence, as agreed upon.

E.   Establishment of a joint Palestinian-Israeli Coordination and Cooperation Committee for mutual security purposes.

F.   An economic development and stabilization program, including the establishment of an Emergency Fund, to encourage foreign investment, and financial and economic support. Both sides will coordinate and cooperate jointly and unilaterally with regional and international parties to support these aims.

G.   Arrangements for a safe passage for persons and transportation between the Gaza Strip and Jericho area.

4.   The above agreement will include arrangements for coordination between both parties regarding passages:

A.   Gaza—Egypt; and

B.   Jericho—Jordan.

5.   The offices responsible for carrying out the powers and responsibilities of the Palestinian authority under this Annex II and Article VI Declaration of Principles will be located in the Gaza Strip and in the Jericho area pending the inauguration of the Council.

6.  Other than these agreed arrangements, the status of the Gaza Strip and Jericho area will continue to be an integral part of the West Bank and Gaza Strip, and will not be changed in the interim period.

ANNEX III—Protocol on Israeli-Palestinian Cooperation
in Economic and Development Programs

The two sides agree to establish an Israeli-Palestinian Continuing Committee for Economic Cooperation, focusing, among other things, on the following:

1.  Cooperation in the field of water, including a Water Development Program prepared by experts from both sides, which will also specify the mode of cooperation in the management of water resources in the West Bank and Gaza Strip, and will include proposals for studies and plans on water rights of each party, as well as on the equitable utilization of joint water resources for implementation in and beyond the interim period.

2.  Cooperation in the field of electricity, including an Electricity Development Program, which will also specify the mode of cooperation for the production, maintenance, purchase and sale of electricity resources.

3.  Cooperation in the field of energy, including an Energy Development Program, which will provide for the exploitation of oil and gas for industrial purposes, particularly in the Gaza Strip and in the Negev, and will encourage further joint exploitation of other energy resources. This Program may also provide for the construction of a Petrochemical industrial complex in the Gaza Strip and the construction of oil and gas pipelines.

4.  Cooperation in the field of finance, including a Financial Development and Action Program for the encouragement of international investment in the West Bank and the Gaza Strip, and in Israel, as well as the establishment of a Palestinian Development Bank.

5.  Cooperation in the field of transport and communications, including a Program, which will define guidelines for the establishment of a Gaza Sea Port Area, and will provide for the establishing of transport and communications lines to and from the West Bank and the Gaza Strip to Israel and to other countries. In addition, this Program will provide for

carrying out the necessary construction of roads, railways, communications lines, etc.

6. Cooperation in the field of trade, including studies, and Trade Promotion Programs, which will encourage local, regional and inter-regional trade, as well as a feasibility study of creating free trade zones in the Gaza Strip and in Israel, mutual access to these zones, and cooperation in other areas related to trade and commerce.

7. Cooperation in the field of industry, including Industrial Development Programs, which will provide for the establishment of joint Israeli-Palestinian Industrial Research and Development Centers, will promote Palestinian-Israeli joint ventures, and provide guidelines for cooperation in the textile, food, pharmaceutical, electronics, diamonds, computer and science-based industries.

8. A program for cooperation in, and regulation of, labor relations and cooperation in social welfare issues.

9. A Human Resources Development and Cooperation Plan, providing for joint Israeli-Palestinian workshops and seminars, and for the establishment of joint vocational training centers, research institutes and data banks.

10. An Environmental Protection Plan, providing for joint and/or coordinated measures in this sphere.

11. A program for developing coordination and cooperation in the field of communication and media.

12. Any other programs of mutual interest.

### ANNEX IV—Protocol on Israeli-Palestinian Cooperation Concerning Regional Development Programs

1. The two sides will cooperate in the context of the multilateral peace efforts in promoting a Development Program for the region, including the West Bank and the Gaza Strip, to be initiated by the G-7. The parties will request the G-7 to seek the participation in this program of other interested states, such as members of the Organization for Economic Cooperation and Development, regional Arab states and institutions, as well as members of the private sector.

2. The Development Program will consist of two elements:

A) An Economic Development Program for the West Bank and the Gaza Strip.

B) A Regional Economic Development Program.

A. The Economic Development Program for the West Bank and the Gaza Strip will consist of the following elements:

(1) A Social Rehabilitation Program, including a Housing and Construction Program.

(2) A Small and Medium Business Development Plan.

(3) An Infrastructure Development Program (water, electricity, transportation and communications, etc.)

(4) A Human Resources Plan.

(5) Other programs.

B. The Regional Economic Development Program may consist of the following elements:

(1) The establishment of a Middle East Development Fund, as a first step, and a Middle East Development Bank, as a second step.

(2) The development of a joint Israeli-Palestinian-Jordanian Plan for coordinated exploitation of the Dead Sea area.

(3) The Mediterranean Sea (Gaza)—Dead Sea Canal.

(4) Regional Desalinization and other water development projects.

(5) A regional plan for agricultural development, including a coordinated regional effort for the prevention of desertification.

(6) Interconnection of electricity grids.

(7) Regional cooperation for the transfer, distribution and industrial exploitation of gas, oil and other energy resources.

(8) A Regional Tourism, Transportation and Telecommunications Development Plan.

(9) Regional cooperation in other spheres.

3. The two sides will encourage the multilateral working groups, and will coordinate towards their success. The two parties will encourage intersessional activities, as well as pre-feasibility and feasibility studies, within the various multilateral working groups.

### Agreed Minutes to the Declaration of Principles
### on Interim Self-Government Arrangements

Any powers and responsibilities transferred to the Palestinians pursuant to the Declaration of Principles prior to the inauguration of the Council will be subject to the same principles pertaining to Article IV, as set out in these Agreed Minutes below.

## SPECIFIC UNDERSTANDINGS AND AGREEMENTS

### ARTICLE IV

1. Jurisdiction of the Council will cover West Bank and Gaza Strip territory, except for issues that will be negotiated in the permanent status negotiations: Jerusalem, settlements, military locations, and Israelis.

2. The Council's jurisdiction will apply with regard to the agreed powers, responsibilities, spheres and authorities transferred to it.

### ARTICLE VI (2)
It is agreed that the transfer of authority will be as follows:

(1) The Palestinian side will inform the Israeli side of the names of the authorized Palestinians who will assume the powers, authorities and responsibilities that will be transferred to the Palestinians according to the Declaration of Principles in the following fields: education and culture, health, social welfare, direct taxation, tourism, and any other authorities agreed upon.

(2) It is understood that the rights and obligations of these offices will not be affected.

(3) Each of the spheres described above will continue to enjoy existing budgetary allocations in accordance with arrangements to be mutually agreed upon. These arrangements also will provide for the necessary adjustments required in order to take into account the taxes collected by the direct taxation office.

(4) Upon the execution of the Declaration of Principles, the Israeli and Palestinian delegations will immediately commence negotiations on a detailed plan for the transfer of authority on the above offices in accordance with the above understandings.

ARTICLE Vll (2)
The Interim Agreement will also include arrangements for coordination and cooperation.

ARTICLE Vll (5)
The withdrawal of the military government will not prevent Israel from exercising the powers and responsibilities not transferred to the Council.

ARTICLE VIII
It is understood that the Interim Agreement will include arrangements for cooperation and coordination between the two parties in this regard. It is also agreed that the transfer of powers and responsibilities to the Palestinian police will be accomplished in a phased manner, as agreed in the Interim Agreement.

ARTICLE X
It is agreed that, upon the entry into force of the Declaration of Principles, the Israeli and Palestinian delegations will exchange the names of the individuals designated by them as members of the Joint Israeli Liaison Committee.

It is further agreed that each side will have an equal number of members of the Joint Committee. The Joint Committee will reach decisions by agreement. The Joint Committee may add other technicians and experts, as necessary. The Joint Committee will decide on the frequency and place or places of its meetings.

ANNEX II
It is understood that, subsequent to the Israeli withdrawal, Israel will continue to be responsible for external security, and for internal security and public order of settlements and Israelis. Israeli military forces and civilians may continue to use roads freely within the Gaza Strip and the Jericho area.

Done at Washington, D.C., this thirteenth day of September, 1993.

For the Government of Israel:                                Shimon Peres
For the PLO:                                                Mahmoud Abbas

Witnessed By:      Warren Christopher        Andrei Kozyrev
                   United States of America   Russia Federation

## EXCERPTS FROM SPEECHES AT THE
## SECRET OSLO SIGNING CEREMONY
*August 20, 1993*

Johan Jorgen Holst, foreign minister of Norway:

History is in the making. In the flow of history sometimes, we register turning points. Turning points must be created. You here tonight, it seems to me, have created a very important turning point. In order to create history, you have to have a sense of history. Making history means making possible that which is necessary. This is what you have done tonight. You have lived through years of confrontation, now you are entering an era of cooperation . . .

The Middle East has, to so many of us, seemed like a powder keg. Now I think it will turn into a laboratory for the creation for a viable, peaceful order. You have so many things going for you in the Middle East, and now I feel confident you will take charge into a zone of stability, cooperation, and openness. I know that it is impossible to capture by means of words what all this means. I think that we all sense that this not only is this important, but it is more important than most of the things that we have had the chance to experience . . .

We are always there if you need our services. But the task is yours and the work has to be yours . . .

Abu Alaa, head of the Palestinian delegation in Oslo:

I cried twice this week. The first time was when we talked by phone [the night before in Stockholm], and at 5:00 A.M. we finished everything. We were six persons: Abu Ammar [Arafat], Abu Mazen [Mahmoud Abbas], Yasser [Abd Rabbo, a senior Arafat aide], Abu Khaled [the patronym of Arafat confidant Muhsen Ibrahim], me, and Hassan [Asfour]. After we finished, really we cried. We congratulated each other. We said now we have to start the big battle for development, for construction, for cooperation. This is the new history . . .

Your Excellency, Mr. Peres, welcome. It is a great honor. I have keenly followed your declarations, statements, and writings that has confirmed to the all the Palestinian people your care to achieve just, permanent, and comprehensive peace. In the name of the Palestinian people and its leader Yasser Arafat, I would like to welcome you and congratulate you on your 70th birthday . . .

Today we have started a new journey towards a new future, in a world whose final form has not yet been shaped and which is open to all sorts of change. The future that we look at won't materialize unless we both together overcome the fears of the past and learn from the past the lessons for our future. Cooperation and enmity don't coexist. Cooperation must be based equity, not domination. It is one of the key [elements] of trust. We should start the process of cooperation, in order to have trust. It is much better than military forces.

We have been parties to conflict. Now we are parties to peace. . . . We can say now that the battle of peace has started today. We are for it. It must be won by both of us.


Uri Savir, head of the Israeli delegation in Oslo:

To the Palestinian delegation, let me say, if I may: We discovered you in Oslo, far away from the region whose future we are negotiating. We were introduced as enemies. We came with good will but yet with a few prejudices. We found men of truth, courage, and depth. Abu Alaa, Hassan Asfour, Mohammed Kosh—you are the neighbors we wish to live with side by side.

Ministers, friends, this day is marked, hopefully, by man changing history. We owe this agreement to the leadership and courage of a few who dare to challenge the illusory comfort of political routine. You have challenged those who are paralyzed by the burden of the past or by the hypnosis of the present. You have indicated with open eyes new yet unknown directions as your sight is set on the good of men and women. Therefore, we can embark today on a new journey—hoping, working, and praying to put an end to suspicion, to violence, hate, fear, pain, [and] suffering. All this, over night, has become the common enemy of Israelis and Palestinian people alike.

It is indeed a new dawn for two peoples plagued by historical tragedies. The Jewish people suffered two millennia of exile and persecution to find a safe haven in its historical homeland, but encountered uninvited violent rejection. The Palestinian people, often caught tragically in the midst of a wider conflict, [were] never able to express the freedom they seek and deserve. The meeting of two tragic histories created the bitter conflict on a small land drenched by historical memory.

Today, all this can be—must be—over. A dark chapter in our common history is closed, shut in the face of those who hoped and even helped to perpetuate our conflict forever and failed. Today is the beginning of . . . . a future where legitimate Palestinian desires for self-government are compatible with Israeli interest in security. It is a test . . .

The needs and aspirations of our young oblige us to succeed. We Israelis have no desire to dominate the lives and fate of the Palestinians. With this agreement, we are not just fulfilling a political interest, but also a moral predicament for our people. We would like our meeting ground to become a moral high ground for peace, democracy, and economic prosperity.

# APPENDIX XVI

## RABIN'S SPEECH AT THE DOP SIGNING CEREMONY
*September 13, 1993*

President Clinton, the President of the United States, your excellencies, ladies and gentlemen. This signing of the Israeli-Palestinian declaration of principles here today is not so easy, neither for myself as a soldier in Israel's wars, nor for the people of Israel, nor for the Jewish people in the *diaspora* who are watching us now with great hope mixed with apprehension. It is certainly not easy for the families of the victims of the wars, violence, terror, whose pain will never heal, for the many thousands who defended our lives with their own and have even sacrificed their lives for our own. For them, this ceremony has come too late.

Today, on the eve of an opportunity for peace, and perhaps an end to violence and wars, we remember each and every one of them with everlasting love. We have come from Jerusalem, the ancient and eternal capital of the Jewish people. We have come from an anguished and grieving land. We have come from a people, a home, a family that has not known a single year, not a single month, in which mothers have not wept for their sons. We have come to try and put an end to the hostilities so that our children, and our children's children, will no longer experience the painful cost of war, violence and terror. We have come to secure their lives and to ease the sorrow and the painful memories of the past, to hope and pray for peace.

Let me say to you, the Palestinians—we are destined to live together on the same soil in the same land. We, the soldiers who have returned from battles stained with blood; we, who have seen our relatives and friends killed before our eyes; we, who have attended their funerals and cannot look into the eyes of their parents; we who have come from a land where parents bury their children; we, who have fought against you, the Palestinians, we say to you today in a loud and a clear voice—enough of blood and tears. Enough!

We have no desire for revenge. We harbor no hatred towards you. We, like you, are people; people who want to build a home, to plant a tree, to love, live side by side with you in dignity, in affinity, as human beings, as free men. We are today giving peace a chance and saying again to you, "Enough." Let us pray that a day will come when we all will say farewell to arms. We wish to open a new chapter in the sad book of our lives together—a chapter of mutual recognition, of good neighborliness, of mutual respect, of understanding. We hope to embark on a new era in the history of the Middle East.

Today here in Washington at the White House, we will begin a new reckoning in the relations between peoples, between parents tired of war, between children who will not know war. President of the United States, ladies and gentlemen, our inner strength, our higher moral values have been derived for thousands of years from the Book of the Books, in one of which, Koheleth (Ecclesiastes), we read, "To every thing there is a season and a time to every purpose under heaven. A time to be born and time to die, a time to kill and a time to heal. A time to weep and a time to laugh. A time to love and a time to hate, a time of war and a time of peace." Ladies and gentlemen, the time for peace has come.

In two days, the Jewish people will celebrate the beginning of a new year. I believe, I hope, I pray that the new year will bring a message of redemption for all peoples: a good year for you, for all of you; a good year for Israelis and Palestinians; a good year for all the peoples of the Middle East; a good year for our American friends who so want peace and are helping to achieve it. For presidents and members of previous administrations, especially for you, President Clinton, and your staff, for all citizens of the world, may peace come to all your homes.

In the Jewish tradition, it is customary to conclude our prayers with the word "Amen." With your permission, men of peace, I shall conclude with words taken from the prayer recited by Jews daily, and whoever of you volunteer, I would ask the entire audience to join me in saying "Amen."

May He who makes peace on High make peace for us and all Israel. Amen.

## ARAFAT'S SPEECH AT THE DOP SIGNING CEREMONY
*September 13, 1993*

In the name of God, the most merciful, the passionate, Mr. President, ladies and gentlemen, I would like to express our tremendous appreciation to President Clinton and to his administration for sponsoring this historic event which the entire world has been waiting for.

Mr. President, I am taking this opportunity to assure you and to assure the great American people that we share your values for freedom, justice and human rights——values for which my people have been striving.

My people are hoping that this agreement which we are signing today marks the beginning of the end of a chapter of pain and suffering which has lasted throughout this century.

My people are hoping that this agreement which we are signing today will usher in an age of peace, coexistence and equal rights. We are relying on your role, Mr. President, and on the role of all the countries which believe that without peace in the Middle East, peace in the world will not be complete.

Enforcing the agreement and moving toward the final settlement, after two years, to implement all aspects of UN Resolutions 242 and 338 in all of their aspects, and resolve all the issues of Jerusalem, the settlements, the refugees and the boundaries will be a Palestinian and an Israeli responsibility. It is also the responsibility of the international community in its entirety to help the parties overcome the tremendous difficulties which are still standing in the way of reaching a final and comprehensive settlement.

Now as we stand on the threshold of this new historic era, let me address the people of Israel and their leaders, with whom we are meeting today for the first time, and let me assure them that the difficult decision we reached together was one that required great and exceptional courage.

We will need more courage and determination to continue the course of building coexistence and peace between us. This is possible and it will happen with mutual determination and with the effort that will be made with all parties on all the tracks to establish the foundations of a just and comprehensive peace.

Our people do not consider that exercising the right to self-determination could violate the rights of their neighbors or infringe on their security. Rather, putting an end to their feelings of being wronged and of having suffered an historic injustice is the strongest guarantee to achieve coexistence and openness between our two peoples and future generations. Our two peoples are awaiting today this historic hope, and they want to give peace a real chance.

Such a shift will give us an opportunity to embark upon the process of economic, social and cultural growth and development. And we hope that international participation in that process will be extensive as it can be. This shift will also provide an opportunity for all forms of cooperation on a broad scale and in all fields.

I thank you, Mr. President. We hope that our meeting will be a new beginning for fruitful and effective relations between the American people and the Palestinian people.

I wish to thank the Russian Federation and President Boris Yeltsin. Our thanks also go to Secretary Christopher and Foreign Minister Kozyrev, to the government of Norway and to the Foreign Minister of Norway for the positive part they played in bringing about this major achievement. I extend greetings to all the Arab leaders, our brothers, and to all the world leaders who contributed to this achievement.

Ladies and gentlemen, the battle for peace is the most difficult battle of our lives. It deserves our utmost efforts because the land of peace, the land of peace yearns for a just and comprehensive peace. Thank you.

## CLINTON'S SPEECH AT DOP SIGNING CEREMONY
### *September 13, 1993*

Prime Minister Rabin, Chairman Arafat, Foreign Minister Peres, Mr. Abbas, President Carter, President Bush, distinguished guests:

On behalf of the United States and Russia, co-sponsors of the Middle East peace process, welcome to this great occasion of history and hope. Today we bear witness to an extraordinary act in one of history's defining dramas, a drama that began in a time of our ancestors when the word went forth from a sliver of land between the River Jordan and the Mediterranean Sea. That hallowed piece of earth, and land of life and revelation, is the home to the memories and dreams of Jews, Muslims, and Christians throughout the world.

As we all know, devotion to that land has also been the source of conflict and bloodshed for too long. Throughout this century, bitterness between the Palestinian and Jewish people has robbed the entire region of its resources, its potential, and too many of its sons and daughters. The land has been so drenched in warfare and hatred that conflicting claims of history etched so deeply in the souls of the combatants there that many believe the past would always have the upper hand.

Then, fourteen years ago, the past began to give way when at this place and upon this desk three men of great vision signed their names to the Camp David Accord. Today we honor the memories of Menachem Begin and Anwar Sadat, and we salute the wise leadership of President Jimmy Carter.

Then, as now, we heard from those who said that conflict would come again soon. But the peace between Egypt and Israel has endured. Just so, this bold new venture today, this brave gamble that the future can be better than the past, must endure.

Two years ago in Madrid, another president took a major step on the road to peace by bringing Israel and all her neighbors together to launch direct negotiations. Today we also express our deep thanks for the skillful leadership of President George Bush.

Ever since Harry Truman first recognized Israel, every American president, Democrat and Republican, has worked for peace between Israel and her neighbors. Now the efforts of all who have labored before us bring us to this moment, a moment when we dare to pledge what for so long seemed difficult even to imagine: that the security of the Israeli people will be reconciled with the hopes of the Palestinian people, and there will be more security and more hope for all.

Today, the leadership of Israel and the Palestine Liberation Organization will sign a Declaration of Principles on Interim Palestinian Self-Government. It charts a course toward reconciliation between two peoples who have both known the bitterness of exile. Now both pledge to put old sorrows and antagonisms behind them and to work for a shared future, shaped by the values of the Torah, the Koran and the Bible.

Let us salute also today the government of Norway for its remarkable role in nurturing this agreement.

But above all, let us today pay tribute to the leaders who had the courage to lead their people toward peace, away from the scars of battle, the wounds and the losses of the past, toward a brighter tomorrow. The world today thanks Prime Minister Rabin, Foreign Minister Peres and Chairman Arafat. Their tenacity and vision has given us the promise of a new beginning.

What these leaders have done now must be done by others. Their achievement must be a catalyst for progress in all aspects of the peace process, and those of us who support them must be there to help in all aspects, for the peace must render the people who make it more secure.

A peace of the brave is within our reach. Throughout the Middle East, there is a great yearning for the quiet miracle of a normal life. We know a difficult road lies ahead. Every peace has its enemies, those who still prefer the easy habits of hatred to the hard labors of reconciliation.

But Prime Minister Rabin has reminded us that you do not have to make peace with your friends. And the Koran teaches that if the enemy inclines toward peace, do thou also incline toward peace.

Therefore, let us resolve that this new mutual recognition will be a continuing process in which the parties transform the very way they see and understand each other. Let the skeptics of this peace recall what once existed among these people. There was a time when the traffic of ideas and commerce and pilgrims flowed uninterrupted among the cities of the fertile crescent. In Spain, in the Middle East, Muslims and Jews once worked together to write brilliant chapters in the history of literature and science. All this can come to pass again.

Mr. Prime Minister, Mr. Chairman, I pledge the active support of the United States of America to the difficult work that lies ahead. The United States is committed to ensuring that the people who are affected by this agreement will be made more secure by it, and to leading the world in marshaling the resources necessary to implement the difficult details that will make real the principles to which you commit yourselves today.

Together, let us imagine what can be accomplished if all the energy and ability the Israelis and the Palestinians have invested into your struggle can now be channeled into cultivating the land and freshening the waters, into ending the boycotts and creating new industry, into building a land as bountiful and peaceful as it is holy. Above all, let us dedicate ourselves today to your region's next generation. In this entire assembly, no one is more important than the group of Arab and Israeli children who are seated here with us today.

Mr. Prime Minister, Mr. Chairman, this day belongs to you. And because of what you have done, tomorrow belongs to them. We must not leave them prey to the politics of extremism and despair, to those who would derail this process because they cannot overcome the fears and hatreds of the past. We must not betray their future. For too long, the young of the Middle East have been caught in a web of hatred not of their own making. For too long, they have been taught from the chronicles of war. Now, we can give them the chance to know the season of peace.

For them, we must realize the prophecy of Isaiah, that the cry of violence shall no more be heard in your land, nor rack nor ruin within your borders. The children of Abraham, the descendants of Isaac and Ishmael, have embarked together on a bold journey. Together, today, with all our hearts and all our souls, we bid them *shalom, salaam,* peace.

## PERES' LETTER TO NORWEGIAN FOREIGN MINISTER
## JOHAN JORGEN HOLST ON THE STATUS OF JERUSALEM
*October 11, 1993*


Dear Minister Holst,

I wish to confirm that the Palestinian institutions of East Jerusalem and the interests and well-being of the Palestinians of East Jerusalem are of great importance and will be preserved.

Therefore, all the Palestinian institutions of East Jerusalem, including the economic, social, educational, and cultural, and the holy Christian and Muslim places, are performing an essential task for the Palestinian population.

Needless to say, we will not hamper their activity; on the contrary, the fulfillment of this important mission is to be encouraged.

Sincerely,

Shimon Peres
Foreign Minister of Israel

## SENIOR ISRAELI OFFICIALS WHO REPORT DIRECTLY TO RABIN

| RABIN |

### as Prime Minister

| Director of the Mossad (foreign security service) | Chief of IDF General Staff | Heads of Delegations to the Bilateral Peace Talks in Washington |
|---|---|---|
| | Head of IDF Intelligence* | • Syria |
| | | • Lebanon |
| Director of Shin Bet (domestic security service) | | • Jordan |
| | | • Palestinians |

### as Minister of Defense

| Deputy Defense Minister | Coordinator of Operations in the Occupied Territories* | Advisor for the Defense Industry |
|---|---|---|
| | | Advisor for Special Projects |
| Director-General of the Defense Ministry | Coordinator of Lebanon Affairs | Advisor for Tank Development |
| | | Advisor for Water and Settlements |

* Reports to both the Prime Minister and the Minister of Defense

# Chronology

## October

30  Middle East peace conference convenes in Madrid.

## December

10  Bilateral peace talks between Israelis and Arabs begin in Washington.

April  Norwegian academic Terje Larsen makes contact with Labor party's Yossi Beilin in bid to broker secret Israeli-Palestinian talks.

## June

20  Larsen, Beilin, and Palestinian leader Faisal Husseini meet at American Colony Hotel in Jerusalem to discuss idea of secret talks.

23  Labor wins Israeli elections under leadership of Yitzhak Rabin.

## July

13  Rabin's government assumes power. Shimon Peres named foreign minister.

**August**

24   Sixth round of bilateral peace talks commence in Washington; first round after Rabin assumed power. Former Likud government official Elyakim Rubinstein retained as Israeli chief negotiator.

**September**

9    Norwegian Deputy Foreign Minister Jan Egeland visits Israel, proposes backchannel Israeli-Palestinian negotiations.
24   Sixth round of Washington bilateral peace talks end.

**November**

3    Bill Clinton elected U.S. president.
16   Peres holds talks in Egypt, asks Egyptians to convey to PLO that he is willing to consider "Gaza plus" approach.

**December**

1    Knesset takes initial step to repeal ban on contacts with the PLO.
4    Israeli academic Yair Hirschfeld and top PLO finance official Ahmed Qurai (Abu Alaa) meet in London to discuss start of secret channel.
17   Rabin announces expulsion of approximately 415 suspected militants (mostly from Hamas) to southern Lebanon in response to the killing of eight Israeli troops within a 12-day period.

## 1993

**January**

19   Knesset repeals ban on contacts with the PLO.
20-23 First round of secret talks are held in Sarpsborg, Norway with Beilin's approval. Shortly thereafter, Beilin discloses existence of talks to Peres, who in turn informs Rabin.

## February

**12-14**  Second round of secret talks held in Sarpsborg. The two sides begin drafting a Declaration of Principles (DOP) for an interim Israel-Palestinian agreement.

**16**  Peres meets with Christopher and urges him to speak to Rabin about allowing Husseini to join Palestinian delegation in Washington.

**26**  U.S. Secretary of State Warren Christopher officially informed about Oslo channel during talks with Norwegian Foreign Minister Thorvald Stoltenberg at NATO meeting in Brussels.

## March

**11**  Rabin meets at the White House with Clinton, who publicly pledges to "minimize risks" of peace between Israel and Arab neighbors. Rabin assents to Christopher's request to include Husseini in the Palestinian delegation. U.S. officials say prime minister admits that no deal can be made without talking to PLO.

**20-21**  Third round of secret talks held in Sarpsborg. Both sides agree to DOP draft that leaves many issues unresolved. Norwegians pass copy of DOP to American officials.

**30**  Israel imposes "closure" of territories after wave of fatal Palestinian stabbings of Israelis.

## April

**2**  Johan Jorgen Holst replaces Stoltenberg as foreign minister of Norway.

**14**  Rabin holds summit meeting with Egyptian president Hosni Mubarak in Ismailiya. Mubarak gives Rabin document indicating that PLO Chairman Yasser Arafat is willing to accept idea of "Gaza-Jericho first" but insists on control of borders and extraterritorial passage linking the two.

**27**  Bilateral talks reconvene in Washington after hiatus caused by deportation of Islamic militants. Husseini joins Palestinian team but is soon recalled by Arafat. Palestinians dismiss U.S.-proposed "bridging" language, complaining that Israelis viewed document first.

29     Fourth round of negotiations in Oslo begins after Israeli precondition—resumption of the Washington talks—is met.

**May**

2      Fourth Oslo round ends.

13     In private meeting with Peres, Rabin agrees that secret talks with the PLO in Norway should be upgraded to official level.

14     Rabin consents to appointment of Foreign Ministry Director-General Uri Savir to conduct Oslo talks. Washington round ends.

21-23  After holding exploratory discussions with Abu Alaa in Norway, Savir recommends that the talks continue at an official level and that Israel should accept mutual recognition of the PLO.

**June**

11     Legal expert Joel Singer joins Savir in Oslo as negotiations delve into greater detail. Shortly thereafter, Rabin authorizes Singer to draft a new DOP.

15     Bilateral talks resume in Washington.

25-27  Seventh round of negotiations held in Norway.

28     United States puts forward second "bridging" proposal.

30     Bilateral Washington talks adjourn.

**July**

4-6    Singer presents draft of new DOP in town of Gressheim.

11     Oslo talks hit crisis when PLO amends its original position.

19     Rabin sends letter to Arafat via Health Minister Haim Ramon and Israeli-Arab Ahmed Tibi.

25     Israel launches week-long bombardment of southern Lebanon known as "Operation Accountability."

25-26  Crisis continues in Norway talks. Savir offers "personal" terms for mutual recognition between Israel and the PLO.

**August**

3      Christopher meets with Rabin to discuss Syrian track.

4      Tibi brings Rabin Arafat's reply to his letter.

| 5 | Rabin continues discussions with Christopher. |
|---|---|
| 6 | Fearful of Israeli progress on Syrian track, Abu Alaa presents Hirschfeld with modified PLO negotiating position. |
| 13-15 | Oslo talks resume. Attorney General Harish calls for Shas party leader Arye Deri to resign due to pending indictment. |
| 18 | Norwegian Foreign Minister Holst holds marathon phone conversation from Stockholm with Arafat and Abu Alaa in Tunis, relaying views of Peres and other Israeli negotiators. Main points of DOP completed. |
| 19 | Peres commits to write a letter preserving the status of existing Palestinian institutions in East Jerusalem. (Letter is actually written on October 11.) |
| 20 | Israelis, Palestinians, and Norwegians initial the DOP at secret ceremony in Norway in middle of the night. |
| 30 | Israeli cabinet unanimously approves the DOP with no amendments allowed. Interior Minister Deri and Economics Minister Shimon Shetreet abstain. |

## September

| 9-10 | After last minute negotiations, Holst obtains signatures of Arafat and Rabin on letters of mutual recognition between Israel and the PLO. |
|---|---|
| 13 | Rabin and Arafat shake hands at signing ceremony on White House lawn. Peres and the PLO's Mahmoud Abbas (Abu Mazen) sign the DOP. The event is witnessed by Clinton, Christopher, Russian Foreign Minister Andrei Kozyrev, and thousands of guests. |

# About the Book and Author

After decades of branding Yasser Arafat an arch-terrorist, Israel has embraced the PLO leader as a partner for peace. In this study of one of the most extraordinary examples of secret diplomacy in the second half of the twentieth century, David Makovsky, diplomatic correspondent for the *Jerusalem Post*, explores the personal, domestic, regional, and international factors that led Israel's Prime Minister Yitzhak Rabin, Foreign Minister Shimon Peres, and other top aides to negotiate the peace accords.

Makovsky traces key episodes prior to the breakthrough in Oslo—including Israel's deportation of radical Islamic activists in December 1992 and its retaliation against Hizbollah rocket attacks from south Lebanon in July 1993—and examines their impact on the fateful decisions that led to the remarkable diplomatic achievement. Working from exclusive interviews with dozens of Israeli, Palestinian, American, and Egyptian officials, Makovsky depicts in fascinating detail the intricacies of the Israel-PLO bargaining. He also examines lessons learned about Israeli decisionmaking from the Oslo experience and assesses the influence of the recent breakthrough in negotiations with Jordan on the Israel-PLO accord.

David Makovsky has covered the Middle East peace process as diplomatic correspondent for the *Jerusalem Post* and special correspondent for *U.S. News and World Report* since 1991. In that capacity, he has traveled to Oslo, Madrid, Cairo, Amman, Beijing, Tokyo, Bonn, Moscow, and Washington.

In July 1994, as a result of the personal intervention of Secretary of State Warren Christopher, he became the first Israeli journalist to report from Damascus. In March 1995, after similar assistance from U.S. officials, he was given unprecedented permission to file reports from Jeddah, Saudi Arabia.

Makovsky was a co-recipient of the National Press Club's 1994 Edwin M. Hood Award for Diplomatic Correspondence for a *U.S. News* cover story on the PLO's finances, and a contributor to *Triumph Without Victory* (Random House/Times Books, 1992), a book on the Gulf War. In January and February 1994, he was a visiting fellow at the Washington Institute for Near East Policy.

He has appeared frequently on the McNeil-Lehrer NewsHour, Cable News Network (CNN), British Broadcasting Company (BBC), and National Public Radio (NPR). A native of St. Louis, Missouri, Makovsky received a B.A. from Columbia University and a M.A. in Middle East studies from Harvard.